SEXUAL GENERATIONS

Sexual

"Star Trek: The Next Generation" and Gender

Generations

ROBIN ROBERTS

University of Illinois Press

Urbana and Chicago

Star Trek, Star Trek: The Next Generation, Star Trek: Deep Space Nine,
and *Star Trek: Voyager* are registered trademarks of Paramount Pictures
Corporation. This book was not prepared, approved, licensed, or endorsed
by any entity involved in creating or producing the *Star Trek* television
series or films.

Library of Congress Cataloging-in-Publication Data
Roberts, Robin, 1957–
Sexual generations : "Star trek: the next generation" and gender /
Robin Roberts.
p.   cm.
Includes bibliographical references and index.
ISBN 0-252-02455-9 (acid-free paper)
ISBN 0-252-06810-6 (pbk. : acid-free paper)
1. Star trek, the next generation (Television program).
2. Women on television.
I. Title.
PN1992.77.S732R63   1999
791.45'72—dc21   98-58090
CIP

1   2   3   4   5   C   P   5   4   3   2   1

To my mother, Shirley Moore Roberts,

with love, gratitude, and respect

CONTENTS

ACKNOWLEDGMENTS

I am grateful to Jane Donawerth and Donald Hassler, both ground-breaking science fiction scholars, for their generous reading of the manuscript. Karen Hewitt at University of Illinois Press was supportive and enthusiastic about the book. Susan Kohler and Leslie Beard assisted me when I needed it most. Theresa L. Sears and Carol Anne Peschke were patient and helpful editors. Elsie Michie helpfully read early drafts, and Nancy Wolff created the index. The Newcomb Center for Research on Women, Tulane University, provided resources and a supportive environment in the fall of 1995. I am grateful to Angeletta Gourdine, Carol Mattingly, and Sharon Weltman, who carefully read each chapter, making helpful suggestions. Their insights have enriched these readings. Pat Day encouraged me to write this book, although he believes that *Star Trek* won't make it to the twenty-first century. Pat, I hope that you are wrong! Rosan Jordan, Frank de Caro, and Emily Toth have been supportive colleagues and wonderful friends. Keith Kelleman shared my love of *Star Trek* before *Next Generation* even began. Mark Benfield and Geoff Clayton have kept me connected to science and been kind and encouraging (not to mention fun). Calvin Johnson's enthusiasm for science fiction and his commitment to writing it have been inspiring; he provided the book's title. Traci Bryant's indefatigable work for feminism has been energizing, and her presents of *Star Trek* paraphernalia spurred me on. Rachel Kahn, Laura, Harry, Izzy, and Sam Schexnayder, the late Lucy, Darcy, Tom, and Bobcat have been very supportive and provided distraction when I needed it most. My mother, Shirley Roberts, and sisters, Gayle, Linda, and Kim Roberts, encouraged this project with their love. I owe a great debt to Peter Fischer, who taught me to love *Star Trek: The Next Generation* and provided innumerable videotapes. Without his encouragement, this book would not have been written.

As I finished this this enterprise, I started on a new one with Les, Dylan, Chelsea, Mrs. Lottie, Bill and Laura Ellen Wade, Marylane, Robert and Meredith Koch, Granny Nash, and Mrs. B. I thank them all for their love and support. As with all projects of my heart, this is for Les.

———

An earlier version of chapter 8 appeared as "Rape, Romance, and Consent in *Star Trek: The Next Generation*" in *Extrapolation* 40 (Spring 1999): 21–35 and is used here with the permission of Kent State University Press.

SEXUAL GENERATIONS

Somewhere every culture has an imaginary zone for what it excludes, and it is that zone we must try to remember *today.*
—Catherine Clément, *The Newly Born Woman*

INTRODUCTION

As its many critics and fans emphasize, *Star Trek* is much more than a television show. For its devotees, it is a way of life, a passion. *Star Trek* exists not only as a televisual text, but also in movies, books, comic books, animated adventures, conventions, and collectible items. Henry Jenkins, Camille Bacon-Smith, Gary Westfahl, and the contributors to *Enterprise Zones: Critical Positions on Star Trek,* among many others, reveal that the incarnations of *Star Trek* and its fans are legion. *Sexual Generations* contributes to this world by closely analyzing the texts of the second series, which ran in syndication from 1987 to 1994. In the world of science fiction criticism, *Star Trek*'s importance has been attested often, most recently in the prominence of articles on the series in Donald Hassler and Clyde Wilcox's anthology *Political Science Fiction* and in a special section of *Science-Fiction Studies* edited by Veronica Hollinger. Recent university press books such as *Enterprise Zones* and Daniel Bernardi's *Star Trek and History,* discussion of race and *Star Trek,* are a part of this dialogue. Mass-market publishers have produced hundreds of *Star Trek* books, but none focus on gender. Unlike Thomas Richards's *The Meaning of Star Trek,* which analyzes a set of themes in the *Star Trek* world, or Jeff Greenwald's exploration of *Star Trek*'s worldwide appeal in *Future Perfect: How Star Trek Conquered Planet Earth,* or Constance Penley's discussion of the parallels between NASA and *Star Trek* in *NASA/Trek, Sexual Generations* focuses primarily on what the show reveals about gender.*

*In *Make It So: Leadership Lessons from "Star Trek: The Next Generation,"* Roberts and Ross reveal how widespread and important the show is. This book, as its title states, uses the fictional characters to teach lessons to aspiring business leaders. Like most of the books about *Star Trek,* this analysis ignores gender.

Since *Star Trek: The Next Generation* has recently ended its highly successful television run of seven years, now is an appropriate time to examine what this tremendously popular science fiction show can tell us about our culture in general and about gender politics in particular. *Sexual Generations* uses the series to explore depictions of the feminine, race as it is dealt with through the metaphor of female aliens, and feminist issues such as rape and abortion. As this book demonstrates, *Star Trek: The Next Generation* reveals American culture's complex and contradictory relationship with feminism. For many viewers and the show's creator, however, *Star Trek* is a positive force for women. Gene Roddenberry, creator of both the original *Star Trek* and its second incarnation, saw himself as highly supportive of women. In the original series, he wanted the captain to be a woman, but this proved too radical a vision for network executives in 1966—it is only in 1995 that a new series, *Star Trek: Voyager* provided us with a female captain. In the original series, an African-American character, Lieutenant Uhura, served as a communications officer and as a role model so important that Martin Luther King Jr. urged her to stay on the show after she resigned. And no less a star than Whoopi Goldberg played a recurring role on *Star Trek: The Next Generation* because of what Lieutenant Uhura meant to her as a child. Although many scholars have discussed the role of women in the original series, the seven years of *Star Trek: The Next Generation* have not yet been examined fully from a feminist perspective.

Two qualities specific to science fiction, extrapolation and defamiliarization, help explain why and how *Star Trek: The Next Generation* raises feminist issues. Science fiction has engendered a tradition of feminist writing, first explored by Natalie Rosinsky in *Feminist Futures*, developed by Marleen Barr in several books, including *Alien to Femininity*, and discussed most recently in Jane Donawerth's *Frankenstein's Daughters: Women Writing Science Fiction*. The same methods used by women writers are used by telewriters, directors, and actresses in *Star Trek: The Next Generation*. Because science fiction customarily uses the future as a setting, the genre must extrapolate. Extrapolation is an important quality of science fiction (and, not coincidentally, the name of a prominent journal in science fiction criticism). Speculating from what exists to what might exist defines science fiction. In science fiction, extrapolation is the process by which an author builds on what already exists, and asks, "What if this continues . . . or doesn't continue?" This essentially is the question called for by French feminist theorists as they envision a new language. Indeed, Monique

Wittig's famous *Les Guérillères* is a science fiction text at the same time that it is a work of feminist philosophy. Wittig imagines a world in which men and women live in literally separate cultures, and her text joins a long tradition in science fiction of representing men and women as alien to each other. Extrapolation keeps science fiction located in issues and ethics that are a part of contemporary human culture, and among those issues are women's concerns such as rape and abortion. In *Star Trek: The Next Generation*, episodes extrapolate from current feminism to a world dominated by women; from advances in reproductive technology to a male character's being raped metaphorically for his DNA. As the rest of this book demonstrates, *Star Trek: The Next Generation* uses extrapolation to comment on feminist issues in American culture.

A parallel to extrapolation, and another defining quality of science fiction, is defamiliarization or cognitive estrangement. Literary theorist Darko Suvin bases this idea on the work of Viktor Shklovsky, a Russian theorist. Suvin has popularized Shklovsky's idea about making the familiar seem new and strange, cognitively different. Although defamiliarization can appear in realistic fiction, this sense of estrangement appears in its most intense and concrete form in science fiction. For example, Octavia Butler defamiliarizes both the biological process and our attitudes toward reproduction and childbirth in a chilling Nebula Award–winning story about a pregnant man, "Bloodchild" (discussed in detail in *Frankenstein's Daughters*). Because a female alien impregnates a human male on her planet, we are estranged from our usual sentimental attitudes toward mothering and are thus encouraged to see the social process in a new light. In its treatment of alien reproduction, *Star Trek: The Next Generation* performs the same estrangement. The reader is thus able to examine a social phenomenon, such as childbearing, from a new angle when, for example, ship's counselor Deanna Troi becomes pregnant by an alien, her entire pregnancy lasts for only days, and she experiences no physical pain during delivery. French feminists' insistence on new ways of looking at the female body and at language are easier to imagine, and can become literal through defamiliarization. Seeing feminine and masculine in alien bodies, for example, allows us to see gendering from a less biased position. Sara Suleri claims, "If realism is the Eurocentric and patriarchal pattern of adjudicating between disparate cultural and ethnic realities, then it is surely the task of radical feminism to provide an alternative perspective" (277). Drawing on its antirealistic qualities of extrapolation and defamiliarization, science fiction can readily create this alternative perspective.

Star Trek and its spin-offs provide an excellent example of the connection between science fiction's alternative possibilities and feminism. *Sexual Generations* builds on the important work done by Henry Jenkins and Camille Bacon-Smith, who, in separate enterprises, examine *Star Trek's* female fans and their feminist revisions of the series. *Sexual Generations* moves from this important ethnographic work to discuss the texts that have generated this tremendous devotion and activity by female fans. As all critics of the original series acknowledge, the show was the first to provoke women's mass participation in science fiction. Although critics differ about what precisely drew women to the original series, women's participation is agreed to be central to the show and crucial to its incredible popularity.

In *Enterprising Women: Television Fandom and the Creation of Popular Myth,* Camille Bacon-Smith explores the female fan community in depth. Her detailed ethnography analyzes what she describes as "rebels in the cause of a women's art/communication system" (3). These female fans appropriate *Star Trek* not for financial gain, but because the text of *Star Trek* (the original series) motivates them to revise the stories and expand its canon. Creating in a variety of genres—fiction, poetry, art—and through loosely organized fan clubs, *Star Trek's* most dedicated female fans help create the *Star Trek* universe and keep it alive commercially. Their unauthorized, underground publications depict what is known as "slash" fiction or K/S fiction—stories using Kirk and Spock, but depicting them as homosexual lovers rather than comrades. Often explicitly erotic, these texts are but one example of the extratextual life of *Star Trek.*

Costuming and discussion groups are other common forms of group activity practiced by women fans. In *Star Trek Fans and Costume Art,* Heather R. Joseph-Witham explores how costuming enables women to assume aggressive or powerful positions not sanctioned in the "real" world; she shows that dressing as Klingons, a fierce warriorlike race, empowers women. In discussion groups, women fans can use the show to focus on issues of concern to them. For example, in *Textual Poachers,* Jenkins describes how one black female fan analyzes the treatment of black characters, "claiming a moral right to complain about producer actions challenging their [fans'] own interest in the series property" (87). In this specific instance, this female fan uses *Star Trek: The Next Generation* to demonstrate "her expertise over the program, the emotional investment she has made in the characters, justify[ing] an increasingly critical stance toward the institutions producing and circulating those materials"

(88). This power, Jenkins convincingly argues, arises from "the consensus of the fan community" (88). Being a fan, then, as Jenkins's and others' scholarship attests, involves much more than slavish devotion to a text. *Star Trek* promotes and invites an interactive and empowering relationship with its viewers.

Jenkins defines and analyzes the fan's use of "poaching," "a subculture that exists in the 'borderlands' between mass culture and everyday life and that constructs its own identity and artifacts from resources borrowed from already circulating texts" (3) such as *Star Trek* and *Star Trek: The Next Generation.* In addition to the printed material analyzed by Bacon-Smith, Jenkins includes more current fan creations, such as music videos. Discussing an audience that is "largely female, largely white, largely middle class, though it welcomes into its ranks many who would not fit this description" (1), Jenkins also points to the feminization of the figure of the fan, using *Star Trek* as an example (10). This feminization has also been stressed by Andreas Huyssen, in *After the Great Divide: Modernism, Mass Culture and Postmodernism,* in which he shows how in relation to high culture, all mass culture is feminized. *Star Trek: The Next Generation* typifies this gendering, both its continuum with classic *Trek* and its situation as a mass culture text—a syndicated, extremely popular television series that participates in fan culture. *Star Trek: The Next Generation* inspires extreme fan loyalty and has already lasted longer than classic *Trek*—seven years versus original *Trek*'s three-year run. And the first *Star Trek* film to feature only *The Next Generation* cast made over $92 million, the highest take yet for a *Star Trek* movie. *Star Trek: Insurrection* opened in 1998 with a weekend take of $22.1 million, debuting in the number-one spot at the box office. *Sexual Generations* closely analyzes the television episodes that produce such financial success and fan devotion, especially in female viewers. In part this devotion can be explained by *The Next Generation*'s use of feminism; as Marleen Barr explains, "*TNG* represents such a desire to represent competent women, to see women as something other than handmaids" ("Things" 232).

As its opening voiceover announces, *Star Trek: The Next Generation* plans "to boldly go where no *one* has gone before." This revision of the original *Star Trek*'s grand claim "to boldly go where no *man* has gone before" draws attention to the inclusion of woman in *Star Trek*'s imperial ambitions to colonize space.* (Gene Roddenberry, creator of *Star Trek*, envisioned the

---

*As Thomas Richards points out, "The Federation can also act like an empire in its relentless expansion into outer space. Here it is worth recalling that one half of the very title of the series, *Trek,* comes from the Afrikaans word meaning a slow and arduous journey toward a

This pulp science fiction cover reveals the identification of space as feminine.

series as a "Wagon Train to the stars"). His vision of the *Enterprise* casts the ship and its crew as pioneers exploring space. Yet, as we will see, the gender implications are more complicated than the mere inclusion of more female characters on the bridge of the starship *Enterprise.* For space itself, after all, is feminized, and so too is the colonial subject.

Space, as a stand-in for America's western frontier, evokes a feminine identity, as discussed by Annette Kolodny, Jane Tompkins, and others. But space already exists in science fiction as a female subject. This depiction of space as a female alien suggests that the female aliens who serve on the *Enterprise* or whom the *Enterprise* encounters in its voyages function as synecdoches for the exploration (and colonization) of space itself. When considered in light of science fiction, Julia Kristeva's famous description of gender differences also takes on a different meaning: "'Father's time, mother species,' as Joyce put it; and indeed, when evoking the name and destiny of women, one thinks more of the *space* generating and forming

new colony. The situation it evokes, that of nineteenth-century Dutch colonists expanding into an African continent already occupied by a variety of tribes, pushing them off their ancestral lands, and nearly exterminating them, serves to remind us that expansion always comes at a cost" (36).

the human species than of *time,* becoming, or history" ("Women's Time" 445). As Claudine Hermann explains metaphorically what becomes literal in *Star Trek: The Next Generation,* "In order to avoid total annihilation, to escape man's habitual urge to colonize, she [woman] must conserve some space for herself, a sort of no-man's land" (169). Outer space can function as a literalization of Hermann's description. So analyzing the treatment of gender in *Star Trek: The Next Generation* draws our attention to postcolonial discourse and to the figure of the female alien.

Science fiction may be especially suited to deal with postcolonial issues. Through extrapolation and defamiliarization, science fiction can draw on the expansion of "postcolonial" *from* (as Sara Suleri explains) "discursive practices produced by the historical fact of prior colonization in certain geographically specific segments of the world" *to* "an abstraction available for the figurative deployment in any strategic definition of marginality" (274). As this book shows, *Star Trek: The Next Generation* uses a postcolonial sensibility and the ship's actual colonial mission "to explore new life and new civilizations" to associate geographic colonization with the colonization of women, gay men and lesbians, and people of color. Though not always self-consciously critical of this parallel, the series nevertheless draws our attention to it, enabling viewers to see the ways in which systems of domination are perpetuated. Through defamiliarization, these groups are represented by aliens and machines. *Star Trek: The Next Generation* uses postcolonialism in the way Sara Suleri describes the category of postcolonialism in general: "both as a free-floating metaphor for cultural embattlement and as an almost obsolete signifier for the historicity of race" (274). As the crew of the *Enterprise* confronts difference in aliens and alien culture, these conflicts inevitably reflect back on American confrontations with other nations and cultures, and on gendered and racial conflict within American society.

Star Trek: The Next Generation grapples with the issues that mark the mid-1980s and early 1990s. As the Berlin Wall and the Soviet Union collapsed, as second-wave feminism experienced backlash and "postfeminism," *Star Trek: The Next Generation* reflected and confronted a postmodern concern about subjectivity, gender, and political power. In its overt representation of an idealized American society projected into the future, *Star Trek: The Next Generation* allows us to examine American preoccupations with power and gender. A major reason for America's ascendancy as a world power has been our preeminence as a scientific power. The race to space, after all, was "won" by the United States when we triumphed over the Russians by landing men on the moon, and this triumph was based on our scientific prowess. And descriptions of the importance of science have been continually couched in terms of the nation's virility and ability to dominate other countries.

Science's cultural preeminence hardly needs arguing. As the authors of *Not in Our Genes,* a widely acclaimed analysis of biological determinism, point out, "Science is now the source of legitimacy for ideology" (Lewontin et al. 29). The connection of ideology to politics is made clear by historians of science such as Donna Haraway and French feminist philosopher Luce Irigaray. In *Primate Visions,* Haraway exposes the gendering of primatology and its national politics. In "Is the Subject of Science Sexed?" Luce Irigaray similarly critiques scientific imperialism and argues that the subject of science is sexed in a number of disciplines, from economics to linguistics to biology. As historians of science such as Stephen Jay Gould show, science has been used to justify the subordination of oppressed groups, especially women. Feminist criticisms of science often focus on language; analyzing language illuminates the gender politics in *Star Trek: The Next Generation. Star Trek: The Next Generation* especially deserves critical scrutiny for what it reveals about attitudes toward women, science, and gender. It is science, after all, that provides legitimacy for many of our social decisions, from schooling to medical treatment. So it behooves feminists to examine popular science fiction texts for the ways in which gender roles are promulgated and also resisted.

Although the gendering of science has been around since Aristotle (and in modern science since Newton), this pattern assumes a redoubled power when, as with America, the gendered language of science is connected to the authority of a world leader. This use of science was especially pronounced in the original *Star Trek,* as the editors of *Enterprise Zones* note: "*Star Trek*'s promises for a better future include more advanced technology, greater political efficiency, and abundant moral and social progress. These assurances rely on Science to meet all human (and most 'alien') personal and social needs" (Harrison et al. 1). In a more subtle form, *Star Trek: The Next Generation* continues to rely on science as moral authority and justification. In *Star Trek: The Next Generation,* the gendering of science depicts women as practitioners of a nonrational intuitive science and male characters wielding a superior power of rationality. Many of the episodes reify the traditional gendering of science as masculine, placing the feminine in a subordinate, colonized position. Even a "woman of science," the ship's chief medical officer, Dr. Beverly Crusher, is shaped more by her femininity than by her medical, scientific training.

The use of Beverly Crusher's name, as well as her function in many episodes, reveals her fundamental femininity. In a move greatly debated in the years when the show ran, Beverly is referred to by her first name, whereas the male characters are referred to either by a role ("captain") or by a last name (Riker). The other two major female characters, Tasha Yar and Deanna Troi, also are tagged by their first names. This book follows this practice, not because I agree with this subordination of women by the use of their first names, but because identifying the characters as they are referred to in the show keeps their status firmly in view. Through gendered language, as with the gendering of scientific discourse, the feminine is reminded of its subordinate place. As viewers, we are encouraged to feel closer, more intimate with the female characters, which may have positive effects, as well as the more obvious communication of disrespect for the female characters' positions.

Sexual Generations draws primarily on feminist theory to analyze issues that emerge from the series. This book emphasizes not only the genre of science fiction germane to the series, especially extrapolation and defamiliarization, but also French feminist theory, particularly that of Julia Kristeva, Hélène Cixous, and Catherine Clément. These theorists became influential in America just before and during the time *Star Trek: The Next Generation* aired, and reflect the same cultural interests that appear in the television show. In her insightful analysis of *Star Trek: The Next Generation,* Lynne Joyrich suggests that the structure of the series itself focuses on the feminine. Although Joyrich does not draw on French feminists, her description of the series uses language that evokes concepts central to French feminist theory: "The show's narrative progression is frequently upset by circularity, multiple identifications, contradictions, and failed closures" ("Feminist" 74).

French feminist theory parallels, perhaps even predicts, *Star Trek: The Next Generation*'s fluid structure. French feminist philosophers Hélène Cixous, Catherine Clément, Luce Irigaray, and Julia Kristeva all share an interest in "revolutionary" language; that is, language that resists traditional hierarchical patterns of power and control. Identifying nascent, as yet incompletely realized language as feminine, these writers stress gender rather than biological difference, though of course the two are related. Because of their subject positions, women are more likely to have access to a new language. Concomitantly, science fiction as a genre that tries to represent what *could* be has more access to the as-yet-uncreated, what Clement identifies as an imaginary zone. More focused on feminine and masculine than male and female, French feminist ideas became quite popular in academic circles during the 1980s. American versions of the same ideas appeared in mainstream publications such as Carol Gilligan's *In a Different Voice* and Mary Belenky et al.'s *Women's Ways of Knowing*. But it is the specifically French feminist emphasis on language and desire and structure that pertains most particularly to *Star Trek: The Next Generation*.

Although Joyrich does not explicitly name the show's similarity to French feminist theory, such a close parallel is not coincidental. That both French feminist theory and *Star Trek: The Next Generation* were popular at the same time (albeit with different groups) suggests that both resonated with the cultural forces at work in America in 1987–94. In her book *Re-viewing Reception,* Joyrich focuses on the fluidity and resistance of women and television, and *Star Trek: The Next Generation* does reflect, as she argues, the qualities this intersection creates in television in general. But *Star Trek: The Next Generation* also comes out of a rich literary tradition that was obsessed with the figure of the Woman from its very beginnings. *Sexual Generations* focuses on this science fiction tradition and the way French feminist theorists' exploration of the feminine helps us understand the show's use of gender.

Sexual Generations is divided into two parts: The first section, "*Star Trek: The Next Generation* and the Feminine," analyzes female figures. Chapter 1, "'The Sensors Are Having Difficulty Penetrating the Interiors': The Female Alien," explores the depiction of feminine power and its containment through the figure of the female alien. A literal embodiment of sexual difference, the female alien can be humanoid, as in "The Vengeance Factor," in which a beautiful woman is unnaturally long-lived and an assassin, or she can be a space monster, as in "Galaxy's Child," in which a giant female alien threatens the *Enterprise*. A few female aliens fall between these two extremes, as in "The Bonding," in which a female alien masquerades as a human female. The female alien may assume a variety of guises, but she always represents an aspect or aspects of human women. Because the female alien usually represents a threat to be conquered, this figure stresses both the power of the feminine and the necessity and justification for male dominance.

Chapter 2, "'A Threat to the Entire Future of the Federation': The Woman Ruler," analyzes a version of the female alien in which she rules societies and even entire planets. "Angel One" depicts a female dystopia in which women rather than men dominate an entire planet. In "Conspiracy," nonhumanoid parasitic female aliens almost succeed in taking over the Federation by infiltrating and dominating human males. And

"The Dauphin" shows a young male ensign falling in love with a beautiful and metamorphic female ruler, whom he must learn to reject. In these episodes the feminine is presented as politically powerful, a force to be respected. Yet, as Marleen Barr notes in her discussion of the series' last episode, "All Good Things . . . ," *Star Trek: The Next Generation* "conveys mixed messages; it simultaneously questions patriarchal power and yet is unable to depict a woman continuing to wield power" (238).

Chapter 3, "'I Am for You': The Perfect Mate," deals with a male fantasy of a woman who is created to reflect and serve a man. The correlative to the female aliens and women rulers of the first two chapters, "I Am for You" depicts the show's use of a male fantasy of a subservient woman to expose the problem with the fantasy. In "Loud as a Whisper," an alien male ambassador uses interpreters who are headed by a female and who are feminized, to speak for him. In "The Perfect Mate" a female alien who bonds with just one man falls in love with Captain Picard accidentally, and both Kamala, the female alien, and Picard must come to terms with her debilitating bonding. In "Man of the People" and "Eye of the Beholder," Counselor Deanna Troi stands in for all women as she is abused by men who take advantage of her empathic reactions to them. Through science fiction tropes, *Star Trek: The Next Generation* extrapolates the effect of gender segregation and exposes the cost to women of their sex-typed roles as reflections of men.

Whereas the first half of the book focuses on the representation of the feminine, the second half of the book focuses on issues in contemporary society of particular concern to feminists, such as homophobia, racism, the treatment of rape, and abortion. "*Star Trek: The Next Generation* and Sexual and Racial Politics" deals with the show's reflection and commentary on social issues. Chapter 4, "'Fully Functional': Machines and Gender," focuses on the parallels between race and sexual orientation in the representation of machine life, especially in the character of Data, the android. This chapter shows how the character of Data is used to explore and criticize sexism and racism. Because he is placed in a subordinate and subservient position, Data is feminized, as are machines in general. In "11001001" a species closely linked to a master computer evokes a metaphorical and stereotypical rendering of the feminine, and in "The Quality of Life," Data risks his career and his captain's life to protect a new, feminine machine species. In "The Naked Now" and "The Most Toys" we see the ugly side of prejudice against the feminine and species (sexism and racism) when Data is unfairly treated as an object, as property.

Chapter 5, "'What Makes You Think You Can Dictate How We Love?': Sexual Orientation," explores the representation of sexual orientation in the two episodes explicitly devoted to the topic. In "The Outcast" Commander Riker falls in love with a female alien from an apparently androgynous race. Condemned for her "feminine" leanings, this alien must fight brainwashing. In "The Host" Beverly Crusher falls in love with an alien who can be either male or female. She meets the alien when he is male, and when that body fails and is replaced with a female body, Beverly confronts homophobia.

Chapter 6, "'We Weren't Meant to Know Each Other at All': Race," analyzes the intersection of race and gender in the series. "Code of Honor" casts a white female character, chief of security Tasha Yar, against a black female alien, Yareena, in a literal fight-to-the-death that illustrates the ways in which black and white women are set at odds with each other. "The Emissary" deals with mulatta politics and what "race" means, both in contemporary America and in the future; the episode extrapolates from and defamiliarizes our sense of "race." In a complementary fashion, "Yesterday's Enterprise" uses the science fiction setting of an alternative timeline to feature Guinan, a wise female alien played by Whoopi Goldberg.

Chapter 7, "'The Right to Exercise Control': Reproductive Politics," reveals the ways in which abortion is discussed and presented in a new defamiliarized aspect. This chapter deals with rape and abortion, as in "Up the Long Ladder" Commander Riker is metaphorically raped when his DNA is stolen. He is allowed to retrieve it and terminate the "pregnancy" that has ensued. In "The Child" Deanna Troi experiences an unplanned pregnancy with an unknown alien rapist; the ensuing debate and threat to the ship posed by the child raise the issue of abortion explicitly. In "The Offspring" Data confronts abortion when he creates a child who cannot survive independent of him. The solutions in these episodes reveal the complex and conflicted nature of American abortion politics.

Chapter 8, "'No, I Won't Let You': Rape, Romance, and Consent," analyzes the way in which contemporary debates about rape appear in the series. In "Violations" Deanna Troi is mentally raped by a male alien. As the episode explores her assault, the show sympathetically deals with feminist issues about consent and rape investigations. In "Sub Rosa" Beverly Crusher survives rape and battering from a male alien. Both episodes depict the female characters' overcoming the assault and wreaking vengeance on their attackers. Although both rapes are psychic, they clearly stand in for the physical assaults that are such a part of women's lives in the twentieth century.

Star Trek: The Next Generation covers topics of central interest to feminists: the representation of women and the feminine, sexual orientation, race, abortion, and rape. As it does so, the show uses science fiction's unique qualities to explore gender and science, women and language, and the definition of difference. Any television show reflects the concerns of its society, but because of its extended run, tremendous popularity, and unique interactive relationship with its fans, *Star Trek: The Next Generation* has a great deal to offer its viewers and feminists. As both a feminist and a fan of *Star Trek* in all its forms, I offer *Sexual Generations* as part of a continuing mission to explore strange new worlds and to discover new life—to boldly go where no one (but *Star Trek)* has gone before.

Part 1

"The Sensors Are Having Difficulty Penetrating the Interiors": The Female Alien

As later chapters on female rulers, the perfect mate, machines, sexual orientation, abortion, and rape demonstrate, *Star Trek: The Next Generation* foregrounds cultural anxieties about gender. But because all these topics work through the figure of the female alien, we must begin with her.

Through the character of the female alien, *Star Trek: The Next Generation* draws on a fascinating and protofeminist tradition in science fiction. From the first modern science fiction novel, Mary Shelley's *Frankenstein*, through the pulp science fiction magazines of the 1940s and 1950s and through contemporary feminist redactions, the female alien always appears deadlier than the male of the species. Science fiction writers reveal an obsession with woman as Other and with specifically feminine traits such as mothering, nurturing, and sexual attractiveness to males. Through such representations, science fiction explores and interprets gender difference. Science fiction, including *Star Trek: The Next Generation*, acknowledges and defines feminine power.*

French feminist theory provides a helpful frame for exploring feminine power in *Star Trek: The Next Generation*. Exploring feminine power and potential power is a central focus of French feminist theory, which became available and much discussed during the mid-1980s, when *Star Trek: The*

---

*The cultural reduction of woman to reproductive organ described by Simone de Beauvoir and other feminist critics helps explain why science fiction has been fascinated with the female alien. Through their reproductive capacity, women have the power to threaten patriarchy, which explains both the fear of women and their oppression. The power of reproduction makes women essential to the human race, but they also control patriarchal lineage because the child is incontrovertibly only the woman's. In her award-winning study of motherhood, *Of Woman Born*, Adrienne Rich explains, "There is much to suggest that the male mind has always been haunted by the force of the idea of *dependence on a woman for life itself,*

Next Generation began its seven-year run. French feminist theory depicts the feminine as powerful and threatening to the patriarchal order. With its emphasis on a new kind of language, *l'écriture feminine*, or "writing the body," French feminists stress the radical and discontinuous nature of the feminine. Focusing on figures such as the hysteric, the witch, and the Medusa, French feminist theorists Hélène Cixous and Catherine Clément especially laud these rebellious enactments of femininity. "The feminine role," Cixous and Clément explain, "the role of the sorceress, of hysteric, is ambiguous, antiestablishment" (5). They celebrate these figures, pointing out that "woman, the periodic being, takes part in something not contained in culture" (8). Women's laughter is depicted as powerful, "like Medusa's laugh—petrifying and shattering constraints" (32). Through the female alien, the figures of the sorceress, hysteric, and Medusa coalesce, but with a metaphorical impact missing in the realistic if utopian visions of Cixous and Clément. *Star Trek: The Next Generation* depicts female aliens who embody the visions of French feminist theory. The phrase "female alien" itself might seem redundant, as in Western culture, female is traditionally cast as Other.

These female aliens embody the Other as the feminine as described by Simone de Beauvoir in *The Second Sex*. Building on her classic work, French feminist theory uses the insights of psychoanalysis to explore how "othered" woman is. As Homi Bhabha describes for the racial other, the feminine functions, especially in *Star Trek: The Next Generation,* as both phobia and fetish. Julia Kristeva describes why the feminine works this way in slightly different but cognate terms. Drawing on woman as Mother, Kristeva sees what she calls "the abject" as being inextricably connected to the maternal. She describes the cultural fascination with the

---

the son's constant effort to assimilate, compensate for or deny the fact that he is 'of woman born'" (xiii). Rich defines motherhood as "the biological potential or capacity to bear and nourish human life" and the cultural power attributed to motherhood as "the magical power invested in women by men, whether in the form of Goddess-worship or the fear of being controlled or overwhelmed by women" (xv). Her interpretation of this gender dynamic is underscored by Julia Kristeva's description of the archaic and all-powerful mother from whom the human infant must separate: "Fear of the archaic mother turns out to be fear of her generative power" (*Powers* 77). Woman's reproductive power is related to her sexual power and attractiveness to men. In many science fiction stories, human males are mesmerized by seductive and dangerous female aliens. Through this female alien, male science fiction writers can discuss the ways in which men feel threatened by their sexual and reproductive dependence on women. In some cases, the female aliens are depicted as evil, in others, beneficent, but their sexual allure always makes them a threat to men and, by extension, to patriarchal society.

"desirable and terrifying, nourishing and murderous, fascinating and abject inside of the maternal body" (*Powers* 54). As she explains, "What we designate as 'feminine' far from being a primeval essence, will be seen as an 'other' without a name" (58). And indeed, some female aliens are nameless others who function as terrifying and dangerous maternal bodies. Repeatedly, in *Star Trek: The Next Generation*, the female alien represents what men both fear and desire.

Episodes of *Star Trek: The Next Generation* stress the changeability and performativity of femininity. In each instance, the female alien has many appearances and tremendous powers usually associated with witches: the power to read minds (telepathy), move objects using only her mind (teleportation), and transform her physical appearance (metamorphosis). Each episode also reveals a tension between the rigid hierarchy of Starfleet, usually represented by Captain Picard and characterized as masculine, and the fluid mutability of the female alien, characterized as feminine and celebrated as such in French feminist theory.

With her strong and assertive sexuality, the female alien belies stereotypes of feminine passivity and stresses, as Irigaray and other French feminists do, the multiplicity of the feminine, especially feminine sexuality. Irigaray's description of woman aptly defines the female alien: "She resists all adequate definition. Further she has no 'proper name'" (*This Sex* 26). The female alien also usually turns out to be part of a collective group or mind: *"She is neither one nor two"* (26). Because she uses telepathy or her body as a form of language, the female alien is freed from the order and hierarchy inherent in the symbolic order, the structure of language that governs and defines society and self from a masculine perspective. Repeatedly the plots of *Star Trek: The Next Generation* show the female alien, as Irigaray calls for, "upsett[ing] the linearity of a project, undermin-[ing] the goal-object of a desire" (30). Perhaps most importantly, through a science fiction setting and a female alien we can see the "jamming of the theoretical machinery itself, of suspending its pretension to the production of a truth and of a meaning that are excessively univocal" (78). By her very existence a female alien draws attention to the otherness of the feminine and the possibility of alternatives to patriarchal society.

As powerful and threatening to the symbolic order as she is, the female alien exists only temporarily. At the end of each episode, the feminine threat to patriarchal structure is defeated. However, the fact that the threats are only temporarily banished, and continually reappear in other episodes, suggests the disruptive power of the feminine. Here too the pattern follows a description by Cixous and Clément of the sorceress and hysteric: "Every sorceress ends up being destroyed, and nothing is registered of her but mythical traces. Every hysteric ends up inuring others to her symptoms and the family closes around her again" (5). In its development of the female alien, *Star Trek: The Next Generation* keeps the specter of feminine power in front of the viewer's eyes. This television show's obsession with the female alien indicates that the apparently liberal culture represented by *Star Trek: The Next Generation* reveals contradictory impulses about gender. The radical feminist potential represented by the female alien shows what liberalism both desires and fears about feminine power. In early episodes, the female alien represents primarily what men fear, as in "Galaxy's Child." In episodes late in the series, the female alien appears as what men most desire, as the episode "The Vengeance Factor" shows. And in between, a balance between fear and desire occurs; "True Q" illustrates this tension.

In some episodes, feminine power appears as a visual spectacle, but in a nonhumanoid form that evokes Laura Mulvey's call for nonrepresentational cinema to free woman from the dominance of the "male gaze." Because the creature is nonhumanoid, she defies conventional sexualization of the female image. Although the captain and others on the bridge are struck by the creature's beauty and size, the plot undercuts the powerful visual spectacle of a nonhumanoid female. An enormous and beautiful female alien dominates the screen in "Galaxy's Child." In keeping with their mission "to seek out new life," the *Enterprise* follows her energy signature in order to study her. A large entity who lives freely in space, she is first admired, but then destroyed by Captain Picard when she threatens the *Enterprise.* The being turns out to have been pregnant, so the bridge crew, with the help of a visiting engineer, Dr. Leah Brahms, devises a way to cut the infant free, but the child in turn threatens the *Enterprise.* "Galaxy's Child," written by Maurice Hurley, first aired the week of March 11, 1991. The episode has two plots. Ship's engineer Geordi La Forge meets the woman of his dreams, Brahms, of whom he has created a fantasy program on the holodeck, and the main plot focuses on a female alien threatening the *Enterprise* with destruction. The two plots intersect as La Forge and Brahms overcome Geordi's obsession with Brahms to work together productively. They must use their intellects to find an engineering solution when the alien's baby attaches itself to the ship. Draining the *Enterprise*'s energy, the alien's child "nurses," but it will destroy the ship and the crew if it continues to do so.

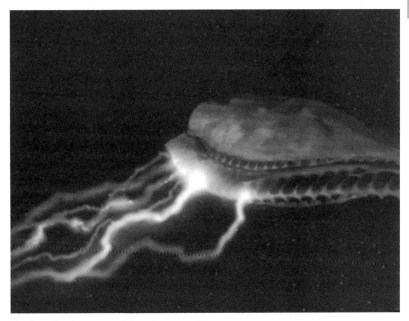

The female alien, powerful and pregnant.

Like the episodes discussed in chapter 7, "Galaxy's Child" raises the issue of reproductive choice. The captain's orders to stun the gigantic female alien accidentally result in her death. Shaken, the captain wants to save the alien's fetus, still trapped inside the mother's body. The operation on the alien female parallels the original cesarean, so called because Caesar was removed from his mother's dead body. The captain's action appears to support Thomas Richards's assertion that "No matter what the species, *Star Trek* always treats the situation of a mother protecting her young very sympathetically" (47). However, a careful reading of the episode reveals that the situation is more complicated than the simple one Richards describes. As he does in later episodes, Worf, as security chief, raises issues of reproductive choice. Should the mother (now the *Enterprise*) be considered before the fetus? Worf argues against freeing the fetus because it may pose a threat to the *Enterprise* as its biological mother did. As usual, Worf turns out to be right. The liberated infant attaches itself to the *Enterprise,* draining it of energy and threatening the entire crew. Here a metaphorical abortion is the issue, for the crew must find a way to remove the infant from the ship as it threatens its new "mother's" existence. Evacuating the air from a shuttle bay and blowing the alien out and away from the ship evokes a suction abortion. But the abortion theme is muted here. The emphasis is far more on the femininity of space and the power of female fecundity.

The seductive power of the female form is also introduced through La Forge's fascination with Leah Brahms and her arrival on the ship just before they encounter the giant female alien. The female alien first becomes visible as "an asymmetrical field of intense energy" (Data). The power and magnificence of the female alien are stressed by her uniqueness and by her positioning in our field of vision. In a number of shots, repeated each time there is a commercial break, we see her floating in space, looking like a giant pierogi. A clam-like object with frilled edges, the entity glides above the *Enterprise,* with a planet looming in the background. The female alien's shape evokes the diagrams of fallopian tubes in anatomy textbooks. Struck by her size and free movement in space, Captain Picard ruminates out loud: "What would it be like," he muses, "no ship, no bulky space suit—just to live between the stars, have the entire galaxy as a home?" His patent envy of the female creature, untrammeled by male-dominated technology, stresses the closeness of the female creature with nature. The captain's inability to know or experience such freedom reveals his inadequacy in comparison to the female alien. It prepares us for a parallel envy and fear of her power of reproduction, as Rich and Kristeva stress of human women in social and psychoanalytic contexts.

The creature also demonstrates her feminine power in another way—by resisting the ship's attempt to probe her. "The sensors are having difficulty penetrating the interiors," Data reports, in language that makes clear the entity's femininity and Starfleet's masculinity. The inability of the sensors reflects the inability of the masculine to comprehend or contain the feminine. Data's language also reflects the pervasive gendering of scientific discourse, as documented by Evelyn Fox Keller, Nancy Tuana, and many others.* Nature is depicted as feminine, resisting the domination of technology, which is coded as masculine. This gendering thus accentuates the play of power, resistance, and control between men and women. Because female aliens' resistance usually threatens Starfleet and the *Enterprise,* the shows emphasize feminine power and strength. Yet the threat the female alien poses justifies using any manner of force to destroy the threat to patriarchy. For a feminist viewer, the message is a mixed one; we are allowed to admire the female alien's strength, but she is eventually destroyed and presented as unknowable.

*See the edited collections by Evelyn Fox Keller and Nancy Tuana, both entitled *Feminism and Science.*

When the creature emits blue rays that strike the ship, the *Enterprise* strikes back, killing her accidentally. Appearing much larger than the ship, the female alien floats aimlessly above the *Enterprise*. Captain Picard is relieved that the existence of a fetus in some way mitigates the loss of the mother. There could be no clearer way of announcing that women's worth exists in their ability to reproduce. Technology must be used to rescue the fetus because technology has caused the mother's death. In language that will echo in other episodes, Beverly Crusher announces that "the offspring is still premature." Using their weapons of war, the phasers, they cut the fetus free, leaving Beverly to declare, "Captain, I'd like to announce the birth of a large baby something." The announcement of "something" where traditionally a sex is identified underscores its sexual ambiguity. Significantly, however, several members of the crew take to calling the baby "junior." Yet because the creature looks just like its mother, it is just as likely to also be "feminine" in that it too could give birth.

Just as dangerous to the *Enterprise* as its mother, the baby latches on to the ship. As Dr. Crusher describes it, "it's imprinted on us. It thinks the *Enterprise* is its mother." But technology can only temporarily replace biology, for the *Enterprise* will be destroyed if the baby does not stop draining the ship's energy. This crisis can be read as reifying the importance of the maternal body. Technology causes problems (the mother's death) and cannot replace her permanently. As Deanna explains, "It's feeding off the energy of the *Enterprise* as it would off its mother." Despite the *Enterprise*'s status as the flagship of Starfleet, it cannot equal a biological mother, and will be destroyed if it remains a surrogate mother to the alien. They try to suck the baby off by creating a vacuum in the shuttle bay it has latched on to, but this operation fails. Where the female doctor fails, the female engineer Brahms and La Forge decide to "sour the milk" of the energy, encouraging the infant to detach by making its nourishment unpalatable. They must persuade rather than enforce its detachment. From a nearby asteroid belt, three adult aliens emerge, presumably to take care of the mewling infant entity. Brahms and La Forge's collaboration is a success, but only in engineering terms. La Forge must relinquish his fantasy of Brahms as a sexual partner. In his holodeck simulation, Brahms is his ideal and willing partner. But technology can only temporarily replace a "real" woman, just as technology can only temporarily replace a "real" mother. La Forge must accept that Brahms is married, and the episode ends with a solitary La Forge staring off into the stars in Ten-Forward, the ship's bar. His failed romance with Brahms parallels the failed union of the ship with an infant alien.

"Galaxy's Child" reifies the representation of maternal femininity as biological. Maternity is part of nature, and thus alien to technology, which can substitute only temporarily for biological mothering. It is the fate of masculinity to explore space only through technology, never completely being a part of what it explores. If maternity and nature are feminine, and technology masculine, space remains a natural space, a womb, a vacuum to be penetrated and then filled by colonization of the patriarchal Federation.

Producer Brannon Braga's fantasy, reported by Jeff Greenwald, is surely pertinent here. Braga explains, "'The female body, as a functional instrument, obsesses me'" (55–56). Directly connecting the female body to science fiction, Braga continues, "'My greatest fantasy is to be with the fifty-foot woman from those schmaltzy 1950s sci-fi films. That would be the ultimate: to actually *crawl up into a vagina*'" (56). Braga's revealing fantasy surely explains the appeal and recurrence of depictions of the female alien, not just because as the show's producer he can realize such visions, but because the science fiction tradition fosters such images of the feminine. But the monstrous fifty-foot woman is alienated from others and others are alienated from her because of her immensity, as the humans on the *Enterprise* cannot communicate with or comprehend the gigantic female alien they encounter.

And as La Forge must accept his solitary state, so must the humans who journey on the *Enterprise*. Almost by definition as a part of Starfleet, they are committed to a masculine ethos of individuality and soldierhood. They define themselves as not feminine, not the female alien. The masculine order invariably kills the female alien simply by contacting her. Having learned this lesson, the *Enterprise* doesn't even try to communicate with the baby or adult aliens, but leaves them (the feminine) abruptly. As they leave, Brahms is congratulated by the captain for weaning the baby and it is a weaning, a separation from the mother, nature, and femininity, that defines all of Starfleet and *Star Trek: The Next Generation*.

Similarly, "The Bonding" uses a female alien to celebrate masculine separation from the mother, and bonding of men. First airing the week of October 23, 1989, "The Bonding" was written by Ronald D. Moore. In this episode, a young boy's mother is killed on an archaeological mission to a planet where war left dangerous mines still active. The mother is killed accidentally when she activates one. Worf, the chief of security, leads the team, but cannot save the woman, Marla Aster. Orphaned himself at the age of six, Worf has strong feelings of guilt and regret over the woman's death. Her son, Jeremy, is left an orphan, too; his father was killed years earlier. A female alien from the planet appears as a cloud of energy and transforms itself into an exact duplicate of Jeremy's mother, attempting to replace her. The female alien tries to take Jeremy to her planet, but the captain, Worf, and Deanna Troi stop her. Jeremy accepts his loss and bonds with Worf in a Klingon ceremony of brotherhood as the episode concludes.

As soon as he learns of the death of Marla Aster, Captain Picard complains that "carrying children on a space ship seems a very questionable policy." He questions the presence of a family on board his ship, which requires him to, in this case, inform a child of his mother's death. Worf also resents the death, and at the beginning of the show asks counselor Troi about his performing the bonding ceremony with Jeremy. Deanna warns Worf that now is not the time, that Jeremy will be angry with Worf for leading the expedition on which his mother died. Worf agrees to wait. What he must wait for, it turns out, is the appearance of the female alien, who enables the captain, Worf, and Jeremy to exorcise the specter of femininity from the ship and their lives.

The specter of femininity appears to be controllable when transferred to video or filtered through a representation such as the holodeck. As we saw in "Galaxy's Child," La Forge is more comfortable with the holodeck fantasy he creates of Leah Brahms than with the actual woman. And Jeremy's mother appears in a home video—it is from that image that the female alien creates the illusion of the woman. These two fantasies contrast sharply with the female alien of "Galaxy's Child," who resists control by remaining nonhumanoid. She can be killed, but not dominated. At first, the female alien who becomes Jeremy's mother appears in nonhumanoid form, but she quickly changes to adapt to the *Enterprise*'s social order. We see energy beams gathering on the planet's surface, and then Deanna senses a presence on the ship. The blue energy field leaves the planet, enters the ship, and assumes the form of Jeremy's mother. As Jeremy watches a video of his mother, dressed not in uniform but matronly clothes, he smiles. Then, magically, she appears just behind him, dressed in the same clothes as in the video. She is dressed like a middle-class mother: short, permed hair, a perky smile, and a peach-colored shirt with a vest and pants. She represents an idealization of the mother as always happy and engaged with her child. Such a vision must be a fantasy, for as Thomas Richards asserts, "The fact is unavoidable: every major character on *Star Trek* comes from a broken or fragmented home" (71).

This female alien, like that in "Galaxy's Child," cannot be detected by the ship's sensors. Such failure reveals the ineffectiveness of technology

The female alien as middle-class mom.

in mapping the feminine. Technology's failure emphasizes that the symbolic order cannot contain or represent the feminine, suggesting that men cannot read or understand woman. In Irigaray's words, the feminine uses "language in which 'she' sets off all directions, leaving 'him' unable to discern the coherence of any meaning" (*This Sex* 29). So the female aliens the *Enterprise* encounters defy the ship's technology and reading capability.

In a number of shots that emphasize her corporeality, the female alien masquerading as Jeremy's mom holds him. The female alien uses the human body of a mother to stress physicality and touch. She promises never to leave Jeremy and tries a number of times to take him to the transporter room, to take him to her planet, where she will keep the fantasy of his mother's presence alive. When he refuses to accompany her, she uses her magic on the ship. The female alien transforms Jeremy's sparse quarters into his home as it appears in the video. She even includes the boy's pet cat, who purrs and rubs against Jeremy when he picks it up. Taking Jeremy in her arms, the female alien explains, "It's your home and it makes you happy." She explains to the captain that she wants to rectify the sad accident of the bomb explosion that killed Jeremy's mother. The ruins that Jeremy's mother was investigating were the remains of a war. The planet had two races: humanoids who destroyed themselves and the energy beings who still survive. The energy beings are a feminized group species who oppose suffering. The female alien asserts that "I will be every bit his mother." She will protect and cherish him. With her superhuman powers, she can provide Jeremy with everything and everyone he desires.

But Captain Picard, Worf, and to a lesser extent Deanna Troi oppose the female alien's vision of maternal love and protection. Picard insists that pain and alienation are "an essential part" of being human. Picard claims the boy by placing his hand on Jeremy's shoulder and calling all of the female alien's representations a "total fiction." His words show a conflict of value systems and representations: the alien's feminine, communal, mother-child-centered vision versus Picard's (and Worf's) representation of the solitary male individual. The masculinity of this view is emphasized when Wesley Crusher is brought in to talk to Jeremy. Wesley's father died on a mission led by Captain Picard; as Wesley expresses his anger at Picard and explains how he now transcends that anger and understands, Jeremy listens raptly to the older boy. Worf then offers to bond with Jeremy and explains how he, Worf, lost his parents. These stories vanquish the female alien, who listens in silence, places a hand on Jeremy's shoulder, mutely walks away, and then vanishes. The parallel movement to Picard's hand on the child's shoulder represents the male-female struggle for control. The narrative of masculine authority, suffering, and death literally silences the female alien/mother. This plot recalls Nancy Chodorow's description of the need for a male to separate from his mother, that being a male adult means distancing yourself from your mother.*

The room changes from the cozy domestic home scene back to the *Enterprise,* and the episode concludes with Jeremy and Worf using phallic candles and sashes to complete the Klingon ritual of male bonding. Here masculinity overcomes species difference, for Jeremy is not Klingon, but human. They light candles together, merging the flames, and Worf places his hand on the boy's shoulder. In Klingon, Worf gutturally makes a series of sounds. When Jeremy asks what it means, Worf explains, "It honors the memory of our mothers. We have bonded and our families are stronger." This ceremony makes it clear that women function better as memories rather than inconvenient actual presences, as the female alien was. The boy repeats the Klingon phrases and the two males smile; the camera cuts to the ship rapidly moving away from the female alien's planet. The meaning of the ceremony and episode is clear. The mother (both his biological mother and the replacement, the female alien) must

---

*I am indebted to Jane Donawerth for pointing out this parallel.

die, becoming only memories for the boy to reach manhood and for the men to bond. They must leave domesticity, love, and nurturing behind. That also means leaving the planet, or nature, far behind. Mothering and nurturing are depicted as "total fiction" and must be rejected. "The Bonding" thus repeats the message of "Galaxy's Child," but does so even more explicitly because it uses a female alien who assumes a humanoid guise. The connections of female aliens to real human mothers and traditional feminine values are thus more concretely depicted and rejected.

Another episode, "Imaginary Friend," takes the idea of a fictional companion and uses the trope to emphasize gender. Here, too, a disembodied female alien represented by a beam of energy takes the shape of a human female to challenge the patriarchal order of Starfleet. The episode first aired the week of May 4, 1992, and the credits reflect the collaborative nature of episodic television; significantly, perhaps, a number of the creators were women. The teleplay was written by Edith Swensen and Brannon Braga, from a story idea by freelancers Ronald Wilderson, Jean Matthias, and Richard Fliegel. Actresses play key parts, as Deanna Troi reassures a father that his daughter Clara's preoccupation with an imaginary playmate is quite normal. Just as the *Enterprise* begins to explore a rare nebula, however, the playmate, called Isabella, materializes into corporeal form. The viewers realize that Isabella is really a creature of pure energy, an alien, who has taken the form of a young girl. Isabella takes Clara all over the ship, getting her into trouble for going where children are not allowed. The *Enterprise* becomes ensnared in strands of energy in the nebula and is in danger of being destroyed. The captain and Clara confront Isabella, and she and her fellow aliens decide not to destroy the *Enterprise*.

This alien is decidedly female. First, we see her as an apparently genderless ball of energy, floating through the ship. But she chooses a flower to light upon, and then, from all the possible lifeforms she could choose, turns herself into a young girl. Her place of transformation is the greenhouse, just as Clara plants seeds—the allusion to reproduction could not be more blatant, as Clara talks to herself about "baby seeds." Her human friend is female, as are the other characters who either had an imaginary playmate, like Guinan, or who take the playmate seriously, like Deanna Troi. But perhaps the most telling aspect of her femininity is Isabella's nonhumanoid form. The red ball may not seem especially feminine, but as the alien's true form is illuminated, we see that it is womblike and that the *Enterprise* is enveloped by blood-red, densely woven strands. That the race is an apparently collaborative group organism also makes it feminine rather than masculine. In science fiction in general as well as *Star Trek: The Next Generation* in particular, masculine is usually human and individual. Our plucky autonomy is what separates humans from other beings. In contrast, female aliens embrace communality and values associated with the feminine, especially the idea of doubleness, or multiplicity, as Irigaray explains. That the female incorporates young into her own body also emphasizes the femininity of any alien who has a group consciousness or body. In a bizarre representation of some folk fears of male castration, the *Enterprise* will be drained of its energy and left inert, impotent. The conflict is clear on a metaphorical level, but it also operates on an explicit level of female versus male characters.

The plot pits two young girls, Clara and Isabella, against the patriarchal order represented first by Clara's father and then by the patriarch of the *Enterprise*, Captain Picard. When the father consults Troi about his daughter's "problem," he patronizes his daughter, disbelieving her tale of playmate and ordering her around in a condescending tone of voice. "It's time for you to go now," the father tells his daughter. Later, when Clara appears in engineering, her father again chastises her and tells her to go back to their quarters. Troi identifies this as a father-daughter problem when she advises Clara's father to make himself more available to his daughter. Worf, the forbidding and ultramasculine chief of security, parallels the ultimate patriarch, the ship's captain, and an encounter with him also underscores the male-female aspect of the show's central conflict. Isabella urges Clara to go to forbidden parts of the ship, and on one such deck, they literally run into Lieutenant Worf. He frowns grimly at them and, reproving them sternly, he tells them children are not allowed in this area. They leave, and Worf harrumphs, grimacing his disapproval. But as soon as he disappears, Isabella leads Clara by the hand back onto the deck area, directing Clara to resist masculine adult authority.

In the same fashion, Isabella confronts the ultimate male authority on the ship, Captain Picard. The aliens keep the ship from moving away, and they plan to eliminate the *Enterprise* in part because, as Isabella explains, "You should be destroyed—you are cruel, uncaring creatures." She has determined that the ship should be eradicated because of how powerless and neglected Clara is. Isabella objects to their confining treatment of Clara: "You wouldn't let her do what she wanted or go where she wanted to." She actually yells at Captain Picard, a quite compelling scene, for Isabella may be a powerful female alien, but she appears to be an eleven-

or twelve-year-old girl. Captain Picard is not accustomed to being chastised, especially by young females or indeed females of any type. The image is quite startling.

Juxtaposed to the male-female conflict is an image of female solidarity. Deanna Troi believes in Isabella and takes Clara seriously, as does Guinan. Isabella sticks up for Clara and leads her to defy her father and masculine authority. Isabella also empowers Clara by making everyone pay attention to her. And Isabella gives Clara the power to save the whole ship. It is because Clara intervenes, saying, "Please don't hurt them," that the ship is spared. Clara and Isabella are best friends and although Clara fears Isabella for a while, the episode concludes with the two of them reconciling. Isabella appears on Clara's bed as the *Enterprise* pulls away from the nebula, apologizes for misleading her, and says, "I never had a friend before," and smiles her first broad, heart-warming smile. She expresses a wish that Clara could return to visit her, and then disappears.

These compelling depictions of feminine power and female solidarity are weakened by the episode's conclusion. The patriarch does have his way, and the *Enterprise* leaves feminine space, with Clara returned to her subordinate status. Yet the image of resistance is clear, and leaves us with the idea that somewhere out in space there may be alternatives to the rigid male dominance of the *Enterprise* and Starfleet. Perhaps Clara will return to visit Isabella sometime in the future. In a sense, Isabella does return—in a variety of other forms as the *Enterprise* encounters the female alien in other episodes. But as a thought experiment, this episode gives its viewers the idea that there will or can be a space for feminine power in the future.

In "True Q," the omnipotent alien race that began the series by putting humanity on trial reappears, this time in a female form. The Q Continuum, as they call themselves, are a group of aliens who have tremendous powers. Simply by wishing it, they can be anywhere, do anything, assume any form. Their powers are so far beyond humanity's that the Q appear magical, even godlike. Although in their first appearances they adopt the form of human men, in "True Q" we meet an apparently human woman who discovers that she is a member of this superhuman race. The title is quite suggestive because it implies that the "true" Q is a female. Amanda Rogers is a young, beautiful honor student who has been awarded an internship on the *Enterprise.* As she takes on various tasks aboard the ship, her supernatural powers become more and more apparent, until she finally saves the *Enterprise* from a core meltdown. The original Q appears to test her and then offer her a choice: Join the Continuum or remain human and refrain from using her powers. Amanda finds her powers too seductive, and after she restores a planet's ecosystem and saves thousands of lives, she decides to join her race. Written by René Echevarria, this episode first aired the week of October 26, 1992.

The Q Continuum itself challenges human notions of gender. Their immense powers make the Q beyond gender—they can assume any form or sex they choose. Yet in their magical powers, they evoke stereotypical notions of femininity. Amanda's female sex makes their femininity more obvious, as the discovery of a Queen Borg does in the second *Star Trek: The Next Generation* film, but like the Borg (discussed in chapter 4), the Q display clues to their femininity.

First of all, the Q Continuum represents a collective. The Q work together and only unusual or deviant Q, such as Amanda's parents or the original Q, separate or try to make individual decisions. The original Q acts hysterically, illogically, and capriciously, and Captain Picard continually contrasts his masculine logic and hierarchy to what Picard sees as the foolishness of the Q's behavior. Second, the Q's powers are depicted as being magical, witchlike. Q describes them as "teleportation, telekinesis," traditional powers of witches. "True Q" makes the femininity of their powers clear through Amanda's casting. The actor who plays Amanda is young, blonde, and traditionally feminine in her appearance. As she performs her magic, she makes hand gestures that evoke Samantha, the blonde witch from the television series *Bewitched.* Not only does the actress look very much like Elizabeth Montgomery, who played Samantha, but even the premise and the body movements are borrowed from the earlier show. Samantha marries a human and decides to renounce her powers in order to lead a "normal" human life. Amanda makes the same decision, but both Samantha and Amanda have trouble sticking to their resolution. The allure of their power and their desire to use their power to help others overcome their resolve. And both are tempted by other "witches" who show them how and when to use their power. The character of Amanda was even called Samantha through several drafts of the "True Q" screenplay (Nemecek 222).

This televisual parallel and the Q Continuum's other qualities reveal that this episode, like so many others, relies on associations with femininity to create the alien Other. In "True Q," as in "Galaxy's Child," the humans express admiration and envy of the female alien's powers. That Amanda is a beautiful, young female makes her seem innocent and worthy of such power. Dressed in a light pink tunic and leggings, she wears her hair up in a bun. She exudes a fresh and modest air through her expressions and minimal makeup. On the edge of adulthood, she represents femininity at its most seductive and powerful. She is depicted as being at a turning point in the feminine—on the cusp of being most vulnerable and most powerful. Amanda's transformation depicts the move from girlhood into womanhood. It is surely significant that as she moves into womanhood—she is just eighteen—that "her powers have begun to emerge," as Q explains. Amanda herself finds the changes she is going through bewildering and explains, "I thought I was going crazy," a normal response to adolescence. The language that Q uses to describe Amanda emphasizes her adolescent appeal and power. She is "a little spitfire," "impetuous," "a plucky little thing."

Sexuality is most certainly a pivotal part of this transition. Amanda must wrestle with her desire for Commander Riker. Demurely, she thanks him for escorting her to her quarters, but as her powers grow, so does her desire for Riker. As Beverly points out, Amanda wants a career and a family; for a family, she needs a male partner. When Riker joins another woman in Ten-Forward, Amanda abducts him; with a gesture, she transforms herself and Riker into nineteenth-century attire on a moonlit evening, complete with gazebo. She makes a pass at Riker, which he gently rejects, explaining, "You can't snatch people and put them in your fantasies and expect them to respond." He explains, "You can't make someone love you," but she does just that, mentally controlling him so that he does love her. But she realizes herself that such manipulation is hollow, and she returns him to Ten-Forward. This scene reveals the power of the feminine to seduce and enthrall, but because she is a beneficent female alien, Amanda renounces this power.

That she has such power over men, however, means that she is a threat to Starfleet, not just as it is represented by Riker. The original Q repeatedly emphasizes the threat she poses to the *Enterprise*. She could control them all mentally. She might even destroy them by not wielding her powers carefully enough. Q reveals the power of a liminal female when he explains, "She may accidentally destroy herself, or all of you, or even your entire galaxy." The female alien, then, can threaten not just an individual man, but the universe itself. As she struggles to come to terms with her identity, Amanda reveals the positive and negative power of the feminine.

In her quest for a female identity, Amanda searches for a role model among the crew and finds one in Beverly Crusher. The support she receives from Beverly evokes the female dyad of "Imaginary Friend." Again, a female alien finds friendship with a human female. With Beverly she discusses her hopes, fears, and desires. Like Beverly, Amanda hopes for a career in Starfleet, and she has already specialized in neurobiology. It is Beverly who stands up to the original Q as he tries to badger Amanda. It is Beverly who insists that the captain inform Amanda about the original Q's plan to try to terminate her. Beverly insists that Amanda be given the information to make up her own mind about what to do. As the original Q argues with Crusher, he turns her into a barking Irish setter and complains, "Crusher gets more shrill with each passing year." Amanda turns Beverly back into herself, but Q's word choice suggests the gendering of the conflict that Amanda faces. As Q tries to abduct her, Amanda gradually realizes her own powers and resists. As Beverly tells her, "Amanda, you are stronger than you think." When Amanda decides to visit her dead parents and then rejoin the Q continuum, it is to Beverly that she makes the announcement, and it is Beverly she hugs good-bye, as she tells her, "I hope I can come back to see you." Beverly pronounces a benediction of sorts as she reminds Amanda: "Amanda, you're a Q. You can do anything you want." And then Beverly smiles.

This fantasy of unlimited magical power seems to promote a strong, positive view of femininity. Amanda's innocence and her insistence on using her powers to help other people show a beneficent side of the feminine. Her very first act of magic is to conjure up, and then tenderly send away, a litter of puppies, and she evokes the maternal when she calls up an image of her parents cuddling her as an infant. She also saves Riker from a falling cargo barrel, saves the entire ship when the core threatens to melt down, and in her final act of magic rescues an entire planet. Amanda complains about a planet where the people use filters to clean the air, instead of preventing the pollution in the first place. Her attitude is ecofeminist; it combines ecology and feminism. Then, as one of the cleaning plants threatens to explode, she not only repairs it, but restores the entire planet to pristine condition. We watch on the screen as the planet's atmosphere changes from an ugly orange red to a beautiful clear blue. Here Amanda associates the female alien with Nature, Gaia. After such a world-saving act, she must leave. When she saves an entire planet, Amanda demonstrates that she is beyond the bounds of patriarchal control. How could Amanda listen to Captain Picard's orders when she can do anything? How could he or any other member of Starfleet be in authority over her? Her departure is more positive than the death of the female alien in "Galaxy's Child" or the forced expulsion of the female alien in "The Bonding," but nevertheless, this episode conveys the idea that there is no safe place for the feminine on the *Enterprise* or in Starfleet.

Her powers, not her beneficence, are almost equaled by another group of aliens who are also superhumanly gifted. In "Liaisons" three apparently humanoid aliens join the *Enterprise* as ambassadors. Each, we discover at the end of the episode, is charged with investigating a certain aspect of humanoid culture: antagonism, pleasure, and love. Like the Q, this race is also genderless, and able to transform itself and space through the powers of its minds. The one charged with exploring love travels with Captain Picard, forces a landing on a deserted planet, and transforms itself into a humanoid female. Written by Jeanne Carrigan Fauci and Lisa Rich, "Liaisons" first aired the week of September 27, 1993.

By focusing on Captain Picard and a female alien instead of Beverly Crusher and a female alien, this episode clarifies the male-female opposition inherent in the figure of the female alien. The scene in which Amanda transports Riker to a romantic setting is here magnified to a major focus of the plot. In "Liaisons," the female alien first masquerades as a male humanoid, lulling Picard into a false sense of security. Once Picard enters the shuttle with the male ambassador, however, his fate is sealed. The alien uses magical powers to crash land the shuttle on a barren planet. Picard takes command, using his jacket to create a pillow for the presumably injured alien and telling the alien he will go for help. As Picard leaves the alien, he transforms himself into a she. Pretending to be a survivor of a crashed freighter, the alien tries to make Picard fall in love with her. She does so in order to understand and experience the (to her) bizarre human condition called love.

As Picard traverses the treacherous landscape, marked by murky atmosphere and lightning strikes, he is knocked unconscious, and we see female hands lift under his shoulders and drag him away. In this one moment, Picard's mastery, captaincy, and potency are stripped away. He wakes up on a makeshift bed and sees a female figure by a fire, dimly lighting the interior of another crashed ship. Picard asks who she is, but he is weak and finally falls back on the red pillows and half closes his eyes. Anna, his "rescuer," tells Picard she has survived on the planet alone for seven years. As she returns to the shuttle to find equipment to make a distress call to the *Enterprise,* Picard asserts himself, getting up and working on escaping. When Anna returns, she helps him to sit down and tells him, "You should be in bed." Anna makes all the right romantic moves, telling him of her loneliness and her desire for him.

Moreover, Picard retains his resolute masculine individuality, pointing out that Anna is overreacting. He keeps the conversation to technical terms and plans for rescue, while she returns to her attraction and love for him. They parody stereotypical male-female positions—the man discussing the practical, the woman the emotional. She finally physically attacks him, kissing him repeatedly, even forcing him to the ground, as he vehemently objects "Anna, NO!" "You should love me now," Anna says, but Picard resists. Realizing her failure, Anna leaves. At this point Picard realizes that he has been duped—that Anna is actually the alien ambassador, masquerading as a beautiful woman. So when he follows Anna, who threatens to jump off a precipice unless he says he loves her, he tells her that she should jump, calling her bluff.

Significantly, the clue to Anna's identity is the necklace she wears. Picard had seen it earlier in the ship, and when she appears with it, he realizes who she is. A necklace, obviously, evokes the feminine because it is a traditional gendered accessory. The episode opens with Worf complaining about the formal uniforms that they must wear to greet the alien ambassadors, which, Worf complains, "look like dresses." Worf's comment reflects an anxiety about being feminized. The necklace and the dress uniforms point to the confrontation with femininity that dominates the episode, most clearly in Picard's encounter. Worf and Troi also escort ambassadors around, but aboard the *Enterprise*. Their dealings with antagonism (Worf) and pleasure (Troi) leave them perplexed. They do not figure out, as Picard does, that they are being experimented with.

Picard's recognition of and rejection of the feminine direct the viewer's attention to the necessity of controlling and expelling the feminine. Because he is the captain of the *Enterprise,* Picard's experience is thus privileged and foregrounded. Like Riker, Picard must first identify the threats posed by the feminine—sexual allure, magical powers, reproduction, maternal control—and then overcome them. The metamorphic nature of these female aliens' bodies evokes the changeability of human women, whose bodies menstruate, reproduce, and then reach menopause. The metamorphic abilities of these female aliens point to the static and individual nature of masculinity as it is constructed in American society. *Star Trek: The Next Generation* reflects and functions like a microcosm of America as it might be in the future. The fluidity of their bodies evokes the French feminist notions of a feminine language. As Catherine Clément argues about a paranoic crime, "The hysteric/sorceress uses her own body to enact rebellion, compelling the male viewer/voyeur to watch repeatedly" (Cixous and Clément 18). In *Star Trek: The Next Generation,* the female alien uses her body to capture male characters and male viewers. She speaks through her body, using it to explore resistance to male-dominated society and technology. The mutable female forms always refer to "real" human women.

Emphasizing a slightly different aspect of the feminine, some female aliens actually have "genuine" humanoid bodies. In four episodes, Captain Picard and Commander Riker confront female aliens who closely resemble human females. These female aliens make the parallel to women quite unambiguous. As with the other female aliens, however, the patriarchal leaders confront these humanoid female aliens only to destroy them and reject femininity. The destruction seems harsher because these creatures' real bodies make them seem human. In "The Vengeance Factor" the cliché that hell has no fury like a woman scorned turns out to be true—but the role is played by a rejected Riker. Vengeance exacted by a man is deadly and final, as it is in real life, where women are in greatest danger from their boyfriends and husbands. The *Enterprise* is on a peace-making mission, trying to reconcile two factions: the government of Acamar III, headed by a female sovereign and representing order and civilization, and a marauding band called the Gatherers, an all-male group representing violence and disorder. A young woman accompanies the female head of state, and Riker falls in love with her. But she is a servant, incapable of love, who turns out to be over a hundred years old and an assassin. At a critical moment in negotiations, Riker discovers the woman's treachery and kills her to preserve the peace. Written by Sam Wolfe, this episode first aired the week of November 20, 1989.

Apparently about the reconciliation of femininity and masculinity, this episode reveals a profound ambivalence about gender separation. The female sovereign of Acamar III, Marouk, is a regal old woman. With gray hair pulled back into an ornate bun, a regal dark yellow gown and sashes, and a large ornamental necklace, Marouk resembles England's queen mother. Her language to the rebel Gatherers evokes family. She offers them amnesty and "a life and a home." She tells them, "It is time to come home." The Gatherers are all male, rough and crude, wearing leather and studs. They appear unwashed and are unshaven. The head Gatherer and Marouk quarrel, and Picard patiently leads them through negotiations, telling them that they are very much alike. The show appears to be about reconciliation despite its title, "The Vengeance Factor."

From the two contrasting societies, both stemming from an original culture, it appears that the feminine (civilization) is to be valued over the

Riker prepares to kill the female alien.

masculine (wilderness/wildness). This apparent reversal of other *Star Trek: The Next Generation* episodes emphasizes the importance of gender and the values associated with masculine and feminine. But although the plot moves these two groups toward a recognition of their need for each other, the narrative reinscribes the masculine through Riker as he destroys the feminine represented by Yuta, a bondservant to Marouk.

However, we discover that, while the "vengeance factor" ostensibly belongs to Yuta as she pursues the extermination of a family who left her as the only survivor of her clan, male vengeance is just as virulent, and finally more successful. Riker's vengeance against Yuta seems all the more vicious because he first pursues her and promises her pleasure. Ironically and appropriately, Yuta, like women in the "real" world, is in more danger from a man who promises to love her than from her sworn enemies.

Commander Riker flirts with Yuta, Marouk's servant, cook, and food-taster. A young pretty blonde woman wearing a high turtleneck and a form-fitting silver, floor-length gown, Yuta seems demure and flattered by Riker's attentions. That the seductive female alien so often is blonde connects with American culture's fascination with the blonde sex object (Isabella and Amanda are also blonde). When the sovereign no longer needs Yuta's help, she goes to Riker's quarters, kissing him and saying, "Tell me what you want William. I will do anything you wish." Riker rejects her slavish devotion, telling her he wants an equal partner. Of course, he does not realize what purpose she pursues in her servitude, but he tries to force her to have a relationship with him on his terms. As she resists, Yuta represents the inscrutability of femininity. Like the Sphinx, she "speaks[s] in riddles," Riker tells her. He tells Yuta that she is entitled to be happy. As he takes her face in his hands and holds her, a security alarm goes off, and their tryst is interrupted by Starfleet duty. Riker is very clearly smitten, but the interruption turns out to be a fortunate timing, for Yuta, like all female aliens in *Star Trek: the Next Generation,* is not exactly what she appears to be.

Her body is her own, and humanoid. However, she is actually well over a hundred years old, despite her apparent youth. The last surviving member of a clan destroyed by another clan on Aramak III, Yuta has dedicated her life to vengeance. To that end, she has been genetically altered to live an extended lifespan and retain a youthful appearance. Youth, especially in women, equals power and desirability. As an old but young-looking woman, Yuta defies traditional categorization of women. She has also been infected with a virus that will kill only members of her rival clan. On the Gatherer outpost, we see her follow a gruff, large rebel. Demure and cute, she seems no threat to him, but she touches his cheek and he falls to the ground, dead. At first the crew thinks the man has died of a heart attack, but the superior technology of the *Enterprise* reveals Yuta's weapon. Using the *Enterprise's* advanced medical equipment, Beverly Crusher discovers the virus in the Gatherer's body, revealing that he was murdered. Technology also exposes Yuta's secret past. Data finds an old picture of Yuta, her face half hidden. They suspect that the image is her, but it is the computer that provides proof. The computer enhances the image of a photo from fifty-three years earlier to reveal Yuta's true age. Yuta's body serves as both her language and her weapon. As French feminists call for, this female alien uses her body to communicate (and to kill). However, technology provides the means to expose and then execute the female alien.

Riker beams down to the conference between the Gatherers and Marouk just in time to stop Yuta from murdering the Gatherer leader. Cruelly and deliberately, Riker shoots Yuta three times; in the last shot she is vaporized. We know that phasers can be used to stun,* yet Riker

*That weapons can be used to stun rather than kill we know from the beginning of the episode. "The Vengeance Factor" opens with the discovery of three Starfleet officers who have been incapacitated during a raid by the Gatherers.

uses his to annihilate Yuta. Is it because she is genetically altered and is not stopped by the first two shots? Is it Riker's vengeance against Yuta for disobeying his order to stop? He tells her, "Yuta, don't do this." Curiously and significantly, Yuta apologizes to Riker as she moves toward the Gatherer leader, telling him "William, I'm sorry." As Riker kills her, he makes no apology. She screams, crumples, and then disappears. The episode concludes with a shot of Riker morosely staring at a drink in Ten-Forward, but he does not express any emotions about killing a woman he cared for.

Age also seems to play a factor here. Often men are fearful about older women, crones, because of their wisdom and experience and association with the maternal figure/body. The lure of the inexperienced virgin is her educability and docility. Certainly Yuta's enemy lets down his guard with her because she is young, beautiful, and apparently no threat to him. In episodes where the Starfleet officer falls in love with a younger woman, she usually survives, as in "True Q." But Yuta's advanced age and deception may make it acceptable for Riker to kill her without compunction. "The Vengeance Factor" details another version of the expulsion of femininity and the dangers of its seductive power over men. Riker must kill that which he desires in order to protect the peace and to serve Starfleet. As with La Forge staring out at the stars in Ten-Forward in "Galaxy's Child," we are treated to another final image of a solitary man, sadly recognizing his need to separate from the feminine.

"Allegiance" features Captain Picard struggling with not one but many female aliens for control of his identity and his ship. Written by Winrich Kolbe, this episode first aired the week of March 26, 1990. Asleep in his quarters, Captain Picard is abducted and taken to a room with three other alien humanoids. They are trapped behind a locked door with unpalatable food. Picard is replaced on the *Enterprise* by a double, who looks and acts like the captain, but whose actions eventually arouse the suspicion of the crew. Meanwhile, Captain Picard tries to organize his fellow prisoners into making an escape. One of his fellow prisoners is a passive, intelligent bureaucrat named Tholl, the other a leonine and fierce fighter named Esoqq, and the third is a female Starfleet cadet called Haro. A silver-skinned alien, she nevertheless is a humanoid female.

As they attempt to break out of their prison, the four represent very different approaches: Tholl wants to wait and be passive, Esoqq wants to fight, and Haro waits for orders. Picard acts like a leader and wins their trust. The Starfleet cadet turns out to be a double female alien in the sense that she is a member of the race that has imprisoned them, an energy being who acts in consort with two others. Significantly, she has chosen to masquerade as a female member of a humanoid-appearing race. Carefully watching their actions, she is nevertheless found out by Picard when she slips, revealing information about Picard that no cadet would know. Picard exposes the alien and says vehemently, "I'm quitting this game." At about the same time, his crew rebels against the impostor taking his place. The prisoners, including Picard, are magically returned to their homes.

Like the female alien in "The Bonding," these all-powerful aliens are feminized. They are represented by sparkling blue light. Like the female aliens in "Conspiracy" (discussed in chapter 2), they have a group identity. Three of them appear as the female cadet disappears; they touch their captives and transport them without technology. The aliens explain their feminized magic: "Our species is telepathically linked. We are all in continual contact. Much more efficient than your primitive vocal communications." These aliens represent a feminine alternative, apparently a more powerful form of intercourse than patriarchal language. They do not have the hierarchy and structure that characterize patriarchy in general and Starfleet in particular. Picard asks them about their difference, inquiring, "Why did you choose to study the concepts of authority and leadership?" The aliens reply, "Because our species has no such concepts. Because we are all identical, distinctions among ourselves are meaningless." These female aliens disrupt and threaten the *Enterprise* and the order of Starfleet itself.

But as is customary, the show depicts female aliens and an alternative to patriarchy only to shut it down. Through nonverbal signals, Picard conveys to the bridge crew that he wishes to imprison the aliens, and he does so. Trapped in a force field on the *Enterprise*'s bridge, the aliens writhe in torment and beg to be released. After giving them a taste of what imprisonment feels like, Picard orders them released, but he threatens them: "We know of your race and we know how to imprison you. Bear this in mind. Now get off my ship." They disappear.

Once again, masculine authority prevails against a feminine alternative. "Allegiance" shows that although there may be alternative possibilities to the military, masculine authority represented by Starfleet and to its technology, finally patriarchy triumphs again. It survives every challenge, even the temporary loss of its leader and his replacement by a female alien masquerading as the captain. That Picard's singing in Ten-Forward finally makes Riker realize that the captain has been replaced by an impostor suggests that unemotional, cold leadership is what is expected and effective.

Captain Picard faces a similar but more serious threat in "Devil's Due," in which a female alien not only abducts him, but also desires him. A more attractive female alien, this protagonist runs an entire world and is hence his equal, if not his superior. "Devil's Due" provides a segue into the metamorphosis of the female alien into a particularly threatening version of the female alien: the female ruler. Written by Philip Lazebnick, "Devil's Due" first aired the week of February 4, 1991. The plot sends the *Enterprise* to the planet Ventax II, where a Federation science station complains that the Ventax people are about to hand over control of their planet to a woman who claims that she is the mythological demon to whom the planet owes its last thousand years of peace. Ardra, as she calls herself, claims that she is the original signatory on a contract that says she will own the planet in a thousand years. Despite her shape-changing and other magical feats, Captain Picard believes Ardra to be a fraud. She makes sexual advances to him, which he rebuffs, and he risks his autonomy in a trial where he must prove she is a fraud or forfeit his own freedom.

Ardra represents the female alien at her most powerful. She has incredible magical powers: to shape-change, to create earth tremors. Apparently immortal, she will own this entire planet, and its people will be her slaves. In her numerous metamorphoses, she impresses everyone except Captain Picard. More successful and deliberately conniving than Isabella, Amanda, or any of the other female aliens, Ardra can change her form at will, appearing at one point as the Klingon goddess and at other times, in an attempt to seduce Captain Picard, as a prim and properly dressed Victorian lady. The head of Ventax II prepares to hand over the planet to her without a murmur of protest, but she is so energetic and powerful that the viewer is not surprised by his ready capitulation.

She is incredibly beautiful and sexually alive. She wears form-fitting outfits that display every curve of her body. At one point, she appears on the bridge of the *Enterprise* in the captain's chair and transforms it into a sexually alluring prop (a use it had not yet been put to). Ardra literally displaces the captain and feminizes the space. She sits provocatively in the chair, with high heels, legs crossed seductively. The piping on her gown emphasizes her breasts. She even does the impossible by changing her attire to a Starfleet uniform and making it appear to be a sexy costume. Her transformations embody what she tells Captain Picard: "I can give you a night that would light fire in your dreams for the rest of your life." Ardra's metamorphic abilities suggest that she could indeed fulfill any fantasy. But her abilities do not appeal to Captain Picard, who says, "You

Ardra, the female alien, captures the captain's chair.

are vulgar and obvious" as she appears in her tarty outfits. Everyone else, including the planet's leader, is suitably cowed by Ardra. They accept her for who she says she is: the planet's devil.

But Captain Picard decides to fight her—another example of female versus male authority. Picard pits his masculine logic and the *Enterprise*'s science against Ardra's feminine appeal and her magic. When Picard first hears the tale of Ardra's contract, he declares, "It's nonsense!" but she chooses that moment to appear, thus refuting him. When she insists on her claims to the planet, Picard angrily declares, "I refuse to abandon this planet to that woman!" His language makes clear the gendered nature of their conflict. So do several sequences: Ardra claims to own Picard because he is on her planet; she says she will take him as her slave if she wins the binding arbitration they enter into to determine who will control the planet.

Picard and Ardra each fight in a gendered fashion. Picard recognizes that Ardra's power stems in part from its feminine presentation. He insists that the *Enterprise* could duplicate all her tricks. "We are capable of recreating all of these events—it's just that she dresses them up and delivers them with dramatic flair." Picard reifies de Beauvoir's famous pronouncement that "women are made, not born." Femininity, as Picard's statement confirms, is a performance, an act. Riker, the captain's "number one," or right-hand man, also staunchly denies Ardra's powers. He says he is not impressed by magic tricks, although Ardra asserts that "We live in a universe of magic which evidently you cannot see." Indeed, the series bears out Ardra's rather than Riker's belief, for the *Enterprise* continually encounters the inexplicable and magical, especially with female aliens.

Although Ardra turns out not to be an actual goddess, she is a female alien who almost succeeds in taking over a planet and confounds Captain Picard and the scientists on the *Enterprise*. She bamboozles them by using her wits, her beauty, and her technology with a flair for the dramatic. At the end of the episode, Captain Picard discovers her cloaked ship, and where she has hidden the *Enterprise* from them. He exposes her by playing the same tricks on her—transportation, shape-changing—that she has earlier played on him. Yet he does not seem to have defeated Ardra. As she is led away by guards, she laughs and walks regally, saying "'Til we meet again, Captain Picard." The implication is that she will escape and confront him again. Although Captain Picard does not encounter the actual Ardra again, he does encounter many other female aliens/rulers, some with powers far more formidable than Ardra's.

The figure of the female alien takes many guises, but she always represents an aspect or aspects of human women. Throughout the series, it is the male senior officers who must confront and vanquish the female alien. When she is literally a creature, nonhumanoid, as in "Galaxy's Child," the captain can feel sorrow for killing her. Yet he quickly abandons her child and makes no attempt to communicate with her people, suggesting that separation between the metaphorically feminine and the embodied masculine—the captain and Starfleet—is desirable.

The situation with the female alien who masquerades as a humanoid woman is more complicated. In some sense, these entities represent the idea that women are duplicitous and metamorphic, and have many guises. The episodes "The Bonding," "Imaginary Friend," "True Q," and "Liaisons" all suggest that the feminine must be exposed, simplified, and subjected to the rigorous male gaze. Only over the destroyed bodies of the female alien do males bond and solidify their ties. A present woman, such as the female alien who replaces Jeremy's mother, poses a threat. She could literally steal the male child away from patriarchy, so the male child must be made to see her as a fiction, an unacceptable alternative.

Finally, the humanoid female alien acts and appears to be a "real" human woman. Like Ardra in "Devil's Due," she may express sexual desires that threaten the male leaders. Or male sexual desire for the female alien may conflict with duty, as it does for Riker in "The Vengeance Factor." The male leaders must resist, as Captain Picard does in these episodes, and capture the female alien in order to escape captivity themselves. That the female alien poses such a threat that she must always be contained suggests the ways in which science fiction literalizes the notion of a war between the sexes.

Star Trek: The Next Generation shows men and women to be two very different species, with different goals, values, and communication systems. Yet it is the raw power of the feminine that seems to make the female alien seem so dangerous. In a number of episodes, her power is so incredible that she is able to rule entire societies and even planets. Chapter 2 explores the female alien as she succeeds where Ardra fails, as a female ruler.

2 "A Threat to the Entire Future of the Federation": The Woman Ruler

A special subgroup of the female alien, the woman ruler has been a staple of science fiction literature since the nineteenth century. Like the female alien, the woman ruler can be traced back to historical and political change in the nineteenth century. As women's roles began to change, fictional representations of what was called "The New Woman" appeared in realistic fiction: "Clever, rebellious, free-spirited, well-educated, independent, and career-minded, the New Woman became the butt of caricaturists, the inspiration for novelists, the model for feminist radicals, and the focal point of the period's [1883–1900] confusion" (Fox v). This New Woman also appears in science fiction, transformed and triumphant. Although in realistic fiction the New Woman can only pose a threat to male-dominated society, in science fiction this figure can rule entire worlds, or even do without men altogether. This figure was especially prominent in the late nineteenth century, in the pulp science fiction magazines of the 1940s and 1950s, and in feminist science fiction in the 1970s. The tradition of the woman ruler is a well-established and venerable part of science fiction,* culminating in several exemplars from *Star Trek: The Next Generation.* As Ferguson, Ashkenazi, and Schultz point out, "the *Enterprise* frequently encounters worlds where women rule" (222).

*Many science fiction critics have noted the pattern of the woman ruler. In "*Amor Vincit Foeminam:* The Battle of the Sexes in Science Fiction," Joanna Russ focuses particularly on the negative depiction of women rulers in dystopias. Pioneering science fiction critic Sam Moskowitz describes and presents a collection of stories about women rulers in *When Women Rule,* and Thomas Clareson's "Lost Worlds, Lost Races: A Pagan Princess of Their Very Own" is a perceptive exploration of women rulers in science fiction. See also my discussion of this pattern in science fiction, especially pulp science fiction, in *A New Species: Gender and Science in Science Fiction.*

The most threatening woman ruler dominates through her reproductive capacity. Woman's greatest power, that of reproduction, is thus turned into a negative, fearful power. This version is perhaps most widely known from the *Alien* movies, in which an enormous and hideous alien uses human bodies to incubate her young. But this formula has its origins in nineteenth-century fiction. In Mary Shelley's other science fiction novel, *The Last Man,* a virulent and unstoppable female *PLAGUE* destroys human civilization. Similarly, the threat posed by the female creature in *Frankenstein* is reproductive. The female alien is far more deadly than the male because of her power to reproduce. The reduction of woman to reproductive organ, described by Simone de Beauvoir and other feminist writers, explains why science fiction writers are fascinated by the female alien.

Through their reproductive capacity, women have the power to threaten patriarchy, which explains both anxiety about women and the reason for their oppression. Sir Edward Bulwer-Lytton literalizes this fear in *The Coming Race,* his best-selling depiction of a female-dominated society that lives in the bowels of the Earth, soon to overtake humanity. Bulwer-Lytton's formulation elides the common connection of female reproductive power with racist fears by emphasizing the Coming Race's matriarchal qualities. The power of reproduction makes women essential to the human race, and women control patriarchal lineage because only the woman's heritage is incontrovertible. In her award-winning study of motherhood, *Of Woman Born,* Adrienne Rich defines mothering as "the biological potential or capacity to bear and nourish human life" and the cultural reaction to motherhood as "the magical power invested in women by men, whether in the form of Goddess-worship or the fear of being controlled or overwhelmed by women" (xv). Her interpretation of this gender dynamic is underscored by Julia Kristeva's description of the archaic and all-powerful mother from whom the human infant must separate: "Fear of the archaic mother turns out to be fear of her generative power" (*Powers* 77).

One common setting for the woman ruler is the female dystopia, or a female-dominated world that is presented as corrupt, evil, or simply misguided. Commonly written by male authors, these books set up a world run by women, only to destroy it as men revolt. One such classic and extremely popular novel is *The Revolt of Man,* published in 1882 by Sir Walter Besant. Set in 2082, the novel depicts a stagnant human culture weakened by the rule of women. Male aggressiveness and action are needed to reinvigorate the society and bring technological advances. The book charts the course of a men's revolt, aided and abetted by a female traitor. This is precisely the plot of "Angel One," an episode from the first season of *Star Trek: The Next Generation.* Three episodes, "Conspiracy," "Angel One," and "The Dauphin," depict the continuation of the female ruler into late-twentieth-century science fiction. Exploring this figure in *Star Trek: The Next Generation* reveals how the series draws on and transmutes a legacy from print science fiction. As it draws on this science fiction tradition, the show continues a century-old representation of woman as alien and other and reveals contemporary anxieties about femininity as well as respect for female power.

The title itself, "Angel One," directs viewers' attention to the angel/whore dichotomy, in which a woman can be either an angel or a whore, but not merely human. The name of this female-dominated planet suggests that women can and should be angels. Instead of Coventry Patmore's "Angel in the House," however, these women rule an entire world, drawing attention to female dominance rather than quiet service and care referred to in the famous Victorian poem. The title of this episode may refer to Beata, the leader of her planet, in that she proves to be an angel and is, in status, the "One." The title identifies the world as a world of angelic dwellers—the beautiful women who are the rulers of their planet. But because the women oppress their men, the title is surely ironic—the women turn out not to be angels at all. The men who are marooned on Angel One at first think that they have died and gone to heaven, but after seven years, they change their minds. It takes Commander Riker only a few hours to make the same determination that Angel One is the abode of termagant women, not "true" angels.

Another well-developed science fiction tradition is that of the attractive and reluctant woman ruler. In this version of the woman ruler, the female is literally an alien being, but one who has an alluring, attractive feminine appearance. This creature can be traced back to Mary Shelley's *Frankenstein* and its many film versions, all of which depict the creature's "bride" as more attractive, intelligent, and gifted than the male monster. Because she is more advanced and able to reproduce, the female monster could create a whole tribe of monsters, who would then threaten man's rule of the Earth. In Shelley's text, Victor Frankenstein destroys the female monster in disgust when he envisions her reproducing and creating a new race that would overpower humanity. Her destruction, then, shows the power of even a potential female ruler to terrify its creator. In the 1940s and 1950s, the golden age of science fiction in which pulp magazines (so called because of the cheap, pulpy paper on which they were printed) flourished, the woman ruler was ascendant. She dominated the covers of these magazines in art that is now highly valued by collectors.

The cover art showed the female alien as powerful and overwhelming—often literally huge, and towering over diminutive male figures. The female aliens were often immortal, with extraordinary magical powers that overwhelmed man's puny technological weapons. Such women ruled entire civilizations, and were gorgeous to boot. Wearing very little, and showing her superiority by needing few clothes even in the Arctic or outer space, the alien female ruler mesmerized human males by her formidable physical attractions. In the stories, the alien female ruler inevitably renounced her powers or sometimes even died saving a human male. This plot appears in "The Dauphin," an episode from the second season of *Star Trek: The Next Generation*.

Examining representative episodes in the use of the woman ruler reveals the continuity of this literary tradition in *Star Trek: The Next Generation*. These episodes—"Conspiracy," "Angel One," and "The Dauphin"—also demonstrate the ways in which women's power can be emphasized through the unique generic qualities of science fiction. Only in science fiction can the power of reproduction be used to threaten a universe-wide, male-dominated government. Only science fiction can show the emptiness of liberal rhetoric of "equality" by showing a male character overthrowing a female-run society. Through a gender role reversal, science fiction can show how reprehensible gender inequality is. We are accustomed to women's oppression, but seeing men in a similar situation can sensitize the viewer to the horrors of oppression. By seeing men limited to the range of roles customarily considered women's, the viewer can see more clearly how narrow and confining such roles are. Although the male characters may complacently feel that women are no longer oppressed, seeing discrimination on the basis of sex in a science fiction setting makes sexism vivid and compelling.

Concomitantly, the artificiality and arbitrariness of femininity and masculinity appear in science fiction settings in which gender roles are reversed. The unfavorable depiction of dominance presented in science fiction has real-life implications and analogues. And only in science fiction can femininity be literally represented as "The Angel in the House." These exaggerations of sexual politics enable viewers to see more clearly the hypocrisy and shortcomings of women's role in contemporary American society. Yet *Star Trek: The Next Generation*'s development of the woman ruler also has a more positive side. Although these episodes display the fear and denigration of woman that is inherent in the figure of the woman ruler, the shows also reflect respect for, and an acknowledgment of, women's power.

"Conspiracy" draws on the characterization of the female alien analyzed in chapter 1. Written by Tracy Torme and aired during the week of May 9, 1988, this episode reflects a crude and unsympathetic vision of the female alien that continues from its origins in print to contemporary television. In this instance the female alien wants to rule mankind, and her reproductive and seductive powers make the domination of Starfleet a possibility. Starfleet's standing orders are to respect all forms of life—the much vaunted Prime Directive that has been an integral part of *Star Trek* since the original series. The Prime Directive, "also known as General Order Number One . . . forbids anyone from interfering with the natural development of an alien civilization" (Schuster 375). Not surprisingly, however, this respect for alien life can be ignored if the alien happens to be female and poses a threat to the masculine individuality/authority/ hierarchy of the Federation. The opening of this episode emphasizes the scientific and exploratory nature of the *Enterprise*, for the crew is on a scientific mission to the planet Pacifica, the very name evoking the peace that the Federation ostensibly stands for. However, the ship takes a detour and never completes that mission because Captain Picard makes the unusual decision to change course. From a close friend, another male captain, Picard receives a message on an emergency frequency. Furtively, Picard arranges a detour so that he can meet this friend, who, along with two other captains, informs him that there is a conspiracy afoot at Starfleet that threatens the very life of the organization. "A threat to the entire future of the Federation," Picard calls it.

This threat is posed in terms of identity; indeed, the entire episode hinges on the question of identity, especially individuality. Before the other captain will confide in Picard, he asks him a series of personal questions designed to ascertain whether he is really Picard, not an impostor. Significantly, the questions all point to relationships but are meant to prove that Picard is actually Picard, a unique individual. His friend, Captain Keel, asks him to prove his identity by answering the question, "Where did we first meet?" and then, "Do you recall the night you introduced Jack Crusher to Beverly?" Appropriately for the episode's theme, his question reveals that a woman's individuality/identity is transformed when she marries—Crusher has changed her last name. And Beverly is identified by her first name alone. Then Keel tests Picard's knowledge of Keel's family by falsely claiming to have a brother. Picard correctly responds that Keel has no brother, to which the captain responds, "We had to be sure you were really you." A number of inexplicable deaths and strange orders throughout Starfleet have led Picard's friend to suspect a conspiracy. He believes that a mysterious something is taking over the bodies of Starfleet commanders, but despite its success so far, the invader/possessor has a weakness: a lack of memory. In an alien invasion that evokes the famous book and film *Invasion of the Body Snatchers,* this episode depicts bodily control and self-mastery as masculine. The masculine/feminine dichotomy is positioned as masculine equals individual, feminine equals collective (or as the show's title has it, "conspiracy").

In her discussion of the film *Invasion of the Body Snatchers,* Nancy Steffen-Fluhr writes of the terror that Becky, the woman who has been taken over by an alien body-snatcher, inspires. When the male lead kisses her, it is a moment of unspeakable horror for him. That Becky is literally alien as well as alien to him because of her femininity makes her doubly dangerous and disturbing. Femininity and collectivity and masculinity and individuality are paired in this film, as they are in so many science fiction representations of female aliens. *Invasion of the Body Snatchers* is most pertinent here because of the filmic parallels between Becky and the pod people and the female aliens who threaten Starfleet. Like the female aliens in the film, those in "Conspiracy" can pass as individual humans: They assume a specific human body but are devoid of the emotions and personality of the real human being whom they possess. The two groups of female aliens resemble each other not only in physical operation, but also in terms of what they represent. Steffen-Fluhr describes the pod aliens of *Invasion* thus: "The pods are associated simultaneously with both a sudden heightening of sexual desire and also with a heightened fear of the consequences of that desire, that sleep: loss of self, loss of individuality, surrender" (141). This conflict between a female alien who represents collectivity and a male human who represents individuality is a science fiction version, as Steffen-Fluhr explains, of "a very traditional version of The War Between the Sexes" (141). Steffen-Fluhr's analysis fits "Conspiracy" precisely. In language that evokes both Shelley's destructive female *PLAGUE* and the pod people of *Invasion of the Body Snatchers,* the alien in "Conspiracy" is described as "a cancer growing within the ranks of Starfleet" and "a subversion within the Federation."

Only men can defeat this feminine menace, by working together but also by maintaining their individuality at the same time. Male bonding may require coordinated action, but it is the antithesis of the blurred and collective nature of the female alien, who may have many parts but only one consciousness. Male bonding is a temporary alliance created between men when they define themselves in distinction to the feminine. Male bonding is critical to all of Picard's actions; it is because he has fought with Captain Keel (and also because they first met in an exotic bar) that he will risk his career to act on his colleague's suspicions. As Picard tells Troi when she objects to his contravening of orders, "Friendship must dare to risk." When the *Enterprise* returns to Earth to explore the contamination or cooptation of Starfleet, it is represented by three male admirals and a junior officer who is male.

In contrast to Starfleet, which is identified as male, and its preservers and protectors (Captain Picard and Commander Riker), the aliens are quite clearly identified as female. "A parasitic being [with] complete control over all brain functions," the female alien has biological implants in key members of Starfleet. We first see the creature when Admiral Quinn brings a specimen to the *Enterprise*. A squiggly insectoid creature, it evokes the femininity of the female alien discussed at length in chapter 1. Insects such as caterpillars metamorphose, and insects are associated with many larval forms and eggs. Because of their metamorphic qualities, insects are especially associated with the feminine. Insects parallel the female body's transformation during pregnancy, menstruation, and menopause. In addition, insects' social structure associates them with female rulers because so many insect species are dominated by the female—the bee and the ant, to name two prominent examples. In their collective nature, too, these species evoke the feminine emphasis on multiplicity and cooperation identified by French feminists such as Cixous and Irigaray.

The visual representation of the creatures also emphasizes their femininity. One of the little creatures escapes, and it runs up the arm and into the mouth of the male officer, Remick, whose body contains the mother creature. Entering the mouth, the alien travels down into a body cavity. Like the human incubators in the *Alien* films, Remick has been turned into a womb. The identification of the alien with the womb and reproduction becomes even clearer as Riker and Picard destroy the officer's body. His head explodes and we see dozens of alien babies milling about in his chest and lower body cavity. The aliens' emergence evokes the bloody process of human birth. Explicitly, however, we learn that the commander of this invasion of Starfleet is, in Picard's words, "the mother creature." So, in metaphorical representation, visual depiction, and overt language, the viewer learns the creature's feminine identity.

The female alien in Remick's chest.

The female alien evokes the insectoid female alien of Donald Woll-heim's *Mimic*. In this chilling story, a female alien hides among human-ity by mimicking the appearance of a human male. The alien's disguise is successful, but only because it never speaks to or approaches human females. The creature has incredible strength, and it lives off human males. The creature poses a further threat in that it reproduces in great numbers, dying as it does so—like a female spider.

Similarly, the female alien in "Conspiracy" has incredible strength, proving that it is, as it claims, "a superior form of life." Just as the female alien will do in "The Dauphin," this alien (inhabiting the body of a frail old man) tosses around Worf, the impressive and powerful Klingon chief of security, as if he were a ragdoll. It takes another female, Dr. Beverly Crusher, to defeat the creature using a laser. And by diagnosing the crea-ture in her lab and providing Riker with a fake alien gill that makes the other aliens believe he too has been taken over, Dr. Crusher facilitates Riker and Picard's destruction of all the aliens. But Beverly uses traditional masculine tools—a laser, a phallic weapon, and the machines of medi-cine—to defeat her female adversary. She must then be considered as acting within the phallocentric authority of the Federation. In this instance, and others throughout the series, Beverly acts as an honorary male, defending Starfleet and her male comrades.

The collaboration of alien and human male is presented in gender terms, with the female as superior. "It's a perfect match—we're the brains, you're the brawn," the alien-inhabited female Captain Scott says. When Quinn tries to implant the creature in Riker, Quinn pushes him toward the alien, saying, "It does like you." Given Riker's propensity for pursuing female companionship, Quinn's language evokes the role reversal in which the ship's Lothario is now the pursued rather than the pursuer. After Picard transports down to Starfleet Headquarters, he is greeted by an admiral whose strange diction should clue him into a gender change in Starfleet. "We are always delighted when the *Enterprise* returns to the nest," the admiral says, using language that evokes the hidden mother alien. Speaking through a male officer, the female alien tells Picard that they "have prepared a special meal" for him. Although she uses male human bodies, the creature betrays her femininity through her words. Using Remick's mouth, the creature claims, "we mean you no harm" and "we seek peaceful existence." The plural suggests the most horrible of prospects: reabsorption into the mother, a communal rather than individual existence. This prospect is what Kristeva identifies as the "power of horror"—what humans most desire and most fear psychoanalytically. Logically and in accordance with the Prime Directive, these words should induce Picard and Riker to negotiate, but instead they decide to kill the creature, responding to the horror and their need to assert their individuality and separation from the female, the mother. First they destroy the body she inhabits. The creature has no words once Remick's body has been silenced. Like Kristeva's phallic mother, the creature can only scream. Locked out of masculine language, she is trapped in the preverbal and cannot argue her way out of the execution. Yet she may have had the last word, for the episode ends ominously with the information that the creature had sent a message to an unexplored quadrant of the galaxy. A homing beacon has been sent, presumably to the female alien's home planet. The episode thus repeats the pattern of pulp science fiction representations of the woman ruler. She is presented as powerful and, though destroyed, still a potential menace. So although this show codifies and justifies misogyny, it also suggests the power of femininity, especially its threat to male-dominated hierarchies.

Similarly, "Angel One" presents a female power, a female-dominated planet, only to set in motion its overthrow. Although the crew should heed the Prime Directive and respect other forms of life and governance, they again interfere. In this case it is Commander Riker who makes a critical intervention. "Angel One" was written by Patrick Barry and first aired during the week of January 25, 1988. The appearance of the woman ruler so early in the show's run suggests its importance. The episode's title hints at the supremacy of women, but it is a supremacy threatened with a rebellion. The *Enterprise* makes a brief stop at Angel One because the crew has reason to believe that survivors of a space freighter disaster may have landed on the planet seven years ago. The freighter is aptly named *The Odin*, after the Norse male deity, a god of war and the dead, for the survivors bring violent conflict to the planet.

Angel One has strategic importance for the Federation, so the crew members of the *Enterprise* must tread carefully and diplomatically in their search. The planet is described as being "similar to mid twentieth-century Earth." Lest we miss the parallel to our Earth, Geordi La Forge, the ship's engineer, muses that for survivors it must be like "being marooned at home." The planet has not been visited by a Federation starship in sixty-two years, and because it is a female-dominated society, a constitutional oligarchy run by elected "mistresses," Captain Picard has Deanna Troi, the ship's counselor, make the initial contact. In this season, Deanna Troi was still wearing extremely short skirts and the low-cut, irregularly shaped neckline that caused many viewers to dub her "Counselor Cleavage." As Lynne Joyrich argues, Deanna "personifies the professionalization of femininity itself" (*Re-viewing* 4). Deanna's seductive attire and her empathic abilities help set up the contact with the female society, which proves to be more unruly and less submissive than Deanna. Despite Troi's female voice and visage, the rulers of Angel One respond that only "a brief visit will be tolerated," causing Geordi to remark, "Ever feel like you're not really wanted?"

In a voiceover, Captain Picard describes the society for an entry in his captain's log: "an unusual matriarchal society where the female is as aggressively dominant as the male gender was on Earth. Here the female is the hunter, the soldier, larger and stronger than the male. An arrangement considered most sensible and natural." Patrick Stewart's reading of these lines introduces the patronizing and humorous approach that the episode takes toward this society. He reads the final line with both a question in his voice and humor as he describes the women's fulfillment of traditionally masculine roles. Of course, no mention is made of the fact that the bridge crew of the *Enterprise* itself reveals that the aggressive dominance of men still continues. A party of two men and two women beam down to the surface: the aggressive and sexually active (and thus prone to sexism) Commander Riker heads the team, accompanied by the android Data, the ship's empathic counselor Deanna Troi, and Tasha Yar, the chief of security.

The *Enterprise* crew wear functional jumpsuits whose colors denote areas of expertise, whereas the citizens of Angel One wear clothes that delimit their gender roles. The men on Angel One wear brightly colored, decorative outfits. The fabrics are shimmery and glitter, and each man sports a large dangling earring. Their pant legs are tightly encircled by rope-like wrappings, and their shirts are open to the waist. In addition, we see one of the Angel One men spray himself with a highly decorative perfume sprayer. To underscore the role reversals, Picard has a voiceover explaining the dominance of women in their society as we first see the citizens of Angel One. That the men of Angel One are all quite a bit shorter than the women reinforces the impression of female dominance and male submission.

The citizens of Angel One are sexually differentiated not only in terms of size, but even more dramatically in terms of their attire and behavior. The women wear somber-hued, loose-fitting, floor-length skorts. Their bodices are cut high, and they wear boots. Most of the women wear their hair pulled back tightly into buns. Significantly, the only exceptions to this hairstyle turn out to be women who fall for the human outsiders. Their unbound hair, then, is a sign of their "true" womanhood. Beata, the Elected One, or head of the oligarchy of mistresses, speaks strongly and assertively. She and the other mistresses stand at attention with their arms crossed in front of their bodies. She immediately takes command of the situation and orders her male servant peremptorily. She explains that the four male survivors of the Odin are now fugitives. At first, they were welcomed into society, but then they "started making unreasonable demands, going against the natural order." Riker volunteers to find and remove the men using Data's assistance to search for clues. The *Enterprise* away team retires to their quarters.

As they do so, a crisis begins on the ship. A virus of unknown origin is turning into a debilitating epidemic. As a sign and parallel of the activity on Angel One, the captain is one of the very first victims of the virus. He is confined to his quarters by the female doctor. At one point, we even see a shot of the captain stripped to the waist, a most unusual shot that evokes the chest-baring of the men on Angel One. As more and more people

Two female aliens taller and more powerful than the males of their species.

become sick, Dr. Beverly Crusher makes the decisions on the ship, disrupting the normally male chain of command. This parallel subplot reinforces Troi's perception of something wrong on Angel One. As the away team must detect and remove the male "invaders" on Angel One, so must Dr. Crusher detect and eradicate the virus making the crew sick. The two missions are given an increased sense of urgency as the *Enterprise* is ordered to get to the neutral zone, where the Romulans threaten an outpost. So the threat of disaster and disorder is multiplied. As the first sign of the unusual, the planet of Angel One itself is somehow implicated in the other problems.

As the captain is "unmanned" by the illness, Riker must assume the attire of a subservient man on Angel One. Mistress Beata sends him a native outfit, complete with earring and the open shirt. He announces his willingness to be diplomatic, but Deanna and Tasha first object, and then burst into gales of laughter when Riker appears in the outfit. Tasha comments sarcastically that the attire is "kind of sexy," and she and Deanna laugh again. Riker sends the others to locate the survivors, while he stays with Mistress Beata. He presents her with a luminous toy that changes its light patterns, and she appears delighted. Then, in a role reversal particularly marked because Riker is the crew member who aggressively pursues women and feeds them seductive lines, Beata comments favorably on his appearance. "I like the way your eyes pick up the color of your tunic," she tells him. Sappy romantic music underscores her, and presumably his, intentions of a romantic physical interlude.

But before they can enter into a physical dalliance, each must proclaim a view of sexual politics. Beata trots out a conventional justification for the subordination of men: "In our society it is the men who are the fortunate ones, enjoying all that life has to offer, while we women devote ourselves to the obligation of making life work." Riker responds with a spirited and inaccurate representation of life in the Federation: "In our society, we share the responsibilities and the pleasures equally." The seduction reveals and parallels what the introduction of "superior" male survivors has already done. Beata tells Riker that he attracts her "like no other man has." They kiss, and Riker responds with the traditionally feminine line, "But will you still respect me in the morning?" However, the line is delivered lightly; because Beata has no power over him, Riker's concern about respect is clearly flippant. His concern about losing her respect if he sleeps with her is playful rather than serious. They kiss, upright, but then Riker rolls over on top of her as the camera cuts to the fire. The symbolism is obvious, as fire traditionally represents passion.

In an overt symbolic move of mastery, Riker inserts a rod into the round crystal globe he has presented to Beata. She responds with "very impressive" as the globe lights up. By inserting a rod into the crystal, Riker stimulates the lamp into lighting and making a beautiful musical sound. The phallic imagery of his actions is obvious, and it reflects the way he dominates her throughout the episode. In a later sequence, Riker stands next to Beata, revealing that he is taller than she is. When she attempts to be on top, he objects—"men are not objects to be possessed, Mistress Beata"—and then their lovemaking ends with a final interruption. Riker's positional dominance represents his dominance on the *Enterprise,* where he is number two in command, but also on this world, where there are no other "real" men, and where Riker commands technological powers far superior to anything on Angel One.

The last interruption occurs when Beata's male servant announces that fugitives have been found and that they refuse to leave Angel One. Data, Deanna, and Tasha have located the fugitives, and they present their view of Angel One—a classic representation of a female dystopia, or an evil, corrupt world ruled by women. As Ramsey, the leader explains, "When we first landed here we thought we'd died and gone to heaven. You've seen the women here. They're tall and strong and very lovely. But after the newness wore off we began to see how the men were treated. There's no votes, no opinions, there's no respect," he complains. The men are from a Federation freighter, but they are not members of Starfleet, so the away team cannot force the men to leave. The survivors have lived on the planet for seven years, formed relationships with women, and had families. Their masculinity is revealed by their decision to stay and fight, a decision re-inforced by the leader's leather and buckskin jacket and the beer-like mug he holds. They are committed to staying and fighting against the evil of female domination over men. The last shot of the rebel Ramsey reveals that his female partner is one of the ruling mistresses. Like Beata, she is shorter than the human male (including her lover Ramsey), and she looks adoringly up into his eyes. Her treachery, it is implied, helped the fugitives elude capture for so long. It is only the *Enterprise*'s superior technology (via a device that locates a mineral trace) that enables the away team to locate the fugitives.

But the woman's treachery has been discovered, and the fugitives are captured and sentenced to death. The sentence reveals the primitiveness of the rulers of Angel One, and their desperation. Riker plans to beam the away team and the fugitives and their families aboard the *Enterprise*, but Beverly Crusher forbids him to do so because of the epidemic. Riker turns to scientific rhetoric to stop the execution. He argues that equal rights are "evolution" and that "no power in the universe can hope to stop the force of evolution." At the last minute, Beata seems persuaded, and she exiles the fugitives instead. But clearly it is Riker's personal advantages as well as his eloquence that persuade her. She turns a beaming smile on him and says, "For a man you can be very clever, Commander Riker." The clever Beverly Crusher has also figured out what caused the epidemic, and the away team is beamed back to the *Enterprise*.

This episode repeats many of the elements of the classic woman ruler. She is shown to be unenlightened and susceptible to masculine charm. Riker's use of evolution to explain and justify the men's rebellion suggests the inevitability of their success, despite their exile. The quick collapse of Beata into Riker's arms, and that of her colleague Ariel into the survivor Ramsey's arms, suggests that this planet of women just needed real men to show up. Women may obtain political power, the plot suggests, but they will always choose to fall into the arms of a "real" man, forsaking that power. The captain's voiceover, the virus on the ship, the trouble at the

Neutral Zone all suggest the disorder of women rulers. It is an unnatural and temporary state. The captain resumes his position in the captain's chair and gives the order to leave the space above Angel One. However, his voice cracks slightly, revealing how he has been feminized by his illness. It is the triumphantly masculine and sexually aggressive Riker who gives the order. No thought is given to letting Deanna give the order, although they were willing enough to use her voice to contact the women on Angel One.*

Perhaps the most troubling aspect of the episode is the fact that Riker seems to genuinely believe that men and women are equal in Starfleet, despite the obvious inequities aboard the *Enterprise.* The women are in traditionally feminine occupations, except for Tasha Yar. Beverly Crusher is a Florence Nightingale, caring for the sick and commanding only in the last resort. Deanna Troi wears humiliatingly revealing costumes, especially in the first two seasons, and her only job is to sense whether someone is lying or angry. She has no command powers. (Beverly and Deanna receive command status only in the last season of the series [Ferguson et al. 224].) Although earlier female dystopias were misogynistic, they at least did not pretend that men and women were equal. In this regard, this episode operates best when it indirectly exposes how like Angel One the *Enterprise* and Starfleet in general actually are, with women in subordinate and ornamental positions.

"The Dauphin" also depicts an attractive female ruler who becomes involved in a romantic affair with a crew member from the *Enterprise.* The title alone suggests a gender role reversal, for "dauphin" was the title of the eldest son of the king of France, but the title here applies to Salia, a beautiful young female alien whom the *Enterprise* transports from an isolated location to her home planet, Daled Four. Written by Scott Rubenstein and Leonard Miodinow, "The Dauphin" first aired during the week of February 20, 1989. Salia is the orphaned daughter of two parents who died in Daled Four's interminable civil war. She has been raised off planet and will return to rule, uniting the warring factions. Only sixteen, she has spent her entire life alone with a governess, Anya, who has educated her thoroughly. Although she has been isolated, Salia knows a great deal about space travel, science, and so on. Wesley Crusher, Dr. Crusher's adolescent son, sees Salia and is immediately smitten. But there is a mys-

*That male voices will give orders is ensured by the placement of men in the roles of captain and second-in-command. To deceive the women of Angel One, Deanna makes first contact, although she and other women have no leadership roles on the *Enterprise.*

tery about Salia: Deanna Troi senses that something is being hidden from the crew of the *Enterprise,* and Anya, Salia's guardian, seems absurdly overprotective.

Salia is the classic female alien—desirable, attractive, alluring, and humanoid. She seems a perfect specimen of young womanhood. With her long dark hair swept behind her head, long straight bangs, and an engaging smile, she quickly captures everyone's attention. She and her guardian, Anya, wear long sweeping gowns that accentuate Salia's attractive figure. But with their medieval ethos—Anya even wears a wimple—the clothes emphasize Salia's romantic position as princess, woman-ruler-in-waiting.

Little wonder Wesley Crusher is so quickly enchanted. In a shot/countershot, we see a close-up of their faces as they see each other for the first time. They smile and gaze at each other longingly. Immediately thereafter, we see Wesley looking at himself in the mirror, brushing his hair. Then he continues his lovestruck behavior when he forgets the part he was supposed to bring to engineering. Wesley inquires about Salia, and then she asks about him. When Geordi La Forge, the ship's engineer, notices Wesley's abstraction, he advises Wesley to go talk to Salia. The advice Wesley is given by various crew members emphasizes the tactical and combative nature of gender relations, even across races of beings.

First La Forge ascribes Wesley's distraction to hormones, explaining that Wesley is just at that age. His biological interpretation is counterparted by the Klingon Worf. We see and hear Worf demonstrate a Klingon mating call (a guttural scream), and when Wesley asks whether he is supposed to scream at Salia, Worf delightedly explains that Klingon females make that hideous sound to attract males, and males read love poetry while the females hurl large objects at them. As Worf pleasurably reminisces about his race's mating practices, we are reminded that Salia is an alien, and human mating rituals may not be appropriate for her. The contrast between La Forge's and Worf's views reveals also that gender relations are social constructions that vary from world to world, culture to culture. The variety of gender roles suggests that they are not natural, but a construction. The implication is that human gender roles and courtship behaviors are not the only possible ways to act. Data reinforces this artificiality by opining that he thinks that Wesley and Salia are biologically compatible. But Wesley points out, "I want to meet her, not dissect her." Then, in a usual universalizing gesture, Guinan, the wise and ancient alien who runs Ten-Forward, the ship's bar, and Commander Riker act out a flirtation—ostensibly to educate Wesley, but they both become so entranced with their flirtatious banter that they tell him to get lost. Fortunately for Wesley, Salia has a better grasp of psychology, so when Wesley arrives at her door, she coyly invites him in, feigning ignorance about the food processor and asking his help.

Since we have already seen that Salia knows everything about the ship's operations, her coy behavior shows her playing the role of the helpless female. (When she first steps off the transporter, Salia identifies the matter-energy conversion controls.) Feigning incompetence and ignorance is a role that she plays throughout their brief courtship, mimicking a traditional human female pattern. Acting like a stupid girl, she asks Wesley to select an entree for her. He chooses chocolate mousse, and as she delightedly sucks it off her finger, she asks him, "Tell me about some of the places you've been." Wesley responds by taking her to the holodeck, which creates on command three-dimensional landscapes and settings. Using this artificial technology, Wesley takes Salia to Saturn and other beautiful planets. Acting scared at the change of scenery, Salia puts her arm around Wesley and clings to him. Alone with her on the top of an asteroid, he shows her the sights of the galaxy. Then, imitating Riker and Guinan, Wesley takes her to Ten-Forward. She oozes, "This has all been so wonderful. I can't believe it's real." Of course, the holodeck hasn't been "real," and as it turns out neither is she. In close-ups we see their faces reflecting infatuation, and Salia says, "I've had a great time being with you." He tells her that she could stay on the *Enterprise,* but to the accompaniment of sappy romantic music she runs away. Guinan advises him to follow and he does, but Salia warns him to stay away from her. She says, "I can't have this life," but Wesley argues, "Salia, nothing is impossible." Like Beata, the all-powerful woman ruler of Angel One, Salia finds a human male attractive and becomes frustrated with her position. Like Beata, Salia acts like a weak human female, easily overcome by her desire for an alien human male.

But unlike Beata, who has political rather than physical superiority, Salia is not what she seems. Her later actions make a mockery of Wesley's protective and patronizing masculinity. There are clues to her power from the beginning of the show. Earlier in the episode, when the crew is informed of Salia's future as the head of state, in charge of a world torn apart by civil war, Riker objects, "She seems too delicate for such a task." But Worf, the perceptive chief of security, warns against being taken in by appearances. "Do not be fooled by her looks," Worf barks out, "The body

Anya and Salia in monstrous form (top); Anya and Salia as humanoids (bottom).

is just a shell." Worf's warning turns out to be more accurate than even he could have suspected. Although Captain Picard and Anya separate the two young lovers, Salia slips out while Anya is having a tour of the ship and goes to Wesley's quarters. She explains, "Anya thought you would corrupt me," but it is Salia who takes the lead, touching Wesley first on the arm, then shoulder. Then she kisses him, saying she wants to do "the normal things people do when they like each other." This moment of bliss is rudely interrupted when Anya enters the room and changes into a huge fanged monster with large red eyes, growling at Wesley and threatening him. Then, unexpectedly, Salia transforms, too. Rather humorously, as she transforms into a monster, she retains the burnt orange of her gown in her similarly colored fur. Hideously ugly and enormous, she growls and swipes at the monster/Anya until Anya relents and returns to the form of an older human woman. Then Salia changes back to her beautiful, diminutive self. Her transformation has been triggered, as it usually is in female aliens, by a desire to protect a human male. Wesley is shocked and repulsed by her transformation, and rejects her. This unexpected turn of events saddens the viewer, who has become invested in Wesley's starcrossed romance. By showing her strength, Salia has shown the mockery of Wesley's protective and patronizing traditional masculinity, and its limits. Romance, this episode suggests, exists only when the male can patronize the female.

We have already seen Anya transform when she thinks that the ship's precautions against infection are inadequate. Anya takes her charge to protect Salia quite seriously, so much so that she demands that an ill patient be killed because his disease is potentially fatal. Anya also has a young, beautiful appearance, that of a humanoid female, that she assumes when she and Salia are in the cabin alone. Anya also appears as a cute, huggable teddy bear–like creature, shorter than Salia. Her metamorphic abilities place her in a long line of formidable female aliens, from Medusa to science fiction versions such as the eponymous aliens in the movie *Aliens.* Linked to women's childbearing capacities, the ability to change her body, as a woman's body changes during pregnancy, defines a female alien. Here, too, such ability is linked with Anya's maternal relationship to Salia. "Emotionally, she's Salia's mother," Deanna Troi explains, and Picard concurs, expressing his worry because "the most dangerous animal is a mother protecting her young." Anya is further identified as belonging to a race distinct from Salia—Anya is a shape-shifter or an alasamorph, who has the power to alter her molecular structure. As Worf says,

"Such a creature would make a perfect protector" and, as he learns, a formidable opponent. Anya criticizes the ship's technology as "primitive," and she easily escapes from her cabin by changing her molecular structure to slip through the walls undetected. In her monster body, she defeats the powerful Klingon Worf very easily. She has proven that her statements such as "Your powers are infinitesimal compared to mine" and "You cannot control *me*" are not empty boasts.

Powerful though she is, Anya is not a ruler. To Salia belongs that distinction. Anya does not accompany Salia to her planet, but lets her go alone. Salia must also face Wesley's adverse reaction alone. She again goes to his quarters, sadder and wiser. While she confesses that she loves him, Wesley says he *loved* her and asks her to leave his room. His use of the past tense conveys the feeling that his love could not survive seeing Salia's other, powerful self. He asks, "What are you really?" and grimaces as she leaves. At the last minute, he reneges and follows her to the transporter room. She then asks *him* to leave, because she wants him to remember her in her human form, and she must change to her "real" form to beam down. He insists on staying, and Riker allows Wesley to give the command to energize the transporter. Wesley's open-mindedness is rewarded as Salia turns into a beautiful, vaguely humanoid shape of glistening lights. With a delighted smile, he watches her dematerialize. At the end of the episode, sitting dejectedly in Ten-Forward, he tells Guinan, "Seeing her on the transporter pad—it was like seeing pure light. I miss her. I feel empty." Salia turns out not to be a monster, but simply "The Angel in the House"—or in this case, ship. Guinan empathizes with his distress and acknowledges that although he'll love again, he will never feel exactly like this again, because each love is different (and presumably his next love will be human).

In this episode, the lessons about the woman ruler are a little less harsh than they are in "Angel One." Salia has more dignity and power than Beata, and her youthfulness probably also softens her position as a ruler. Salia is more like a fairy-tale heroine, such as Mopsa, the Victorian fairy from Jean Ingelow's *Mopsa the Fairy.* This fantasy novel depicts a miniature female fairy kissed into transformation by a young boy. Like Wesley's transformative kiss, this boy's kiss sparks Mopsa's transformation into the Queen of Fairyland. And like Salia, Mopsa must return to her kingdom and reluctantly leave her human lover behind. Unlike Beata, but like Mopsa, Salia doesn't seem to want to rule. In this regard, Salia and Beata can be read as complementary reinforcements of male dominance. If you want to rule, you must do without "real" or human, desirable men. Even in the twenty-fourth century, the price of power for women is heavy indeed, and really no different from that of nineteenth-century fiction.

Examining the depiction of women rulers in *Star Trek: The Next Generation* reveals that this pattern is little changed from the nineteenth century. As a television series, however, *Star Trek: The Next Generation* has the time and space to explore different versions of the woman ruler. "Conspiracy" reflects the woman ruler as she appears in horror/science fiction: the nonhumanoid and disgusting rendition of femininity. This version of female power must be exterminated at all costs. Metaphorically, however, this female alien represents femininity, which must be repressed in favor of masculinity. The traditional values of femininity—an emphasis on community played out through cooperation and an undifferentiated self—are contrasted to the typical values of masculinity—individuality and direct action. Dr. Crusher enacts this division when she kills the female alien with a phaser and tricks it through medical science. The episode thus suggests to its female viewers the advantages of assuming masculine values and behaviors. This message continues in "Angel One" and "The Dauphin," but more subtly. These two episodes focus on conversion or seduction narratives, in which the woman ruler converts to a masculinist ideology. Sexual politics is played out through the narrative of heterosexual romance. All three episodes reveal that *Star Trek: The Next Generation* goes where science fiction *has* gone before: to a denigration of femininity through the figure of the woman ruler.

Yet even as it repeats misogynistic science fiction patterns, there are moments of resistance and pleasure for feminist viewers of these texts. "Conspiracy" presents so negative a view of femininity that it is almost humorous. We can easily see how masculine the hierarchy of Starfleet is. And this awareness can help us interpret the choices that Beverly Crusher had to make to become chief medical officer. Similarly, in "Angel One" we can see in the oppression of the males on the planet a reminder of the ways in which women were and still are denied full parity in our society. And there is pleasure in seeing a female-run society, even if it may be overthrown in the future. Salia's clever manipulation of Wesley and her metamorphic body also suggest a more positive view of femininity than that shown in "Conspiracy." Because it appears a season later, we might see this as "progress" in the image of woman presented in the series. Salia is likable and her various bodies—even that of the monster—are attractive. And we can take delight in the fact that she will rule a planet and end its divisive civil war. Like Wesley, viewers of *Star Trek: The Next Generation* may learn to respect and admire femininity.

3

"I Am for You": The Perfect Mate

The figures of the female alien and the woman ruler present powerful but negative images of women. This chapter's title comes from another recurring depiction of woman and the title of one key episode, "The Perfect Mate." Literary science fiction contains many representations of an idealized female, the perfect mate for a man. Perhaps the most widely known version is *The Stepford Wives,* a popular 1974 film based on a novel by Ira Levin in which real, opinionated, and demanding wives are gradually replaced by androids, machines that duplicate the actual women's bodies but replace their personalities with docile and submissive programming. The perfect mate is a horrifying version of convenience, woman reduced to responding only to her male partner's needs. *The Stepford Wives* was a science fiction film, meant to shock and provoke, but even more upsetting is science fiction that uncritically depicts the perfect mate as a desirable role model for women. *Star Trek: The Next Generation* repeats but also criticizes the portrayal of the perfect mate.

Although I admire the sophisticated analysis of this episode by Lee Heller, I disagree with her conclusion that the desire for a perfect mate "is affirmed rather than successfully called into question" (233). Viewing "The Perfect Mate" through the lens of popular writing about heterosexual relationships makes sense, but this frame also makes the episode look more negative than it is when you place it in a science fiction context. In part, I disagree with Heller because reading the episode through French feminist ideas emphasizes the more subversive aspects of "The Perfect Mate."

Exploring *Star Trek: The Next Generation*'s depictions of the perfect mate enables us to analyze how these characterizations have changed and how her representation dovetails with that of the female alien and the woman ruler discussed in chapters 1 and 2. The perfect mate reflects and responds to her male partner; she is empathic and sympathetic and has no desires of her own. A perfect mate is a version of a perfect wife: attentive to her husband's needs, self-sacrificing, always available, always willing to serve. Perhaps most importantly, she revels in this role, deriving her pleasure and satisfaction from subordinating herself to others. Not surprisingly, Deanna Troi, the ship's counselor, who as a Betazoid has an enhanced ability to read others' emotions, features prominently in these episodes. Even the one episode that does not focus on Deanna Troi evokes her through the figure of a female alien who has abilities like Troi's, only magnified. Reading the pattern of the perfect mate, then, allows us to see more clearly how conventions of traditional femininity, as represented by Deanna, figure throughout the series.

As a half-human, half-alien being who is empathic, Deanna Troi has qualities that make her a perfect mate. Because of her empathic abilities, she senses others' moods and needs. For this reason, her job as ship's counselor makes her the perfect mate for everyone on the crew. Of course, she serves in a special position with the captain, advising and counseling him when no one else can. Attractive and desirable, Troi represents a version of traditional femininity. For this reason, perhaps, she functions as the focus of many more plots than the only other female on the bridge crew, Dr. Beverly Crusher.* Deanna Troi's central role in plots that focus on the perfect mate is usurped only by a female alien whose empathic powers are even greater than Troi's. Comparing the eponymous perfect mate to Deanna reveals that she carries the same function throughout the series.

Deanna's most important function is to serve as a conduit for communication. When the captain meets with aliens, she analyzes the emotions and feelings behind their words, enabling the captain to better understand them. Deanna functions in part as a translator; in this way she becomes a part of the captain. Her job reflects the perfect mate's desire and ability to become one with her partner. An alternative form of communication, Deanna's ability to sense and reflect emotions is a form of feminine language called for by French feminist theorists. She exemplifies a science fiction version of the preverbal, harnessed to the use of patriarchy to better colonize and dominate alien species.

Applying French feminist ideas to *Star Trek: The Next Generation* makes sense, despite their disparate settings, because both became popular in

---

*The tough chief of security, Tasha Yar, lasted only one season, and her job was filled by the ultramasculine Klingon, Lieutenant Worf.

America about the same time—the mid-1980s. The emphasis on language, an interest in the feminine, and focus on the psychological mark both this popular television series and French feminist theory. Julia Kristeva's identification of a stage she calls the preverbal and her emphasis on the association of the feminine with the maternal helpfully illuminates the female alien and the woman ruler, as discussed in chapters 1 and 2. The emphasis on communication and reflection, so crucial to the perfect mate, can be seen in Kristeva's analysis of language formation. "Discourse is being substituted for maternal care, and with it a fatherhood belonging more to the realm of the ideal man" (*Powers* 45). Cixous and Clément echo this formulation: "A stage that is scarcely constituted in human development, it is to return to the disordered Imaginary of before the mirror stage, of before the rigid and defensive constitution of subjective armor" (33). It is within this stage that the perfect mate exists, to her peril. And the plots of the episodes that focus on the perfect mate reify the importance and power of discourse through male characters.

Hélène Cixous and Catherine Clément's focus on the power of the sorceress and the hysteric can be applied to the female alien; the perfect mate is a self-destructive female alien, the counterpart to the threatening female alien discussed in the first two chapters. The perfect mate follows the path of the sorceress as they describe her—"The history of the sorceress oscillates . . . and often ends in confinement or death" (8)—and the hysteric, "a prisoner inside the family; or else in crisis, she bears the brunt of producing a medical spectacle" (8). These descriptions of two incarnations of the feminine conflate in the figure of the perfect mate. Both sorceress because of her witchlike powers and hysteric because of her uncontrollable behavior, the perfect mate disrupts the patriarchal order of the *Enterprise*. As a character, she presents a spectacle that can be interpreted only through psychoanalysis.

Although this figure appears to be presented as an ideal and attractive character, the plots of these episodes reveal that performing the role of perfect mate leads to violence and subjugation. The plots function to warn viewers of the insidious and seductive dangers of being a perfect mate. Read in conjunction with the episodes that deal with female aliens and women rulers, these episodes make a powerful feminist statement about the problems with the construction of traditional femininity. In these episodes, the powerful female alien is subdued, unhappily and hazardously harnessed in the service of men.

Although the four episodes that focus on the perfect mate use different settings and plots, all draw on woman as a reflection of man. In "Loud as a Whisper," an episode from the show's second season, a hearing-impaired alien mediator uses three interpreters, a chorus, to communicate his thoughts and desires. The title of the episode implies that women's voices should be muted, that women should be seen but not heard, but the actual representation of the feminine is more complicated. The only woman interpreter serves as the head of the chorus and the multiple voices of the chorus represent a feminine mode of speaking. This chorus exemplifies the *chora* that Kristeva describes, as well as feminine language, "speaking with a thousand tongues," called for by Hélène Cixous. The interpreters function as a feminine alternative to the masculine symbolic order; they represent an alternative form of language and communication. Together, this chorus functions as the perfect mate. A woman is presented as a peace offering from one planet to another in "The Perfect Mate," from the fifth season. An empathic mesomorph, she bonds with a man and can anticipate and fulfill his every need and desire. Traveling on the *Enterprise*, this perfect mate falls in love with Captain Picard, creating a dilemma for them about honor, duty, and love. This episode seems to valorize the function of woman as mediator and passive reflection. "Man of the People," by contrast, exposes the seamy consequences of using a woman as a receptacle. The episode appeared in the sixth season, and it shows another mediator who uses women, this time to channel his negative emotions. And finally, in the show's last season, "Eye of the Beholder" features Deanna suffering from a psychometric assault as she picks up murderous and suicidal emotions from a particular room on the *Enterprise*. A love triangle ends in murder, and Deanna unwittingly begins to reenact the tragedy. In all four episodes, women reflect, and suffer for their reflection of, men's emotions. In this way, the perfect mate can be read as the concomitant impulse to that of the female alien and the woman ruler. Like the other two figures, the perfect mate provides a site from which to explore gender roles.

Perhaps most prominent and classically feminist is the attention to women's voices—or the lack thereof. In all four episodes, the plots focus on women using their voices to allow men to be heard. Their ability and the right to speak for themselves is appropriated by male speakers. Instead of speaking for themselves, women, especially Deanna, use their extraordinary abilities to empathize, to sense others' emotions, not to communicate themselves, but to allow men to communicate. "Man of the People" shows the man's mother and Deanna raging for him, expressing emotions the man chooses to suppress. In "The Perfect Mate" the female alien becomes a symbol of a treaty, wiping out her own desires and voice.

A woman serves as the receptacle of a man's negative emotions in "Eye of the Beholder." When she expresses herself apart from him, he kills her. Reflecting this control almost kills Deanna Troi, too. "Loud as a Whisper" depicts a woman who has no voice of her own, but literally gives it over to a male ambassador. In addition to being sexually alluring, self-sacrificing, and passive, women give over their voices and are silenced, with horrific consequences.

The first episode to deal with woman as reflection of male thoughts and desires draws on the real-life parallel of signers, interpreters for the deaf and hearing-impaired. Increasingly familiar to television viewers as disabled Americans pressed for their rights to equal access, signers are virtually unknown in the Federation. The Federation's advanced science has corrected most such disabilities. In America, most signers are women. Many Americans' common contact with a signer may be during speeches or ceremonies in which a usually male politician or leader speaks, with a female signer in the foreground, to the left or right. So in casting the alien mediator as deaf, the telewriters draw on an already gendered tradition. Not coincidentally perhaps, this episode was written by a woman. "Loud as a Whisper" first aired the week of January 9, 1989; the episode was written by Jacqueline Zambrano.

Sent to ferry the famous and always successful mediator Riva to Solais V, a planet that has been at civil war for centuries, the *Enterprise* picks up not only Riva, but also his chorus of three interpreters. In a version of signing, the three speak for Riva. Each has a particular function and name: One is the Scholar, another the Warrior/Lover, and the third simply the Woman. That she has no assigned role, as the others do, suggests her centrality, as well as the notion that every being contains a feminine side. The Woman describes herself as "that which binds all of the others together." She speaks literally about the chorus, but her words also apply to the function of women in society. The chorus of interpreters, then, can be read as reflecting both an internal psychological dynamic and a social one. Although the signers are not all biologically female, that they are headed by a woman suggests that they represent the feminine. (Because they serve a man, they reinforce their feminine function as handmaids as well.) The chorus functions as a feminine alternative to the symbolic order; in place of language, heard and interpreted through verbal and aural signals, the chorus uses a preverbal communication, telepathy, to understand and communicate with and for Riva. In both, this configuration suggests, Woman is the key, and a positive one. The Woman explains, "I am harmony, wisdom."

Riva with his chorus.

The centrality of Woman is reified through Deanna Troi's actions. She is the only one of the bridge crew who immediately understands and identifies Riva's unique method of communication. She describes it as "elegant and quite beautiful." He is drawn to her, as well. They serve parallel functions as sensitive individuals whose job it is to counsel and mediate. Just before the crew beams down to the planet to meet Riva, Deanna shows her empathic side as she reads Lieutenant Worf's emotions about this assignment. Deanna's parallel function prefigures her own parallel and replacement for the signers. As Riva tells Deanna, "Much of what we do is similar. We are both learned in how to allow people to examine feelings hidden deep within their psyche." Riva's insistence on this parallel also suggests that he, too, is feminized, a position underscored by his female interpreter's physical resemblance to him. Both have similar reddish-gold hair. As Riva and Deanna share a romantic dinner, Riva describes communication in a way that evokes a French feminist perspective on language: "Sometimes we must allow the surroundings to flow over us, to dwell in each separate part, how it feels. Allow it to fill you." As he emphasizes the importance of "writing the body" through his language that stresses reacting to the world through the body, he also points to the futility of words. "Words are here on top. What's under them, their meaning, is what's important," he explains, but she voices for him, as his last interpreter has left the room. As he gestures, Deanna utters his thoughts for him. She exemplifies a male fantasy of a woman who understands him perfectly; he does not have to explain himself because she can do it for him and she understands him intuitively, with no effort on his part.

Through images, too, the episode directs the viewer to the difficulties with traditional and technical forms of communication. The video that beams up to the ship from the war-torn planet is fuzzy, bisected with lines, and finally breaks down altogether. The *Enterprise*'s viewer screen does not work well under the atmospheric conditions of Solais V. Similarly, just as Deanna and Riva begin to move beyond words and reach a deep intimacy, they are interrupted by Commander Riker's voice, communicating through Deanna's badge. These difficulties with conventional forms of communication point toward the need for an alternative form.

But the alternative form of communication is literally exterminated in the course of the episode, suggesting its vulnerability. Lieutenant Worf, Commander Riker, and Riva transport down to the surface to begin the negotiations, but they have not even begun when one of the Solai natives tries to kill Riva. Riker pushes Riva away from the line of fire, exposing the three interpreters, who are killed instantly. Devastated and incommunicado, Riva refuses to continue negotiations without his interpreters. He cannot communicate clearly, emotionally, and effectively. Through sign language and facial and body gestures, he conveys the idea that he must be returned home. Frustrated, Captain Picard grabs Riva's arms and yells, "You are not alone!" But of course, Riva is alone—for the first time. Without his feminine chorus, he must enter the symbolic world and learn how to express himself through sign language. Medical science can do nothing, as Dr. Pulaski, the ship's doctor,* informs the captain, because Riva's brain cannot receive auditory information.

This reinscription of the patriarchal symbolic order appears also through Picard's actions, which close the show. Deanna persuades Riva to use his disadvantage as an advantage in negotiations by drawing the participants into learning a new common language. Riva will teach both factions his sign language; assured of his success, the *Enterprise* leaves Riva on Solais. Because it is gestural, sign language represents a bridge between the symbolic order, verbal language, and the body. As Riker says in his log entry, "We leave the Solais system confident that Riva will help

---

*A short-lived character like Tasha Yar, the gruff and tough Kate Pulaski replaced the more feminine Beverly Crusher, but lasted for only one season.

the Solais achieve a lasting peace." But the last word is Captain Picard's. He calls Deanna to his ready room to compliment her on her work in language that reveals the importance and gendering of this dynamic. Using verbal language, he reveals his power to command and elevate her through his words. As her captain he has the power to promote her. Although she knows what he feels, Captain Picard uses language to assert his authority to pass judgment on her. Acknowledging Deanna's power to "read" him, he nevertheless insists on pronouncing her achievement in words. "I just wanted to say the words—thank you. Well done." And Deanna beams at this praise bestowed by the father. The symbolic order thus dominates the intuitive through Picard's commendation of Troi. "Loud as a Whisper" thus ends with the replacement of the feminine alternative—empathy and Riva's feminine chorus of voices—with traditional hierarchical and patriarchal language. The reflective and multiple-voiced feminine has been displaced, replaced, and abandoned.

In "The Perfect Mate," Captain Picard must fall in love with and renounce the feminine, as embodied by a beautiful and exotic female alien, Kamala. "The Perfect Mate" first aired the week of April 27, 1992, written by Gary Percante and Michael Piller. This chapter takes its title from this episode because "The Perfect Mate" exemplifies the depiction of woman as passive reflection of a male partner. Using the figure of the female alien, this show extrapolates the qualities of traditional femininity—self-abnegation, empathy to the other's needs, even erasure of self in the pursuit of nurturance—to an extreme. This extrapolation, a standard technique in science fiction, enables the viewers to see more clearly the dangers of being a perfect mate. Kamala's extremism also sheds light on Deanna Troi's role as a perfect mate in other episodes. Although Deanna Troi does not figure in this episode, Kamala's every action recalls Deanna's role as the ship's counselor and empath and the dangers Deanna will experience in other episodes.

The *Enterprise* is carrying "rare and valuable cargo" accompanied by an ambassador who is on his way to cement a treaty ending centuries of war. Ambassador Briam from Krios has an object in a stasis field that is intended as a gift for the ruler of Valt Minor, named Alrik, and Captain Picard orders it to be held in a secured cargo bay. An acquisitive Ferengi, member of an alien race known for its greed,* enters the cargo bay; through a series of mishaps, the stasis field is ruptured. As the large, glowing, egg-

---

*Daniel Bernardi (171–75) discusses the charges of anti-Semitism that circulate around these aliens, and Jeff Greenwald reproduces an article about the issue and also discusses Klingon and Vulcan "Jewishness."

shaped cocoon slowly drifts to the ground, bright light emanates from it. Itself an object of beauty and reverence, the cocoon dissipates as the Ferengi, members of the crew, and the ambassador watch in awe. Bathed in the soft light of the cocoon, a beautiful woman appears. She is the gift intended to seal the treaty. Elegant and regal, she walks directly over to Picard, smiles, and says, "I am for you, Alrik of Valt." Picard explains her mistake, and the rest of the episode is spent coping with her powerful presence on the ship.

Kamala, the gift, is a genetic rarity among her people; she is an empathic mesomorph. Like Deanna Troi, Kamala has the ability to sense what others want. A highly sought-after mate, she goes through a process in which she permanently bonds with a man, becoming whatever he most desires in a woman. Such a woman caused the war between Krios and Valt Minor when two brothers, rulers of their people, fought over an empathic mesomorph. Picard and Riker immediately object to the use of "a sentient being as property," and Picard orders that Kamala be given quarters on the ship. From the very beginning, Picard sees and treats Kamala as a person.

Yet he advocates the Prime Directive, the doctrine of noninterference, in regard to Kamala. In "Conspiracy," when a female alien is a ruler, the Prime Directive is ignored, and the female alien destroyed. Here, when a female alien is in the service of men, the Prime Directive is invoked to maintain her subservience. It remains for a female human to object to this exchange in women. In her regular breakfast with Picard, Beverly Crusher vehemently objects to the way Kamala is being treated. Beverly asks Picard, "How can you simply deliver her to an arranged marriage—it's like prostitution!" Picard replies that Kamala has chosen this path, but Beverly rebuts him by pointing out that "She has been bred from birth." By pointing out how socialization operates, Beverly makes a feminist point about the conditioning of all women to be perfect mates. Kamala is merely an extrapolation or exaggeration of what exists in the real world— the way in which a woman is raised to believe that having a man and pleasing him should be the focus of her existence. Kamala is Deanna Troi, ratcheted up a notch. Kamala is more rigidly controlled, but her confinement represents the confinement of all women in a male-dominated society. Crusher makes an explicit parallel to slavery when she informs Picard, "That slave trader who calls himself an ambassador has her confined to quarters." Making the connection between slave trading and ambassadorial politics makes it clear that men's politics are made at the cost of women's lives. For example, during the Gulf War, America defended a country that doesn't allow its women to vote, drive, or function as full citizens. It is the Prime Directive again cited in real-life politics. If women's rights are involved and valuable oil products are to be protected, America will not interfere in a country's domestic policies. Not coincidentally, perhaps, "The Perfect Mate" aired shortly after the Gulf War, in April 1992.

Even Kamala's name reflects her adaptability and subordination to a patrilineal system. Her lack of a surname signals her availability—she has not yet become the property of a husband. She was separated from her mother at age four and educated to become the perfect mate. Isolated from others and equals, she has been conditioned for her role as a gift. She does not resent her role, but embraces it. Still, her commitment is suspect, for she has never known another possibility. Only her journey on the *Enterprise* offers the glimpse of another choice. Her journey allows the viewers, too, to contemplate how limiting gender roles are for women. The episode implicitly evokes the idea of compulsory heterosexuality. Kamala is biologically drawn to men, and goes through a three-stage process in which she ultimately and permanently bonds with one man. Her physical process parallels human women's socialization and eventual marriage (90 percent of all women in America marry). And Kamala's journey ends up with a marriage, too. Clad in a traditional white wedding gown, complete with a net veil, Kamala is given away in marriage by Captain Picard, who by this time has fallen in love with her himself. He cannot help himself because Kamala wields power over all men through her sexual allure and her entrancing adaptability.

Kamala emerges from her cocoon in a form-fitting, diaphanous satin gown. Like her personality, the gown tastefully hints at her powers of seduction, providing glimpses of her breasts, her legs, her body. At this stage in her development, she exudes powerful pheromones that all males find irresistible. She has a bewitching smile that she produces as soon as she emerges from the cocoon. And her words are as pleasing to the male auditor as her appearance. When she directs herself to Picard, but addresses him as Alrik, she tells him, "I apologize [for the mistake in identity]; as an empath, I could sense your authority." While she reflects to the captain his need to be in charge, she reflects to Riker his sexuality. As Riker escorts her to her quarters, she acknowledges his sexual curiosity by kissing him. She then informs him, "We [empathic mesomorphs] learn so quickly what stimulates a man that the second time is even better than the first." With two passionate kisses, she turns Riker, a ladies' man, into jelly. He backs away, explaining, "I make it a policy never to open another man's gift." Only the patriarchal hierarchy protects her and him—and Riker is shown immediately after rushing to the holodeck to quench the sexual passion Kamala has generated. Significantly, he does so in the holodeck, with another version of the perfect mate, a projection of a woman that he creates. "Whew," he says, and he wipes his brow.

Picard suffers even more from Kamala's power. Significantly, her actions are not presented as wiles, but as quintessential feminine qualities that she cannot help. Her character reinforces the idea that women are sexual distractions to men. Picard tells Kamala that it bothers him that "a sentient being can live only to be what someone else wants them to be." But many women dress and act in ways to catch and keep a mate. Of course, this is what is expected of human women. Kamala is a more extreme version of traditional femininity, but she echoes the plight of some single women when she answers his question, "What about when you're alone?" with "I am incomplete." She explains to Picard that she is "exactly the way you would want me to be." She proves her extreme adaptability by showing that she is knowledgeable and interested in archaeology, one of Picard's passions. She serves men by becoming devoted to them and their interests. But while she tempts Picard into violating a Federation directive of noninterference, Kamala also has a powerful effect on all other males on the ship, except Data, the emotionless android.

Unable to be in her presence for long, Picard assigns Data to be Kamala's chaperon. As they explore the ship, Kamala's behavior reveals that she desperately needs a chaperon. Like Deanna Troi in other episodes, Kamala acts out, creating havoc wherever she goes. She alters her behavior to please whatever male she is physically closest to. As she and Data enter Ten-Forward, the ship's bar, she undergoes a series of transformations, being the perfect mate for a wide range of males. Getting close to a non-Federation roughneck, she proclaims, "I just want to have a good time" and orders a drink, acting like a bar girl. Her metamorphosis is not restricted to humans, for when Worf intervenes and protects her from the louts, she exits the bar with a Klingon growl at him, a sexual invitation in the lexicon of Klingon mating. Worf growls back, then shakes his head at this outburst that appears to have been involuntary. She becomes whatever a man wants, and this is her defense for her behavior. When she begins to seduce Picard, he asks her, "Why are you doing this, Kamala?" and she replies, "There can only be one reason—because some part of you wants me to." Picard also blames Beverly for this entanglement, telling her, "It's all your fault. You insisted I look into her situation." Picard's blaming Beverly fits perfectly into the idea of the perfect mate; it's always the woman's fault.

Looking is key to this situation, as the presence of mirrors suggests. Evoking Jacques Lacan's description of the mirror stage, in which infants become aware of their autonomy by identifying themselves as separate from the mother, the mirrors in this episode show that Kamala, despite her adult body, is psychologically an infant, unformed and undifferentiated. Kamala's constant gazing at herself in a mirror shows that she is on the verge of developing a self. When she is alone, she gazes at herself and smiles. The camera angle reminds the audience that the viewers are implicated in this male gaze, too. We watch as Picard enters her room, and we see her at first only in a mirror. Then the mirror image blurs as Picard speaks to her, reminding us that this creature exists only to reflect back to man. As Picard enters her quarters, we see Kamala reflected in a mirror three times. Each shot reminds us that Kamala serves to reflect back to men their desires. At the same time, the shots remind the viewers that we too are participating in a fantasy, a representation. The mirrors evoke the holodeck's more sophisticated representation of fantasy. But for women, a mirror functions as a check: Have we created the image of desirable femininity? Kamala's last glance into the full-length mirror occurs after Picard exits, suggesting that she can, and perhaps should, develop the ability to look at and examine herself and her life reflectively.*

What happens is that Kamala bonds with Picard, completing her third and final stage of metamorphosis. In so doing, she becomes the woman who would be his perfect mate—intelligent, strong, fascinating. As Picard's ideal mate, however, she acts as he would have her act. Instead of asking him to violate Federation rules and risk his career, she sacrifices herself, allowing Picard to give her in marriage to Alrik, for whom she has been intended. By insisting on following through on her role as gift, Kamala both follows Picard's principles of honor and protects him, at great cost to herself. For Kamala has learned to love Picard and his interests, and the ruler she is to marry has been revealed as a Philistine who tells Picard that he is "far more interested in the trade agreement than the mesomorph." "I will never truly love him," Kamala tells Picard. But Alrik will never know that

---

*Heller reads the mirrors very differently, suggesting that "the blocking of the scene acts as a visual metaphor for the function that Kamala performs for Picard over the course of the episode . . . he is attracted to what she supplies—a looking-glass in which he can admire himself" (235).

Kamala's image in the mirror as Picard enters her quarters.

she has not bonded with him, for as Kamala reassures Picard, she will use her empathic abilities to act out whatever Alrik desires. "He will never know—I only hope he likes Shakespeare" is her pathetic expression. Because Alrik has already declared his passion for trade agreements to Picard, the viewers realize he is unlikely to share Kamala's dedication to Shakespeare—an interest she has picked up from Picard.

"The Perfect Mate" shows the cost to both Kamala and to Picard of this dangerous type. A perfect mate is born to suffer, for existing only for another will inevitably leave the woman wanting. Picard fulfills a male fantasy of being loved by the perfect, but unattainable and hence undemanding, woman. But because his job requires all his attention and dedication, the perfect mate for him is unavailable. Appropriately, the wedding ceremony takes place on the holodeck, the place where fantasies can be embodied. After all, it is to the holodeck that Riker flees when he feels overwhelmed by Kamala. And the holodeck represents the artificiality of the perfect mate, for all the women there are constructs, real only in the holodeck space and acting only on the orders of the male characters who have created them. (See the discussion of Minuet in chapter 4.) As Joyrich explains, "More than just providing viewers with a futuristic diversion, the holodeck then reiterates the logic of television (and *The Next Genera-tion*) itself, providing the *Enterprise* crew with the ability to actively en-gage with illusionary characters" (*Re-viewing* 7). That so many of these characters are female reminds us of the constructed nature of the femi-nine, a theme of this episode.

Donning a traditional white wedding dress and veil makes Kamala's transformation and parallel to real women even clearer. Again, we see an-other shot of her in a mirror, reminding the viewer we are seeing woman as reflection. Kamala has become a "normal" woman because she is no longer in process of being bonded. As a fixed mesomorph, she can expe-rience unfulfilled desire, in this case for Picard. And she will have to work on pleasing her new mate, Alrik, just as real women are encouraged in books and women's magazines to please their male partners. "The Per-fect Mate" shows how serving as a reflection of men's desires makes a woman a miserable slave. As Cixous and Clément explain, to woman, "each story, each myth says to her 'there is no place for your desire in our affairs of state'" (67). "The Perfect Mate" epitomizes this dynamic. As Joyrich describes it, this episode "thus carries TNG's social and semiotic tensions to their farthest extremes, proclaiming women masters of their fate even while circumscribing femininity as total reflection and service for the heterosexual male" ("Feminist" 68).

"Man of the People" complements the previous two episodes by show-ing the cost to women of serving as the reflection of men's needs, desires, and emotions. The title is ironic: Alkar, the man of the people, a mediator like Riva, exploits women. Women are obviously not considered "people." "Man of the People" first aired the week of October 5, 1992; the episode was written by Frank Abatemarco. As in "Loud as a Whisper," Deanna Troi, the empathic ship's counselor, plays a pivotal role. Representing tra-ditional femininity, she provides the perfect victim for the "man of the people." His exalted title suggests that behind every successful man there is a woman. However, the episode shows, in horrifying detail, the cost to the woman behind the man. Like Kamala, Deanna has all the qualities of the perfect mate: She is beautiful, sexually alluring, intelligent, and em-pathic. Her alternative form of language proves critical to the man of the people and dangerous to her.

Like Riva and Captain Picard, Alkar seems to deserve the perfect mate. Of course, women never seem to deserve the perfect mate; it is only men, in important leadership positions, who are depicted as needing and de-serving someone who serves their needs exclusively. This is an idea embedded in the original *Star Trek,* where Captain Kirk had Yeoman Rand, whose only job was to wait on him. But *Star Trek: The Next Generation* complicates the simple sexism of the original series. The tradition of femininity changes, as it does in the real world, and *The Next Generation* reflects the influence of feminism in its portrayal of a perfect mate. Deanna Troi appears as the victim of a powerful man—his victim because he exploits her. An extremely successful negotiator and apparently devoted son, Alkar seems an altruistic and attractive man. However, his very success has been built, literally, on the bodies of women. As the plot unfolds, we realize that Alkar's extraordinary peace and calm exist only because he projects all negative emotions into a female partner. This episode's feminist message is more obvious than in the previous episodes because the male is not a sympathetic character here. Instead, he is depicted as a vampire who destroys likable women. His victims absorb his negative emotions, raging and aging rapidly, finally dying. The perfect mate, as this episode reveals, functions as a *tabula rasa,* a blank slate onto which the man's emotions can be written. Literally and figuratively, the perfect mate becomes her male partner, reflecting and absorbing his hostility and anger. She absorbs the negative part of the man, the part of himself he wants to subdue and control. The perfect mate's death thus makes perfect sense, for in dying she negates his evil self, and completely loses her self.

Alkar's vampiristic actions unfold gradually; at the beginning of the episode, the viewer, like Deanna, feels drawn to this appealing character. As in "Loud as a Whisper," however, a clue to Alkar's misdeeds appears in the damaged communications that mark the episode's opening. Alkar and his mother must be rescued from a ship, attacked because he, the mediator, was on it. Transported to the *Enterprise,* Alkar beams affably, but his mother acts like a shrew, turning on Deanna in a rage. "You think he's attracted to you. But he isn't. You offer him nothing!" the extremely aged woman shrieks. With her frail old body dressed in a flowing gown over a tight body suit, her long gray hair spread down over her shoulders, the mother seems a stereotype of a witch or a shrew. Her inappropriate attack and Alkar's gentle remonstrance make her seem old and crazy, and Alkar a devoted son.

Despite his bizarre and troubling mother, Deanna is attracted to Alkar. We see the two of them in a t'ai chi–like class, both attired in white, performing stylized exercises. Alkar stares at her; she returns his gaze. After the class, they discuss the importance of the mind-body connection. Prefiguring her later disintegration, and her femininity, Deanna laughingly says, "Sometimes my body has a problem conforming to my mind's wishes." Walking with him to his quarters after this conversation, Deanna again faces an attack from Alkar's mother. This time, although it is still inappropriate, we see that there is some basis for her concern. Screeching, Alkar's mother asks, "Have you mated with him yet? . . . I can always tell. If you do, you'll regret it for the rest of your life." Her words prove prophetic, for Alkar almost kills Deanna. Recounting the incident to Riker, Deanna explains, "She frightens me. . . . She's evil," but the episode reveals that instead of being repulsed by the mother and attracted to the son, Deanna should listen to the woman. The plot reveals the importance of listening to women's voices—even, or perhaps especially, the voice of the crone-mother. The story of the perfect mate, of the woman who sacrifices her needs to serve her mate's, is here used to corroborate the need for women to work together, with each other, against male dominance and manipulation. Falling into the trap of being a perfect mate for a man, as Deanna does, can prevent women from listening to each other as their attention focuses on a man. At the same time, the plot warns of the danger of falling for an attractive man with a persuasive and engaging manner. Such externals may hide evil.

Deanna's traditionally feminine qualities of care and nurturance lead her into dreadful danger. The evil appears after Alkar's mother dies in a most unexpected and insidious way. The mother dies suddenly, and we see her on the floor of Alkar's quarters, her hands clenched like claws, her face a hideous grimace. Deanna makes a tragic error when, acting in accordance with traditional feminine precepts, she asks the grieving Alkar, "Is there anything I can do?" This offer leads Deanna into terrible danger. Innocuously enough, he asks Deanna to perform a funeral meditation with him. As an empath, he explains, she is "the only person on board who could perform this ritual with me." With traditional feminine nurturing, Deanna responds warmly, "I'd be glad to help."

The ritual involves two rocks and some kind words about grief, but it is in essence a grotesque parody of a sexual exchange that is vampiristic. Alkar pulls the rocks out of a small casket-shaped box. The box provides a clue as to their deadly nature. Holding two rocks close together and closing their eyes, Alkar and Deanna touch the rocks together. A blue light leaps from Alkar's rock into Deanna's and into her body. She looks terrified and overwhelmed and we see her eyes open wide with shock. She has been violated, as she is repeatedly throughout the series (see chapter 8).

The episode demonstrates that becoming a perfect mate involves a brutal erasure of the female self. The perfect mate may be a man's dream, but it is a woman's nightmare. Deanna loses control of herself, her focus on what is important to her (her job), and her identity. As with Alkar's mother, Deanna's every waking moment is a torment. She is bedeviled by a need to be with Alkar and to prevent him from forming attachments to other women, whom she sees not as potential allies, but as enemies. Divided from other women and her own identity, Deanna quickly deteriorates. Her breakdown works as a science fiction extrapolation of the isolation and torment experienced by women who are victims of domestic violence, in which the abuser separates the woman from her friends, family, and job. A victim of domestic violence finds that her abuser forces her into existing only for him through a process of isolation. She is forced to respond to his every whim, no matter how absurd, and she endures his abuse as he vents his negative emotions on and through her. The perfect mate parallels precisely the battered women's experience. The process works more slowly in real life, so the science fiction setting enables *Star Trek: The Next Generation* to expose the suffering caused by male violence in a condensed and vividly compelling fashion. Alkar can take Troi over and subdue her in a matter of days, whereas real-life batterers take months or even years. Compressed, this narrative takes on even more power and impact. The conventions of science fiction are thus used to extrapolate and expose the hideous exploitation of domestic violence. As victims of domestic violence are often raped, so Deanna Troi shows signs of this metaphorical rape, a mental invasion and violation.

Like a rape survivor, Deanna immediately changes her way of dressing and behaving. Her body reflects the cost of carrying Alkar's negative emotions almost immediately. As Picard finally realizes by the end of the episode, Deanna has been brutalized, and she goes through dramatic changes that reflect her suffering. We see Deanna in her quarters, gazing into her mirror. Already she has circles under her eyes and many wrinkles. We see her alone, seeking repose practicing the t'ai chi–like moves; significantly, we see in the mirror four images of Deanna—she represents everywoman and she is fragmenting, disintegrating. A sign of her distress appears in her attire. Instead of her uniform, she begins wearing outrageously sexual outfits. She attempts to seduce Alkar, blatantly and incompetently. He rejects her; she doesn't realize he is already using her body in another way. Like survivors of sexual abuse, Deanna acts out her pain by wanton and random sex. She picks up a young engineer in an elevator, and then has him in her quarters when Will Riker, her former lover, comes on a scheduled work appointment. Wearing a white, very revealing gown, she behaves rudely to the engineer and to Riker.

Counselor Deanna Troi has changed her appearance, and Riker and Data notice.

Deanna's distress even affects her work. We see her in a counseling appointment, chastising and haranguing rather than comforting a young, visibly upset cadet. Even Commander Data, the unemotional android, notices the dramatic change in her looks, commenting with his habitual understatement, "Counselor Troi has altered her appearance." This comment accentuates the extreme alteration in Troi's dress, for Data makes the statement as Deanna staggers in on high heels, wearing a sequin-studded fishnet dress that leaves nothing to the imagination. With her hair swept up and wearing heavy makeup, Deanna looks like an aging tramp, for her hair has begun to turn gray. Echoing Alkar's mother, Deanna attacks the female colleague who is meeting with Alkar, saying, "You want him but you have nothing to give him." Finally, Riker leads Deanna back to her quarters, where she first passionately kisses him and then violently scratches his face and neck, leaving marks that ooze blood. In her acting out of sexual aggression and negativity, Deanna uses her body to perform and complain about the assault on her mind. Deanna Troi explicitly carries negative emotions that abused women carry. Her behavior becomes inappropriate and seems inexplicable and indefensible to others. She shows no external signs of abuse, so she seems to be the problem, not

Alkar, her abuser. In this way, she resembles the hysteric described by Cixous and Clément in *The Newly Born Woman*. As Cixous and Clément call for, in this plot Deanna Troi "open[s] up the space where woman is wandering, roaming, (a rogue wave), flying, (thieving)" (91). Deanna Troi's actions, "exasperating, immoderate, and contradictory, destroy laws, the 'natural' order" (96). Through her altered appearance and disruptive behavior, "her appearance caus[es], if not revolution, harrowing explosions" (98).

Fortunately for Deanna, another woman, Dr. Beverly Crusher, comes to her aid. Suspicious about the demise of Alkar's mother, Beverly asks permission to do an autopsy. Alkar refuses, but Beverly persists, examining transport and medical tricorder logs to find discrepancies in Alkar's accounts. Beverly discovers that the woman was only thirty years old, despite her aged appearance, and that genetically, she was not Alkar's mother. Beverly slows down Deanna's aging and finally fakes her death in order to fool Alkar into releasing Deanna from bondage. Female solidarity, then, provides the release for the female survivor of male aggression. In an act that again recalls *The Newly Born Woman*, Beverly "kills" Deanna with a shot, and then resuscitates her thirty minutes later, a newly born woman, free from the clutches of the male predator. This plot reveals that abuse will be the lot of the perfect mate. It's not that being a perfect mate justifies abuse, but that giving a man that much power over her and abnegating herself can lead to disaster.

The plot emphasizes that the cycle of violence will merely continue until the male predator is stopped. Alkar "releases" Deanna after he thinks she is dead, but he immediately locates another victim, the female colleague Deanna had tried to warn as she herself had been warned. Alone in his quarters, the woman naively asks Alkar, "Is there anything I can do?" He repeats the ritual with the rocks but is stopped when the crew transports the woman away from Alkar before he completes the transference of his negative emotions. The emotions rebound upon him, and he ages with great rapidity, screams, and drops to the floor. He attempts to speak, lifts one finger in an impotent gesture, and then dies. In poetic justice, Alkar bears and dies from all the rage and anger he has transferred to women for so long. In this way, the plot reveals the cost to men and women of the perfect mate. Male projection, then, can also destroy the man if he attempts to create and live through a perfect mate. Transferring all his aggression to women makes Alkar unbalanced, and vulnerable too. The plot suggests that men can and should be responsible for their own emotions and violent impulses. As he falls dead, Deanna's youthful appearance, abundant dark hair, and fresh young skin are restored. She lifts her hand and smiles. The feminine, untrammeled by male aggression, survives.

"Eye of the Beholder," from the show's last season, finds Deanna Troi again in a pivotal position. Again the plot reveals the dangers of an extreme version of traditional femininity that emphasizes a woman as a reflection of male desires; Deanna's empathic responses put her in danger of losing her life. "Eye of the Beholder" first aired the week of February 28, 1994; the episode was written by René Echevarria. The episode's title suggests that the beholder, a man, should determine what is beautiful or desirable, and he does so based on his own needs. Like the other episodes, however, this one puts a twist on this familiar notion. Viewers see through Deanna's eyes the horror of male dominance and violence. As in "Man of the People," male violence is exposed as a danger to women. The story opens with a young crewman committing suicide by jumping into a plasma stream. Oblivious to Commander Riker, who is trying to stop him, he looks right into the stream and leaps into it. Investigating this mysterious and unprecedented suicide, Lieutenant Worf, as chief of security, and Deanna, as the ship's counselor, try to discover why Kwan killed himself.

One clue exists in Kwan's heritage. His mother was an empathic Betazoid, like Troi's mother. So although he was male, Kwan has been feminized by empathic sensitivities. The show explores telemetry, an empathic trait associated with witches: the ability to read emotions from objects. This power kills Kwan and almost results in Deanna's death as well. Again, an extreme sensitivity to the emotions of others, a traditional trait of the female, is presented as literally dangerous. So through a male character, as through Alkar's mother's death, we see that the qualities of a perfect mate can be deadly for those who possess and cultivate them. The plot reveals that being a receptor, or receptacle, makes the female highly vulnerable to violence.

As she is with Alkar in "Man of the People," Deanna relates how she is "suddenly overwhelmed by a flood of emotions, rage, fear, and panic." Whereas Alkar, a man, projected these negative emotions onto her, in this case, it seems to be the setting itself that has retained the images and feelings associated with a man murdering his former lover and her new beau. As she tells Worf how she feels, the warlike security chief reifies her view by soberly agreeing, "There are things we do not understand but nevertheless exist." The support for her emotional response to an empty room from the most masculine of all the characters aboard the *Enterprise*, a Klingon warrior, makes the support especially compelling. Deanna Troi's reaction to an empty room that contains strong emotions evokes the notion of the perfect mate—here so perfect that she can sense masculine rage in a blank space. Meanwhile, Deanna's quarters, where they are speaking, show her at her most delicate and feminine—a delicate pink floral arrangement dominates her coffee table and she daintily sips tea. Worf, of course, feels or sees none of what almost kills Deanna.

What Deanna witnesses is a sexually inspired double murder; the murderer a jealous male partner. Significantly, however, she sees a woman screaming "no—no—please" as she cowers in a corner, helplessly trying to avoid her attacker. However, Deanna sees the incident not from the woman's perspective, but as she did with Alkar, from the man's perspective. Deanna feels and sees the murderer's negative emotions. As a perfect mate, she experiences what he experiences and, as in the other episodes, it damages her. She sees him, too, in a reflection. But when she confronts the murderer, Lieutenant Pierce, he denies everything and she cannot read his current emotions. To continue the investigation, Deanna must turn again to Beverly Crusher for help. Beverly provides an inhibitor that enables Deanna to investigate without being overwhelmed by the negative emotions she encounters.

Although the double murder is horrible and provoked by jealousy, it suggests the power of a woman's laugh. Pierce has come upon a former girlfriend and her new lover, who nervously laugh at him, driving him into a murderous rage. Their bodies and their murder had not been discovered for eight years. The lapse of so many years suggests the permanence of such negative emotions that persist and cause continuing damage. Pierce continues to displace his emotions onto Deanna, despite the inhibitors. Having just begun a sexual relationship with Worf, Deanna is at a vulnerable point. She begins to feel jealousy and sees Worf with another woman. Her hallucinations drive her crazy, so that she finds herself about to commit suicide as young Kwan had done. Deanna imagines that she has discovered Worf with another woman and killed him. Despondent, she prepares to throw herself into the plasma stream. At the very last second, Worf saves her. Yet she has the last word, by revealing to him that she had killed him in her hallucination. He looks puzzled and worried as she reminds him, "Hell hath no fury like a woman scorned." Deanna Troi's comments are in perfect synchronicity with the figure of the perfect mate. By experiencing the male murderer's emotions, Troi effectively becomes him, reenacting the crime in her own life. Yet the experience, once resisted, restores Deanna to a position of power. She has been powerless, prey to emotions because of her empathic ability. But having been warned, she can and does regain her equanimity. Kwan, the young man who commits suicide, does so because he has not been warned. "Eye of the Beholder," like the earlier three episodes, can be read as a warning to women of the dangers of traditional feminine qualities such as nurturing or care for others, especially when these equal self-surrender. Carried to an extreme or applied to the wrong man, these are the very qualities that can destroy a woman. Deanna Troi's experience implicitly warns the female viewers of the dangers of being a perfect mate, just as Alkar's "mother" explicitly warns Deanna Troi (and by implication other women) to stay away from a man who desires a perfect mate, a woman to possess and reflect himself.

The figure of the perfect mate, then, is far more complicated than a sexist depiction of a male fantasy of a woman who exists only for him. That this fantasy exists and is powerful for both men and women is evident in all four episodes. The likable and admirable character of Deanna Troi finds herself endangered every time she succumbs to the pattern of the perfect mate. Exploring the perfect mate through science fiction convention allows *Star Trek: The Next Generation* to examine some of the same issues it deals with through the female alien and the woman ruler, but from a different angle. Whereas French feminist notions about feminine power and language dominate the depiction of the female alien and the woman ruler, the perfect mate shows what can happen if women do not exercise the power of the feminine. Embodying traditional feminine qualities such as nurturing, self-abnegation, and existing vicariously through the achievements of male partners brings suffering, self-destruction, and perhaps even death. The episodes use the qualities of the perfect mate to reveal how repugnant and debilitating these notions can be for women. But the fact that Deanna Troi escapes, with her self, energy, and identity restored, also provides the hope that no matter how trammeled women are by such sexist conventions, they can and will escape.

Part 2

4

"Fully Functional": Machines and Gender

The gendering of machines has a long history, not only in science fiction, but also in the culture at large. Ships, for example, often are designated female, and their captains are male. Although there is no intrinsic reason to gender machines, nothing in their makeup that requires it, humans do so. *Star Trek: The Next Generation* presents the gendering of machines in a number of fascinating and revealing ways, showing a great deal about gender, technology, and the relationship between the two. Androids especially draw on the science fiction quality of defamiliarization to enable us to see human problems from a new perspective. An android is a specific version of a cyborg—a being defined as part human, part machine; it is not quite human, but it looks and acts humanoid. Because of its separation from, and subordination to, mankind, an android can effectively function as a stand-in for women.

Data, a member of the bridge crew who has been created to imitate human beings, appears at the center of most episodes about gendering of machines. An android because he has been made to resemble humans, Data presents a contrast to robots, machines who may be sentient but who do not look like humans. Data can almost pass for human, so his presence also brings up many of the issues of race and gender discussed in chapter 6. In an insightful article on Data as racial other, "Dating Data: Miscegenation in *Star Trek: The Next Generation*," Rhonda V. Wilcox explores the ways in which this android functions as a stand-in for issues of racial difference. Data's treatment in "The Mismeasure of Man" is discussed in Daniel Bernardi's book on race, *Star Trek and History,* and is mentioned in Ferguson et al.'s "Gender Identity in *Star Trek.*" Data's treatment as Other overtly reflects on the issue of difference in contemporary

American society. But in part because Wilcox and Bernardi so skillfully cover the territory of race, this chapter focuses on the way in which Data serves a parallel function for gender, as a feminine stand-in. Because women are also an oppressed group, much of what Wilcox argues about race can be applied to gender.

Because of his position as racially other, Data stands in for woman. In this regard, the character parallels the monster in Mary Shelley's *Franken-stein*. As many feminist critics such as Jane Donawerth have pointed out, the monster shares many similarities with women. Like the monster, Data is presented sympathetically, engaging the viewer's concern. In this re-gard, as in many others, *Star Trek: The Next Generation* draws on a long-standing science fiction trope that has a feminist angle.

In too many episodes to enumerate, Data serves a plot function to re-mind us of sexual difference. But in several key episodes, his position is central; the plot revolves around the issues he raises about gender. The gendering of machines has been a focus of *Star Trek: The Next Generation* from the very first season. In "The Naked Now," from that season, Data demonstrates that he is "fully functional" sexually. Yet the woman he has sex with rejects him after she escapes the influence of the powerful intoxi-cant that has infected the crew. The plot suggests that Data could be found desirable only by a human under the influence of drugs. In "11001001," a race closely linked to a master computer evokes a stereotypical and meta-phorical rendering of the feminine. As in the episodes discussed in chap-ters 1 and 2, these female machine-connected aliens threaten patriarchy by taking over the *Enterprise*. In "The Most Toys" Data is reduced to a collect-or's possession, reflecting the position of trophy wife. In "The Quality of Life," Data encounters a new machine lifeform and risks his career and his captain's life to preserve it. Finally, in "Inheritance" Data confronts his own femininity and that of machines when he meets his "mother."

Each of these episodes reveals Data's metaphorical femininity, but there is more evidence for Data's femininity in the depiction of other machines as feminine. The Borg are an alien collective race that has superior weap-onry and fighting skills, in part because they are a collective entity. Each Borg sees itself as part of a larger whole, so the individual Borg will sacrifice itself for the greater good of the Borg as a unit. Another version of the feminized, collective machine appears on the *Enterprise* itself in the holodeck characters. The holodeck is a virtual reality simulator that al-lows a crew member to create any scene he or she wishes. All, including simulated humans, appear and feel real, and are so, within the holodeck itself. Significantly, most of the holodeck characters who have personality or are featured in an episode are female (one exception is Professor Moriarty, but even he is complete only after a female companion is created for him). As Rhonda V. Wilcox explains, the sexist depiction of women on the show appears in "the crew's fascination with synthetic women as opposed to real ones—in particular, with holographic, computer-created women" ("Shifting" 56). She argues that whereas women's rare interactions on the holodeck are presented as fantasies, the male characters are often depicted as "engag[ing] themselves emotionally with the unreal" ("Shifting" 57).* These characteristics of the holodeck point toward the femininity of computer-generated reality and computers in general. This casting is not essential to the technology, but is a cultural creation drawing on the identification of ships, cars, and planes as feminine and of interior space, cyberspace, as womblike. This gendering is further emphasized by the ship's female computer voice. Although the Borg, an alien race that is part organic, part machine, and the holodeck women characters seem to have little in common—for example, the Borg are hideously ugly and the holodeck women are unrealistically gorgeous—both creations emphasize the femininity of the machine and thus throw Data's femininity into sharper relief.

The cyborg, or half-organic, half-machine creature, also points toward a feminization of the machine. The cyborg is itself feminized. As a machine, the being is personified as female; in many instances, a cyborg is given a feminine gender. Women and cyborgs share many overlapping qualities in terms of their expected position of service, their willingness to serve and sacrifice themselves for others, their commitment to community over self. As Lynne Joyrich claims, "A connection between figurations of women and cyborgs certainly exists, particularly on television, in which cyborgs are feminized and women cyborgized" ("Feminist" 66). This parallel can be fruitful for feminist critics. What the cyborg does that is helpful for feminists, according to Anne Balsamo, is to "foreground the constructedness of otherness" (33). Like the female body, as Balsamo explains, the cyborg is "an intensely fascinating yet threatening object of cultural control" (28). Appropriately, one of the most famous essays of feminist criticism is Donna Haraway's "A Manifesto for Cyborgs," in which she demonstrates the usefulness of the cyborg for feminist theory. Stressing how the figure of the cyborg encapsulates hybridity and muta-

*Wilcox notes, "For the *Enterprise* women, romances on the holodeck (the holographic entertainment area) are rare" ("Shifting" 56).

bility, Haraway calls for feminists to embrace the figure in her liminality and her potential to challenge existing patriarchal and capitalist social structures. In a number of episodes, *Star Trek: The Next Generation* uses the cyborg and the feminized machine to question traditional femininity. By exposing the connection between machines and the feminine, the episodes expose sexism through displaced feminine characters, machines, and androids. That this is a central theme in the series is emphasized by the early and repeated appearance of machine-based lifeforms.

The Borg exemplifies this function of the cyborg. The Borg is a collective entity, itself feminine when contrasted (as is shown in chapters 1 and 2) to the rugged and insistent masculine individuality typified by the male members of the *Enterprise*. The Borg ship evokes a womb and the alien from *Aliens*—the interior is dark, womblike, as each Borg nestles into a crevice in a wall. (Recall, too, that the computer on board the ship in *Alien* is called Mother.) As Borg are created from organic "units" such as humans, the ship is a vast site of reproduction. Although the Borg themselves are not the focus of this chapter, their similarity to Data and affinity to him and his brother Lore is critical to an understanding of Data. Lore, Data's evil identical brother, even affiliates himself with the Borg in "Descent," an alliance that suggests the androids' affiliation and sympathy for the Borg. In this episode, Data himself appears to have joined his brother in allying himself with the Borg. Like Data and Lore, the Borg collective and its tremendous technological power pose a threat to the Federation. As a machine-based lifeform, Data is like the Borg in his potential immortality, flawless efficiency, and ability. This parallel and gendering were emphasized in *First Contact*, the first *Star Trek: The Next Generation* film. The movie reveals that the Borg are ruled by a queen, who seduces Data to join the Borg. As Taylor Harrison argues in another context, "The cyborg as a textual figure points to and stands in for other fusions. Such a strategy is not one of masking, but of replacing" (246). What is replaced here is the female, as the feminine is represented by the machine. Data and other machine-based lifeforms evoke the feminine, and their treatment by the Federation points to the ways in which human women are marginalized and controlled. *Star Trek: The Next Generation*'s use of feminine machines reflects the promise of the cyborg for women, but not its fulfillment.

The gendering of machines dominates the first episode after the pilot, "The Naked Now." Drawing heavily on a classic *Star Trek* episode, "The Naked Now" explicitly refers to the original *Enterprise*, the ship itself characterized as feminine and hence setting up the theme of gender and machines. The episode was written by J. Michael Bingham and aired the week of October 5, 1987. The current *Enterprise,* like its predecessor, encounters unusual gravity fields, which have the effect of an intoxicant on the crew. Rendezvousing with a research vessel that is investigating a supernova, Captain Picard explains, "Something has gone wrong with the research vessel." Just after his pronouncement, we hear a transmission from the science ship. Peals of female laughter disrupt the staid and masculine bridge of the *Enterprise.* A sensual, husky female voice intones, "Well, hello, *Enterprise.* I hope you have a lot of pretty boys on board because I'm willing and waiting. In fact, we're going to have a real blowout here." In seconds, we hear an explosion, and then dead silence. The message is that female sexuality can literally blow a ship apart. Eighty people have been killed by, in the captain's words, "madness, mass hysteria." This introduction sets up the association between femininity and hysteria, unbridled female sexuality and death. Significantly, this intoxicant provides the only time Data indisputably experiences sexual relations in the seven-year run of the show. His femininity emerges through this uninhibiting substance that reveals the inner desires and personality of each crew member.

As Data represents femininity, though he is a "fully functional" male android, so his sexual partner, Tasha Yar, represents masculinity. The *Enterprise*'s chief of security, Tasha is seen only in the same unisex Starfleet uniform that the men wear. With her hair cropped quite short, wearing no makeup, Tasha repeatedly demonstrates her machismo. Yet when affected by the intoxicant, Tasha reveals her "true" feminine self. Sashaying and swiveling her hips, Tasha exudes female sexuality and furthers her transformation by entering Deanna Troi's quarters. As discussed earlier, Deanna is the most obvious and consistent symbol of the feminine on the show, and her wardrobe reflects this. As Joyrich points out, Troi is "noticeable for her extravagant hairstyles and (at least before the last season) her singular neglect of regulation uniform in favor of low-cut costumes that emphasize her body" ("Feminist" 63). One critic has even devoted an entire article to the significance of Troi's fashions (Hastie). Naturally, Tasha finds the most seductive and flimsy dresses that Deanna has and begins trying them on. When Deanna appears, Tasha asks her which she likes best. Deanna takes these typical feminine queries as evidence that Tasha is ill and says she should go to sickbay.

Deanna's actions suit her stereotypical feminine role as ship's counselor, but they also emphasize how women can be used to control and monitor other women's behavior. Because the feminine (Deanna) cannot quell the feminine (Tasha), Captain Picard sends another version of the feminine, Data. But Data too catches the "strange contaminant," and he too behaves in a flighty, feminine fashion. In his case, Data acts like a giddy girl, demonstrating emotion and high-spiritedness. When Tasha seduces Data, he does not resist her or follow orders to escort her to sickbay. As in French feminist theory, the feminine is marked in this episode by hysteria, a disregard for order and hierarchy, and acting out through the body. This feminine malady breaks down the patriarchal social order, causing the hyperloyal Data and Tasha to disobey orders, to mutiny. They do so in part by engaging in sex. In an exchange that signifies the breakdown of gender categories, Tasha seduces Data. Both characters abandon their rigidity and Tasha acts out a masculine role of aggressive seducer while Data acts the role of acquiescent female.

When Data comments on her seductive attire, Tasha replies, "I got out of my uniform for *you*, Data." Wearing a harem-type outfit that leaves her midriff down to her groin completely bare, Tasha has also slicked back her hair, softening it with a curl in the front. She's wearing heavy eye makeup, too. In a direct address, Tasha explains her needs: "What I want now is gentleness and joy and love. From you Data. You are fully functional, aren't you?" He explains that "I am programmed in multiple techniques, a broad variety of pleasuring." Sighing "Ooooh," she exclaims, "You jewel, that's exactly what I had hoped." Calling him a jewel feminizes him, as her direct request for sex masculinizes her. As a "jewel," Data is objectified, as women are traditionally cast as sex objects for a male gaze. The role reversal continues as she takes a slightly smiling Data by the hand and leads him into her bedroom. She embraces him, and then turns around, throwing him down on her bed. This maneuver reveals that her top is alluringly backless. Then the door abruptly closes. Afterward, coyly positioning himself in the doorway to the bridge, Data returns to duty, bragging to the captain that he is "fully functional." In a statement that could apply to gender differences, he tells the captain, who imagines the android to be immune to the intoxicant affecting the rest of the crew, "We are more alike than unlike, my dear captain." The phrase "my dear captain" appears next on Beverly Crusher's lips as she tries to seduce the captain, the repetition again stressing Data's femininity.

Yet Beverly Crusher develops an antidote that puts an end to all the feminine disorder and unbridled sexuality. Things return to their rigid, controlled state. Just how rigid the symbolic order is appears at the beginning of the outbreak when Data begins to recite a limerick: "There once was a young lady from Venus / Who had a face shaped like a—" The "p" word cannot be uttered on the bridge, so Captain Picard hurriedly cuts Data's vocalization off. Patriarchy elides the ever-present phallus and its importance, its unutterability emphasizing its sacredness. Similarly, restored to her masculine self, Tasha Yar enters the bridge and rejects the feminine disorder of the previous hours. Data sees Tasha enter and looks, then looks down and away. She strides over to him and says, vehemently, "Data, I'm going to tell you this just once. It never happened." Repudiating her encounter with him, she stalks to the front of the bridge room. Picard announces to the ship in general, "I put it to you all. I think we should end up with a fine crew—if we avoid temptation." So the feminine has been repressed and patriarchal order restored. But Picard's phrasing, "if we avoid temptation," suggests that the feminine disorder remains a threat to the ship and must be guarded against in the future. As the first episode after the pilot, "The Naked Now" signals the ways in which the feminine and the masculine will appear on the show. Securely identified as subordinate, different, and feminine, Data shows that the machine is and will be kept under control. His position as representative of the feminine is paradoxical because his logic and lack of emotion should make him masculine, but his subordinate position and plot functions associate him with the feminine.

"11001001," another episode from the very first season, repeats this theme using an alien race. Written by Maurice Hurley and Robert Lewin, "11001001" first aired the week of February 1, 1988. The *Enterprise* returns to a starbase to have a computer upgrade. As mentioned previously, in *Star Trek* and *Star Trek: The Next Generation*, computers are gendered female through a decidedly female voice. Updating the computer will be performed by aliens known as Bynars. Their race has grown so dependent on computers that they work in pairs and communicate in a high-pitched binary language. In a sense, they function like organic extensions of a computer. The four actors who were cast as Bynars were all female dancers, but the casting alone does not make them a feminine race.

Smaller than human males, with high-pitched voices, their pairing as well as their physical appearance associates them with the feminine. They work with the *Enterprise*'s main computer, which throughout the series has a female voice. Computers themselves are seen as feminine, containing within themselves multiple consciousnesses. In this sense, they evoke the female aliens and woman rulers of chapters 1 and 2. These aliens, like those discussed previously, reflect a French feminist characterization of the feminine, especially through language. The Bynars make computing's femininity clear. Their group language appears when they speak English. Instead of speaking in separate sentences, they weave in and out of feminine language, sharing each declaration and utterance. This race enacts what Cixous describes as *l'écriture feminine:* "These waves, these floods" (Cixous and Clément 246), "a language of 1,000 tongues which knows neither enclosure nor death" (260). Riker is suspicious of them because they are "acting so excited," or feminine. Furthermore, when they decide to steal the *Enterprise,* they do so not by force, but by guile, using a holographic computer projection.

In a creation who evokes "The Perfect Mate" discussed in chapter 3, the Bynars devise "Minuet," a holographic projection, a computer simulation, who entrances and distracts both Commander Riker and Captain Picard. Riker appears to be in control as he enters the holodeck and orders a setting from New Orleans, a jazz club on Bourbon Street. But despite his overt mastery, he is soon entranced and bamboozled by Minuet. The Bynars watch from the doorway as Riker puts the moves on Minuet, oblivious to the Bynars. Wearing a tight, short, red strapless dress, Minuet sits perched on a bar stool, ready to massage Riker's ego. Overwhelmed by her beauty and attentiveness, Riker exclaims that she is "too real." He asks, as Tasha has asked Data a few weeks before, "How far can this relationship go? How real are you?" She assures him, "As real as you need me to be," and they kiss passionately. Captain Picard enters at this moment and soon he too falls under Minuet's spell. Picard says that she is "very impressive" as she speaks French to him. "You're very different. You adapt," he comments. He tells Riker that Minuet is "more than intuitive," and Riker replies, "She already knows what I want her to say before I'm aware of it myself. It's uncanny." These descriptions recall the female alien, woman ruler, and perfect mate analyzed in the first three chapters. Like those figures, Minuet presents a feminine threat to the order of the *Enterprise,* but this time a technological, computer-based one.

"An exquisite example of a computer product," as Wilcox ("Shifting" 57) styles her, Minuet is created to distract Riker from the computer-dependent Bynars as they take over the *Enterprise.* As she distracts first Riker and then Picard, the *Enterprise* is evacuated under a false alarm and then stolen by the Bynars. They kidnap Picard and Riker because they need help on their home world. Their all-powerful mainframe computer is threatened by an electromagnetic impulse from an exploding star. In-

The seductive Minuet.

stead of asking for help, they sneak away with the equipment and personnel they need. In a stereotypical feminine fashion, they manipulate rather than confront, just as Minuet manipulates Riker.

Picard and Riker soon figure out the plot to take over the *Enterprise*. Their awareness begins just after Picard renounces love and the feminine. "Doesn't love always begin that way, with the illusion more real than the woman?" he asks, rhetorically. And the illusion begins to unravel. Minuet cannot keep them on the holodeck, and Picard angrily asserts the importance of regaining control of the ship, which itself is feminine. Even at the cost of their lives, "We've got to regain control of the ship," he tells Riker. To the sounds of military music, they stride through the *Enterprise*'s empty corridors. They cannot communicate with the bridge. "If we don't regain control then no one else should have it," Captain Picard declares, explaining to Riker why they must activate the self-destruct sequence. Significantly, the voice to the self-destruct countdown is male, in contrast to the usual female voice of the ship's computer. On the Starbase, the hypermasculine Klingon, Worf, declares, "Someone else has control of the ship."

But as throughout the series, the threat to patriarchal order is defeated. Picard and Riker make it to the bridge and halt the self-destruct sequence because they find a pile of Bynars, unconscious and in a huddle. Pathetically, they weakly speak together, "Please try to help us." As powerful as they seemed, this feminine race still needs men to rescue them. Picard and Riker discover that the Bynars have performed a core dump of information from their computer into the *Enterprise* computer. But they are not sure how to help the Bynars until they realize that Minuet was the "note" the Bynars left for them. She explains what happened, and they return to the bridge to reboot the Bynar computer. The Bynars stir and wake up. Apologetically, they offer to return to the Starbase "for whatever punishment your system requires of us." They acknowledge and accept the patriarchal order. Picard communicates with the Starbase, reiterating "Everything's under control" and "Everything's in order."

Yet although the feminine has been subordinated, it still retains power. That the Bynars could steal Starfleet's head ship attests to their power, and so does Minuet's continuing influence on Riker. He returns to the holodeck, but she cannot be activated because she was "part of the Bynars." Riker tries variations in the program, but still Minuet cannot be recreated. Captain Picard tries to reassure Riker and comfort him with banalities. "You know, Number One, some relationships just can't work." Riker replies, "Yes, probably true. She'll be difficult to forget."

This episode repeats many of the themes of "The Naked Now": the destructive and disordering power of the feminine, the need for men to beware feminine guile, the power females have through their sexuality, the masculine nature of traditional language and discourse, and the femininity of technology, especially computers. This same message is repeated from another perspective in "The Most Toys," in which Data's feminized position is made clear.

In "The Most Toys" Data reflects the subordinate status of women, especially as trophies. Written by Shari Goodhartz, this episode first aired the week of May 7, 1990. In this episode, Data is abducted by a trader who specializes in collecting rare and unique artifacts. Kiva Fajo, the trader, has arranged for Data's shuttle to explode after Data has been immobilized by Varria, a woman who has been a slave to Fajo for fourteen years. The plot follows Data's attempts to bond with Varria and to make an escape.

Data has been knocked unconscious, frozen in a submissive and degrading posture. As we saw Deanna in "Man of the People," the camera zooms in on Data from above. We see Data supine on a red sofa, his legs spread apart, his arms up, as though to ward off attack. Gradually Data's consciousness returns, and his captor appears. In language that reflects

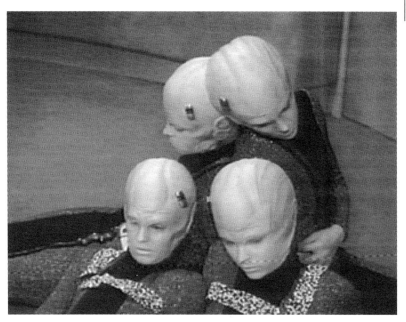

The Bynars, collapsed in a helpless heap.

the gendered nature of their interactions, Fajo responds to Data's query as to why he is being held. "You have been brought here for my enjoyment and appreciation," Fajo explains. Like a caged bird, Data is supposed to enjoy his captivity. He will be "catered to, fawned over, cared for. Your every wish will be fulfilled," Fajo says, justifying Data's imprisonment. The similarity of Data's position to that of a a battered woman is striking.

Fajo pretends to care for Data and cater to his needs, but really Fajo revels in the control he has over Data. Fajo's fawning language evokes the language of love and desire. In a controlling gesture of domestic violence, Fajo even tells Data what to wear and insists that he sit in a particular chair and entertain Fajo's guests. "Put on the lovely new clothes," Data is instructed. When he refuses, Fajo applies an acid that eats away at Data's Starfleet uniform. This move is classic in battering; the batterer destroys his victim's belongings, often her clothes. Data then has the choice of appearing naked or wearing the designated new outfit. Fajo taunts him, again in words that evoke dominance and men's traditional control of women. "Personally I'd be delighted to see you go naked," he informs Data. Fajo's language adds sexual dominance to the power and control he already exerts. And when all other inducements to be controlled fail,

Fajo uses another move characteristic of batterers; he tells Data that he will kill Varria, someone Data has grown attached to, if he refuses to comply with Fajo's wishes.

Fajo's word choice invariably suggests Data's feminine position. "You are the crown jewel of my collection, a treasure beyond comparison," he tells Data. The words recall Tasha's similar description of Data as "a jewel" in "The Naked Now." Fajo insists that Data should not resent, but enjoy his subordinance. "I think you should be flattered," he tells Data, in words that evoke a dominant male's attitude toward a woman he oppresses.

Lest we miss the parallel to women, however, some of the other objects Fajo collects point to Data's feminine status. The only other living creature in Fajo's collection is female, "the last surviving member of her species," Fajo explains to Data. One brief shot shows Data feeding the creature and speaking to her, revealing Data's nurturing maternal side, also revealed by his pet cat, an animal traditionally a woman's pet. In another sequence, Data stares at the *Mona Lisa* by Leonardo da Vinci. He appears mesmerized and tries to imitate that famous smile. The sequence suggests the *Mona Lisa* as a mirror for Data—a feminine reflection of his enigmatic, and hence feminized, character.

Varria, the alien woman whom Fajo threatens to kill in order to make Data comply with his wishes, finally rebels. She helps Data escape but is herself killed by Fajo during the attempt. Using a barbarous weapon that tears the body apart, Fajo tortures Varria before she dies. Data, who as a machine is not supposed to feel emotion, turns on Fajo. Firing the same weapon, long outlawed by the Federation, Data almost kills Fajo in the same barbarous fashion. But a simultaneous transport back to the *Enterprise* saves Fajo from this hideous death, preserving him to be tried for his crimes.

The episode exposes the awfulness of treating any living being as a possession, for centuries the legal the status of women. "The Most Toys" suggests that such attitudes persist, for although Fajo behaves illegally, he has gotten away with his treatment of women (and feminized objects) for decades. Only because Varria decides to work with Data does Data escape. The plot suggests that women must work together to resist subjugation. But Varria's death shows that such resistance can come with a high price: life itself. In this regard, Varria can be read as a stand-in for the thousands of women killed each year by abusive men, just as they attempt to escape. Through Data as a feminized machine, *Star Trek: The Next Generation* protests against notions of females as possessions and

Data with the Mona Lisa, practicing her smile.

suggests that the feminine can and should revolt against masculine control. Data's release of emotion, shown by his firing on Fajo, is justified. In a final confrontation, Data asserts that he can take no pleasure in Fajo's imprisonment, but unlike Fajo, we know that Data did fire on him. And as viewers, we can experience satisfaction in the collector's now being collected himself. This is the same pleasure that viewers receive in films such as *Sleeping with the Enemy,* in which a battered wife, played by Julia Roberts, turns a gun on her abusive husband.

In "The Quality of Life" Data again assumes a prominent role in the defense of a machine lifeform that is presented as feminine, but rather than protecting himself, Data intervenes to save the lives of a new sentient machine race, the Exocomps. Created as a tool, cute like the Dirt Devil, a small vacuum cleaner, the Exocomps are treated as expendable items by their female scientist-creator. Problem-solving smart computers, Exocomps work together and appear to communicate telepathically with their mates. "The Quality of Life" was written by Naren Shankar and first aired the week of November 16, 1992.

The episode opens with a poker game, a recurring scene in *Star Trek: The Next Generation.* The poker game often is used to air gender differences, and this particular scene is quite blatant. The poker game evokes the notion of the frontier, a logical association for the series because classic *Star Trek* was described by Gene Roddenberry as "*Wagon Train* in outer space." The poker game reinforces the sense of frontier life and its rough and ready masculinity and competition. It is at poker games that some of the most specific comments about gender are made (see for example, the discussion of the poker game in "The Outcast," chapter 5). And this game proves no exception as Beverly provokes a passionate defense of beards by the men—beards that are a sign of frontier life and removal from feminine civilization.

Worf, Geordi La Forge, Riker, and Beverly are in the middle of a poker game when the discussion turns to beards. Worf asks whether La Forge will continue growing his beard, and Riker nods approvingly, saying that he likes the beard. Interrupting and ridiculing their male bonding, Beverly comments that men with beards may be trying to hide something, and that after all, beards are simply a "fashion statement." Worf insists that "to Klingons, a beard is a symbol of strength." Riker takes umbrage, too, and angrily contradicts Beverly: "Don't be ridiculous. The beard is an ancient and proud tradition. A sign of strength." La Forge objects mildly, saying that Beverly seems to be implying that growing a beard is "no more than an affectation." Beverly replies that she sees nothing wrong with that: "I just think it's time that you men admit it." She compares beards to makeup. As they are in the middle of a hand of the poker game, Beverly suggests that they bet—if she wins, they all shave their beards off. If she loses, then she will dye her hair brown (Riker's suggestion). Beverly raises, and seems confident of winning, when abruptly the captain's voice calls them to work. The voice of the father intervenes to protect masculinity from symbolic castration.

Seemingly unrelated to the plot that follows, this introduction actually introduces the notion of gender difference and appearance quite crucial to the new computer lifeform they discover. The poker game itself represents a masculine activity, a warlike competition. The conversation about beards reveals the arbitrariness of gender difference, at least in terms of its external manifestations. The men's spirited defense of their beards reveals that they need a visual, external show of male difference. As Worf and Riker defend beards as a sign of "courage" and "strength," Beverly points out that men grow beards because women can't. The beards also point to Data, who normally plays poker with the other members of the bridge crew. He cannot grow a beard and thus is feminized further. Data's pivotal position in the plot appears indirectly through his absence of a beard.

The captain calls Geordi La Forge, the ship's engineer, to evaluate a project to create a particle stream. The project, headed by a female scientist, has had many problems and is in danger of being canceled. Here the gendering is quite explicit: All the power belongs to Geordi La Forge and the captain, who will make a decision about the project based on La Forge's report. Almost incidentally, the female scientist, Dr. Farallon, reveals that she has created a new tool, the Exocomp. These creatures are feminized in three ways. Cute little machines, the Exocomps seem to communicate with squeaks, endearing high-pitched noises that evoke the Bynars' rapid speech that is incomprehensible to humans. As the Exocomps are computers, their femininity has been established by "11001001." They are also feminized not only by their creator's sex, but also by their behavior. They work together like the Bynars. Their language is feminine. Their most unique quality is a minireplicator, which enables them to produce a tool for any task. The replicator suggests that they are reproductive and metamorphic, feminine qualities of the female alien. They are creative and collaborative.

Significantly, Data, who has himself been oppressed and feminized, first recognizes the Exocomp's sentience, and he fights for their rights. They fail a test of their intelligence, but Data quickly realizes that it was the mechanical test that was faulty rather than the Exocomps. And it is the female doctor, Beverly, who is with Data when he makes his momentous discovery. Data is overwhelmed because he realizes this new lifeform is like him. "Suddenly, the possibility exists that I am no longer alone." Acting on his belief, Data refuses to allow the Exocomps to be transported to the project to save Picard and La Forge. He risks court-martial to prove their right to life. "I do not believe it is justified to sacrifice one lifeform for another," he proclaims, taking solidarity with the Exocomps. When given a choice, they demonstrate their femininity by sacrificing one of their number to rescue others. With their new status, the Exocomps are free, perhaps to reproduce, but certainly to explore a new role as sentient beings. They also save their female creator's project.

This episode reinforces the notion of machines as feminine and subordinate, but as in "The Most Toys" and "11001001," the plot suggests that if females work together, they can find a place for themselves in the patriarchal social order. As in "The Most Toys," and to a lesser degree in "11001001," in which the Bynars voluntarily return to a Starbase to accept punishment, a death is the price for freedom. The one Exocomp sacrifices itself to save Picard, La Forge, and the other two Exocomps. So "The Quality of Life" can be read as pointing to the oppression and cost to women of their subordination.

"Inheritance" continues the theme of the female machine. Like Data's daughter, Lal, discussed in chapter 7, the protagonist of "Inheritance" is a female android, superior to Data in her humanoid appearance. Although Lal could not "pass" because of her social maladjustment, her "grandmother," Dr. Juliana O'Donnell, is so humanlike that she herself is unaware that she is an android. Created by Dr. Soong to be an exact replica of his wife, Juliana leads a perfectly normal, happy, human life. We know already that Dr. Soong created Data and his brother Lore, but Juliana is a different case because she is a duplicate of a once-living person, his wife. "Inheritance" was written by Dan Koepel and René Echevarria and aired the week of November 22, 1993.

Data encounters Juliana when the *Enterprise* goes to her planet to assist with a geological mission to stabilize the planet's core. The mission reflects ironically on Data's discovery of his "mother," for his solitary stability is again shattered by another female machine. Data suspects almost immediately that Juliana may be an android by her quickness at calculations, her precise and mechanical way of playing the violin, and her blinking pattern. These are signs that only another android could identify.

Although she is unaware that she is an android, Juliana does identify with her human predecessor's experiences of creating Data. She tells him stories of his early childhood and seems quite fond of him. She explains how he came to be gendered. "Your father insisted upon a son," she tells him. "He had made it [Data's head] in his own image." She claims credit for Data's creative side—his painting, his musical interests (he, too, plays the violin). "Giving you the creative aspect was my idea," she tells Data. Data responds by telling her that "I believe that it is during my creative endeavors that I come closest to experiencing what it must be like to be human." Juliana's insistence that a woman caused those features to be included and Data's identification of the arts as "most human" reinforce their femininity, and his.

An accident reveals that Data's suspicions about Juliana's humanity are correct: She falls unconscious when her mechanical arm separates from her body. In her mechanical brain, Beverly discovers a chip that literally contains Dr. Soong—a holographic image of him that explains that Dr. Soong built a protect-program into Juliana. He asks Data not to reveal to Juliana that she is an android. In a meeting with Captain Picard and the bridge crew, Data ponders his choice. Should he reveal to his mother that she is an android? He dislikes being unique, the only sentient android, but as Troi points out, to tell her would be "robbing her of the one thing you have wanted your whole life—to be human." Data magnanimously refrains, and they bid each other a tender farewell, making tentative plans to meet during Data's next leave. Data's sacrificing his emotional needs for Juliana's also situates him as feminine.

This episode shows again the femininity of the machine. Juliana is female, and as she claims, literally Data's "mother." This female android exemplifies that on television, "cyborgs are feminized and women cyborgized" (Joyrich, "Feminist" 66), for this woman does not even know that she is a machine. But the viewers know, and our sense of machines as feminized, or in this case feminine, is confirmed. What Data has inherited, as the episode's title suggests, is a subordinate position in a society that privileges the masculine. An android or a machine is to be put into service for the patriarchy, and both Data and Juliana reflect their secondary status as a machine and a woman. Unlike the Bynars or the Exocomps, Data has no inclination to work with Juliana to resist Starfleet or Dr. Soong's hierarchy and designs. In fact, Dr. Soong literally appears when they remove a chip from Juliana's brain. He explains how he deceived Juliana into thinking that she is human, and asks Data's help in continuing the deception. The deception enables her, as a real woman does, to think that she is a fully equal member of her society, making choices and acting independently. But this facade is an elaborate deception. Like the female characters on the holodeck, like Minuet, Juliana dances a dance not of her own choosing. And "Inheritance," like the other episodes of *Star Trek: The Next Generation* that focus on the feminine machine, finally reflects back on human woman, reminding us that our own positions are no more secure than the female machine's. Chapter 5 reveals how *Star Trek: The Next Generation* draws on ideas about femininity to discuss sexual orientation.

"What Makes You Think You Can Dictate How We Love?": Sexual Orientation

Sexual orientation remains a divisive and controversial topic in American society. We still live in a society that practices what Adrienne Rich calls "compulsory heterosexuality," a series of customs and behaviors that not only encourage, but actively prescribe heterosexuality as the norm. Although gays, lesbians, and bisexuals have made some small legal gains and increased acceptance in American society, these advances have occurred slowly and met with great resistance. The years *Star Trek: The Next Generation* aired, 1987–94, were years in which homosexual rights were the subject of great public debate. The rights of gay men and lesbians to serve in the military, for example, were the subject of presidential inquiry and congressional debate, resulting in the infamous "don't ask, don't tell" compromise of 1993 that satisfied no one. At the same time, Hawaii and other states debated legalizing same-sex marriages, a right that would not only legitimize gay and lesbian unions, but also provide gay men and lesbians with economic benefits such as health insurance similar to those accorded married heterosexuals. These highly publicized controversies found their way into *Star Trek: The Next Generation*, as did public concerns about abortion and rape, discussed in chapters 7 and 8.

As it does with other social concerns, *Star Trek: The Next Generation* reflects social anxieties about sexual orientation in subtle ways. That so many of the *Enterprise* crew are single suggests an indirect resistance to compulsory heterosexuality. Unlike many television programs, *Star Trek: The Next Generation* does not present an advertisement for the nuclear family. Like classic *Trek*, in which a subculture of fans posits the homosexuality of Kirk and Spock in so-called slash or K/S fiction, in *Star Trek: The Next Generation*, fans interpret clues about certain characters to mean that they are homosexual, such as Geordi La Forge's difficulty with women or Tasha Yar's somewhat butch appearance. That there is no explicit mention of characters' sexuality provides a space for interpretation. As Jenkins explains, "For these fans, the text's silences about characters' sexuality or motives can be filled with homosexual desire, since, after all, in our society, such desire must often go unspoken" (Tulloch and Jenkins 259).

Both Jenkins and Joyrich repeat the often-cited story about Gene Roddenberry's promise to include a gay or lesbian character in *Star Trek: The Next Generation* (Tulloch and Jenkins 238; Joyrich, "Feminist" 68). Roddenberry died before he could fulfill this commitment and the failure of the show's producers to follow up on the promise led Joyrich to pronounce that the absence of a major gay or lesbian character "disturbingly suggest[s] that even in the twenty-fourth century, 'infinite diversity in infinite combinations' does not include sexual diversity" ("Feminist" 68).* Joyrich dismisses the two episodes that deal explicitly with sexual orientation. Although I agree with her assessment that the episodes "The Host" and "The Outcast" are "extremely problematic," I disagree that the shows "fail to represent anything that might be seen as 'earthly' constructions of queer sexuality" ("Feminist" 68). As this chapter demonstrates, these two episodes raise issues about sexual orientation in a direct and concrete fashion.

Using defamiliarization and extrapolation, *Star Trek: The Next Generation* displaces homosexuality onto alien characters. By defamiliarizing the site—alien society rather than American society—the viewer can attain some distance and perspective on our own culture's homophobia. When the alien characters are presented sympathetically, as they are in both "The Host" and "The Outcast," even a homophobe may find him or herself rooting for a metaphorically homosexual character. Extrapolating on technological advances in surgery and reproductive technology as well as inquiring into the nature of sexual orientation, each episode explores "what if?" What if humans could be either male or female (an extrapolation of transsexual surgery and the new interest in transgendering)? What if sexual orientation is biological? Can social pressure or psychological techniques be used to alter sexual orientation? Should such powers be used, if available? These are some of the questions raised by these episodes.

The series' use of defamiliarization and extrapolation evokes the issues raised by French feminist theorists about language and the body. The fe-

*Fans are still waiting for the fulfillment of that promise (see Greenwald 197).

male aliens in these episodes expose the gendered nature of the symbolic order. Through an alien who can be either male or female, like Le Guin's Gethenians, *Star Trek: The Next Generation* asks its viewers to consider the effect of the body on our perceptions and social position. Through an androgynous alien and her struggle to understand humanity, the show reminds us of our language's gendered nature. The alien has an androgynous pronoun that describes its people, but Commander Riker struggles as he explains to the alien the limitations of human language (English). Both episodes privilege disorder and change, feminine qualities according to the French feminists, whereas order is seen as confining and claustrophobic.

Viewing these episodes through the filter of French feminist theory makes their more positive qualities emerge. I agree with Lee Heller, who argues that these shows are not entirely satisfactory, nor are they progressive. However, as the rest of this chapter argues, the episodes do provide some resistance to compulsory heterosexuality. Using science fiction's quality of defamiliarization enables the show to raise questions about how human sexuality is overly controlled. As Heller acknowledges as she compares *Star Trek: The Next Generation* to accounts of frustrated heterosexuality in the popular press, the series "repeatedly asserts the inability of men and women to find in each other the satisfaction of their needs and desires" (230). In its destabilization of heterosexuality, accompanied by its exposure of rape and abortion, *Star Trek: The Next Generation* does not present a solution, but it acknowledges the problems of heterosexuality for women while suggesting that its characters' compulsory heterosexuality limits them.

The first, titled "The Host," shows Beverly Crusher falling in love with a Trill, a race that has a humanoid body that periodically is replaced. The essence of the individual is a nonsexed symbiont that is placed in bodies of different sexes over time. The individual Trill, then, will change sex over its long lifetime. The second, "The Outcast," depicts the virile Commander Will Riker falling in love with a deviant member of a race without gender. Both shows use an alien race to explore social mores and human reactions to sexual orientation. Like the other themes explored in *Star Trek: The Next Generation*, the theme of sexual orientation draws on a tradition of literary science fiction. As Donna Minkowitz points out, "In a culture that treats homosexuality as another 'planet,' some of the best explorations of gay and lesbian identity have, appropriately enough, taken the form of science fiction and fantasy" (67). More specifically, as Jenkins explains, "Many fans trace their commitments to feminism, gay rights, vegetarianism, pacifism and/or multi-culturalism to *Star Trek*'s 'IDIC' philosophy ('Infinite Diversity in Infinite Combinations')" (191). This chapter explores how these episodes of *Star Trek: The Next Generation* do and do not live up to such descriptions of science fiction's and *Star Trek*'s progressiveness.

Most discussions of science fiction and sexual orientation, including Jenkins's brilliant analysis, "Out of the Closet and into the Universe: Queers and *Star Trek*" (in Tulloch and Jenkins), focus on gay and lesbian fans of the shows. *Star Trek*'s popularity with gay and lesbian fans, and their subversive appropriation and resistant readings of the various series from classic *Trek* through *Voyager,* justify such ethnographies. In his study of the Gaylaxians, the Boston chapter of an international organization of gay, lesbian, and bisexual science fiction fans and their friends, Jenkins describes the group's national convention and the letter writing campaign in which they urged the acknowledgement of a gay presence in *Star Trek: The Next Generation* (Tulloch and Jenkins 237–38). Ironically, the very activism of gay and lesbian fans has resulted in more critical emphasis on fandom than on the ways the texts invite such an active participation of gays and lesbians. This chapter attempts to fill out the picture of *Star Trek: The Next Generation*'s relationship to gay and lesbian culture by analyzing the texts closely.

In lesbian and gay science fiction, the figure of the alien is often used to encourage the reader to sympathize with a nondominant sexual practice. Because the character is alien, the heterosexual reader especially can feel less threatened by his or her or his/her sexuality. After we are induced to identify with the character, relevant parallels to human homosexuals are revealed. This use of defamiliarization may enable the reader to overcome social conditioning against homosexuality. In another technique, gender is so completely altered that such divisions as male and female and gay and straight have no meaning, thus questioning our society's rigid enforcement of such social mores. For example, in Ursula K. Le Guin's award-winning novel *The Left Hand of Darkness,* a human male encounters an alien race in which individuals have no fixed gender or sexuality. Instead, they go through a process in which they temporarily become male or female and fertile. Over a lifetime, these aliens are both male and female at different times. In the novel, the protagonist, a human male, has to reconsider completely his understanding of gender, and eventually he falls in love with one of the aliens. His love for an alien shows that feelings such as love can transcend arbitrary boundaries such as sex.

Two anthologies of gay and lesbian science fiction, *Kindred Spirits* and *Worlds Apart,* exemplify the ways in which the genre can be used to explore sexual orientation sympathetically. *Kindred Spirits* and *Worlds Apart* present a wide range of well-known science fiction writers' stories about sexual orientation. Only in science fiction can one create an entire world populated by lesbians who have never known a man, as in Joanna Russ's "When It Changed" or James Tiptree Jr.'s "Houston, Houston, Can You Read?," redefining the human subject as female and the female subject as lesbian. Only in science fiction can a writer imagine a planet that contains a guild of lesbians who swear an oath of fealty to each other, as in Marion Zimmer Bradley's Darkover series. Only in science fiction can John Varley or Tanith Lee depict a society in which sex change and bodily alterations are as easy and accepted as changing clothes is today. The characters in John Varley's "Eight Worlds" stories, for example, easily transcend our limitations of compulsory heterosexuality. That alternative sexuality continues to be an important use of extrapolation and defamiliarization can be seen in a bibliography of works edited by Eric Garber and Lyn Paleo, *Uranian Worlds: A Reader's Guide to Alternative Sexuality in Science Fiction and Fantasy* (revised and updated in 1991 to include horror), and by anthologies such as Nicola Griffith and Stephen Pagel's *Bending the Landscape: Fantasy,* the first in a series of books focused on homosexual science fiction and fantasy. Literary science fiction deals quite radically and explicitly with homosexuality, and the impress of such thought experiments can be seen in "The Host" and "The Outcast." Nevertheless, neither episode is as radical as the literary treatments of homosexuality.

"The Host" first aired the week of May 13, 1991; it was written by Michel Horvat. *The Star Trek: The Next Generation Companion* describes the episode as "Another tale that could only be told in science fiction, [because] Horvat's script gives Gates McFadden [the actress who plays Dr. Crusher] the opportunity to show Beverly as a woman of passion, and even dallies with homosexuality" (Nemecek 165). Beverly Crusher falls in love with an ambassador named Odan, whom the *Enterprise* is ferrying to an important negotiation needed to prevent war between two moons. From the opening frames, the viewer sees a strong expression of physical attraction between Beverly and Odan.

The depiction of physical passion also separates this episode from most others; rarely does the series show or even hint at sexual contact. Quite abruptly and surprisingly to the regular viewer, "The Host" opens, not with the captain's log or an action scene (the customary opening), but with

Beverly Crusher reading her personal log aloud. Immediately, the rhetoric tells the viewer that this episode will be different from all the others. Beverly recounts the details of her life: a letter from her son, and the surprising announcement, "There's someone new in my life." Her words preface a graphic visual representation of the usually asexual Beverly embracing someone. She recounts no more details; in keeping with television's focus on the visual narrative, we know that we will be shown the "someone new." At that second, we see an extreme close-up of Beverly and a man, kissing passionately. The shot of their profiles and their energetic kissing makes it quite clear that Beverly Crusher is a sexual being. Because Dr. Crusher has always been presented as a loner, still not quite recovered from her husband's death in the line of duty many years ago, this scene is striking. In addition to her solitary and dedicated nature, Beverly has also been depicted as a devoted mother. But as her announcement of her son's letter reveals, he is away at Starfleet Academy, and Beverly is finally allowed to have a sex life. That she has an adult son but is still entitled to express her sexuality also shows a positive aspect of *Star Trek: The Next Generation*'s depiction of women. In contrast to our culture's (and especially television's) neglect of older women's sexuality, this episode shows that even a mature woman can be sexual. The different structure, giving Beverly a voice for the introduction, signals an attempt to give women in the series more focus. Significantly, giving women a voice also means, in this episode anyway, giving voice to sexual orientation.

Beverly's lover, Odan, belongs to a mysterious race named the Trill. They are a secretive people, and not much is known about them. However, Odan is quite a handsome humanoid. Sporting shoulder-length hair and a form-fitting uniform with a long tunic, Odan behaves in a considerate and devoted manner to the woman he addresses as "Dr. Beverly." In part because of his courtly behavior, he seems to deserve her love. The episode makes it clear that his intentions are serious and honorable—he asks Captain Picard if the captain thinks that Beverly would ever consider leaving Starfleet. The context implies that Odan is thinking of asking Beverly to make such a drastic move, for him. As a successful ambassador and negotiator, Odan has a prominent position, and his query to Captain Picard signifies that something might be amiss. As Beverly finds later in the series in "Sub Rosa" (discussed in chapter 8), the price of sexual passion is her career.

Another sign of Odan's difference from the other characters is the strange movements in his stomach. We see him stand before the mirror in his quarters, rubbing his hand over his stomach, which bulges out strangely. He grimaces, and then shoots a green light into his stomach, and the bulge subsides. He also refuses to be transported, preferring instead to travel to the moon's surface via a shuttle craft. Odan rationalizes the refusal to "beam down" because he doesn't want to have his molecules rearranged, but because most characters on the *Enterprise* travel through the transporter and because the transporter scans the bodies of those transported, his refusal suggests that Odan may be hiding something. The bulging stomach suggests that what he is hiding is actually in his body.

In science fiction film, a bulging stomach, especially after the tremendously popular *Aliens* films, immediately evokes the idea of a parasite or, more specifically, an alien fetus. Like the humans who carry the aliens' young in those movies, Odan too may be carrying a parasite. And after an emergency transport, that is what Beverly Crusher tells him—that he is infested. But of course, the infestation is of a particular kind that makes him symbolically female. As his long hair and tunic reinforce, Odan has qualities that make him feminine—most notably, his carrying of a wormlike symbiont in his abdomen. That is the secret that he has been keeping— a sort of permanent pregnancy that parallels him to a pregnant woman.

Although symbolically he is pregnant, as the representative of his people, his condition suggests that the Trill as a race are feminine. Considering the hearty masculinity of the Federation and Starfleet, it is no wonder that the Trill have kept their feminine bodily functions a secret. Along with their metaphorical femininity comes one of the qualities associated with female aliens: virtual immortality. As I discuss elsewhere ("'No Woman Born'"), female aliens characteristically threaten patriarchy by their immortality. In a tradition of female aliens that can be traced back to pulp science fiction magazines of the 1950s and 1950s, the female alien, as in Philip Jose Farmer's "The Lovers," for example, will live forever unless she gives birth. Because female aliens are associated with mythological goddesses, their magic and powers are allied with a goddess's imperviousness to human mortality. As in "The Lovers" and other science fiction treatments of the female alien, it is pregnancy or a romantic relationship with a human that threatens her immortality. So, too, does Odan face death, in a parallel plot.

In an ironic reversal of pregnancy, Odan's essence is not the handsome humanoid body, but the rather gross wormlike symbiont that is transferred to another humanoid body when the old one fails. Odan, then, can be either male or female in its humanoid form, and during the episode,

Odan changes "his" body and sex. But the alternating (or possibly alternative) sex of its humanoid body does not alter the creature's fundamental femininity. Although the symbiont appears rather phallic and masculine, the combination of fetuslike creature and humanoid encasing for it inevitably evokes the image of a pregnant woman. As with a pregnancy, the symbiont and the humanoid body work together. The Trills always appear humanoid; the only sign of their difference is a tattoo-like patterning on their faces. Although they can use human bodies as hosts, such a pairing can work only temporarily because of genetic differences. Furthermore, the Trill host bodies welcome the symbiotic relationship, just as women are socialized to welcome romantic liaisons with men that subordinate women to the men. The Trill host is clearly subordinate to the symbiont, and the symbiont's personality dominates, although altered by the new body. Odan retains "his" name, although "he" is now a "she." However, the Trill live like permanently pregnant women—the symbiont cannot survive without a host body. Beverly, then, has fallen in love with a member of a feminized race. Because she had been unaware of Odan's intrinsic nature, she feels betrayed at first.

The plot line forces Odan's symbiont into Commander Riker's body as a short-term expedient until another Trill host can be sent, and Beverly performs the surgery. That she performs the operation stresses its significance as a kind of reverse-cesarean delivery—in this case, the fetus is implanted into a new body. That as the ship's chief medical officer Beverly performs the operation implies an openness to difference on her part. After all, her job requires her to deal with and treat an immense variety of alien species with diverse bodies and from diverse cultures. With some difficulty, Beverly accepts that Odan inhabits Riker's body, and they make love. Beverly's love for Odan allows her to overlook what body he is in, even though it is the body of a close colleague. Although Riker is her friend, he is still male, and their embrace poses no challenge to the system of compulsory heterosexuality. But when the host body arrives, Beverly is shocked to discover that Odan will become female. After the transfer, the female Odan still expresses love for her. His/her position suggests an acceptance of gender change and sexual orientation in Trill society. And the female body looks remarkably like the male Odan—same color hair, similar features, similar voice. But Beverly finds herself unable to love Odan as a woman. The literal transfer into a female body proves too much for her homophobic prejudice. Beverly represents a part of society that espouses tolerance and acceptance of sexual difference until it gets too close.

Odan, in its female body, kisses Beverly good-bye.

In a cloying scene, Beverly rejects Odan. Beverly seems to be justifying and reaffirming heterosexuality in her speech to Odan. Ironically, Beverly has performed the operation that transfers the symbiont to the new host body, and she announces the operation's success by saying, "There were no difficulties in assimilation." Although there are no difficulties for the Trill, there *are* for Beverly. Odan asserts his, now her, continued love for Beverly, but Beverly replies, "Perhaps it is a human failing. But we are not accustomed to these kind of changes. . . . Perhaps someday our ability to love won't be so limited." Odan accepts her rejection, says, "I will never forget you," kisses her hand passionately, and then walks out of her office. The scene seems to suggest that Beverly is justified in rejecting a woman as a lover, even a woman she loves passionately. Yet the tinge of sadness in both actors and Beverly's words of regret for the future suggest that there is a loss in prejudice against same-sex unions. Still, the rejection is justified within the plot, and "The Host," while presenting an alien race that can accept same-sex love, shows humans rejecting lesbianism.

As with other controversial themes on *Star Trek: The Next Generation*, the issues surrounding sexual orientation seem more comfortably and radically dealt with when they are worked through a male character rather than through a female character such as Beverly. In the only other episode that deals overtly with sexual orientation, Will Riker assumes a central role. In their response to these two episodes, the group of gay, lesbian, and bisexual fans called "the Gaylaxians were sharply divided about 'the Host'" (Tulloch and Jenkins 253), some approving of the show's treatment of sexual orientation, others disapproving and disappointed. As the producer and writer of the episode, Jeri Taylor, explains, "'The Outcast,' though, is a gay rights story. It absolutely, specifically and outspokenly dealt with gay issues" (Tulloch and Jenkins 255).

"The Outcast" first aired on March 16, 1992. In this episode, the J'naii, an androgynous race, lose a shuttle in "null space," a pocket of space that nullifies technology, stranding the crew in their nonfunctioning shuttle. Soren, a member of the J'naii, teams up with Commander Riker to rescue the stranded shuttle. Working together in close proximity in a high-pressure situation makes the two close friends, even intimate. Soren confides to Riker about "her" deviancy: having female tendencies, which are looked upon as an illness by the J'naii. If Soren is discovered, Soren faces brainwashing to make "her" conform. Soren and Riker fall in love, but are discovered by Soren's superior, and Soren is tried for the crime of deviancy. Riker attempts to rescue "her," but he is too late: Soren has already been converted to the androgynous state believed to be "normal." Soren calmly assures Riker that s/he is all right, and Riker leaves, bitterly disappointed.

The awkwardness of describing this situation without an appropriate pronoun is evident. Unlike Marge Piercy, who provides a nonsexist pronoun, "per," in her novel *Woman on the Edge of Time*, this episode provides no such word, even though Soren explains that the J'naii have a nonsexist pronoun. Although *it* may appear to be a neutral pronoun, the word applies to inanimate objects, not people. This usage suggests that people are defined by their gender. So our language forces us to choose a gender identity for Soren. Our socially/culturally constructed language forces humans into binarisms, but this episode invites us to imagine a world that is nonsexist, with nonsexist language. This human linguistic difficulty should alert us to the overdeterminancy of gender roles: Not only social mores but our language itself forces us into either/or binarisms. In addition to this pronoun difficulty, there are other clues to Soren's femininity. Soren's furrowed forehead sports V-shaped crests, suggesting the femininity of the vagina. Although the J'naii are supposed to be androgynous, their physical makeup provides not-so-subtle clues as to their race's gendering. In a marked contrast, Worf, the excessively macho Klingon, has ridged brows—a row of phalluses on his forehead reinforces his masculinity. The raised crests that run across his forehead are impossible to ignore. (Klingon females sport ridges, too, but it is a sign of their equally aggressive, macho nature). So even alien creatures must be feminized or masculinized. In this way, the special effects of alien makeup are used to reinforce gendering. Again, this emphasis implies overdeterminancy.

The most telling cooption, however, occurs in the casting of performers. Women play the role of Soren and Soren's superior. And although the characters wear attire that seems neutral, their voices and visages depict thinly disguised female characteristics. Although casting Riker as the character who falls in love with a differently gendered alien is more radical than Beverly's namby-pamby rejection of a female lover, casting the aliens in this episode with female actors undercuts the show's message of acceptance of sexual orientation. A more radical choice would have been to cast men in the roles, thus making the theme's parallel to homosexuality clearer and more convincing. Jonathan Frakes, the actor who plays Riker, criticized this casting: "'I don't think they were gutsy enough to take it where they should have. Soren should have been more obviously male'" (Tulloch and Jenkins 285n).

Although these two structural problems weaken the case the show makes for appreciating differences in sexual orientation, the bare bones of the plot suggest that the episode argues for sexual tolerance. After all, Riker is a sympathetic character, and Soren's plight is a moving one. As Larry Nemecek points out, however, "For over twenty-five years Trek's two television series had pioneered the intelligent and fair-minded depiction of various sexes, races, and ethnic groups, including aliens. One notable exception, though, was homosexuals" (194). Until "The Host" and "The Outcast," *Star Trek* had avoided the issue of homosexual rights. This avoidance suggests an ambivalence that was deep and long-standing, and indeed this episode and "The Host" both reveal an unwillingness to embrace sexual orientation in its totality. The show's creators and writers may have avoided the issue earlier because of its sensitivity and volatility, and in "The Outcast" they have at least taken a major step, which then displays ambivalence.

However, the plot overtly challenges the idea of social norms for sexuality through a role reversal. Whereas in human society we are forced into being either male or female, and men are expected to be physically attracted to women and vice versa, the J'naii are forced into having no preference. All J'naii are equal and undifferentiated sexually. Such a planet might have been seen as a utopia in the 1970s, when androgyny was seen as a solution for the problem of sexism. Carolyn Heilbrun's influential *Toward a Recognition of Androgyny* was published in 1973. But by the mid-1980s, androgyny itself was presented as oppressive. Cultural feminism, championed by Carol Gilligan and others, celebrated gender difference by emphasizing the positive qualities of the feminine. Androgyny was presented as escapist and as denying the feminine. "The Outcast" takes a cultural feminist position in that the episode suggests that freedom comes from accepting your own sexuality, even if your society disapproves. And this freedom can be seen as paralleling the freedom for homosexuals and lesbians to openly declare their sexual orientation. Soren's fear of being brainwashed into denying her sexual orientation has its analogue in horrific psychological abuse and reconditioning of homosexuals in our own society. Her fear is justified by her recounting the terrifying story of a child abused by its peers for being different, the child's clothes torn and its body bleeding. Again, hate crimes occur on Soren's world as well as ours. And Soren's moving account of this abusive incident surely is intended to make the series' viewers recoil from the increase in such violence against gays and lesbians in our own world. This increase, too, occurred during the years that *Star Trek: The Next Generation* aired. For example, "In the five major cities with agencies that monitor hate crimes against lesbians and gay men, reports of anti-gay and anti-lesbian incidents increased by 172% between 1988 and 1992" (Rosenbloom 207).

Most compelling in its declaration of tolerance for sexual difference, perhaps, is the trial scene. Riker tries to provide Soren with an escape by declaring in court that he forced and misled Soren. But Soren rejects this cover story, asserting the right to innate sexual orientation. In ringing tones, she asks the court, "What right do you have to punish us? What makes you think you can dictate how we love?" As Riker looks on approvingly, Soren makes a speech strongly reminiscent of Shylock's speech in Shakespeare's *The Merchant of Venice.* The camera angle has the viewer literally look up at Soren. This camera work reinforces our sympathy for Soren and presents her as a passionate defender of her own and other sexual "deviants'" rights.

In a time when the expulsion of lesbians and gays from the military was becoming a national crisis, this trial scene presents the cruelty and short-sightedness of expelling people from the military because of their sexual

Soren pleads for tolerance.

orientation. Setting this scene up in a military-style courtroom emphasizes the parallel between Soren's situation and that of gay and lesbian members of the armed forces. Such trials have become more and more common, and have been well covered by the media. Like many of those discharged for their sexual orientation from the military, Soren is a hero for rescuing the shuttle crew, and as her actions show, an extraordinary pilot and brave individual. Her society has much to lose by rejecting her.

In addition to the plot, other science fiction characteristics help point to gender-related problems in our society. The show uses defamiliarization to pose questions about gender roles and homosexuality. Riker and Soren's friendship allows the alien to question Riker about human gender roles from the point of view of an outsider. Soren inquires about "the strange division in your species—males and females" and asks about sexuality. Riker, usually quite loquacious, stumbles badly, citing nursery rhymes that nonsensically explain gender difference—"girls are sugar and spice" and boys are made of "puppy dog tails," generally being inept in justifying and explaining human sexual difference and behavior. He finally admits that her questions about gender roles "would take a lifetime to answer." When Soren asks what Riker looks for in a mate, he lists intelligence and a willingness to laugh at his jokes. Through these exchanges, human gender roles are made to look foolish and arbitrary. Gender roles cannot be logically explicated because they are not logical, and of course, the qualities of humor and intelligence apply to both male and female.

The theme is explored further when Soren also asks a woman about human femininity. After an injury in null space, Soren receives treatment from Beverly Crusher. Soren comments that human females sport longer hair and more elaborate hairstyles, and apply color (makeup). The language Soren uses makes women's styles seem bizarre and foolish. Asked about the difference between men and women, Beverly explains that men and women are equal, and that both try to attract mates. Although the plot and dialogue explicitly call for understanding and tolerance, in its setting, camera angles, costume, and use of science, the episode remains a conservative exploration of the toleration of sexual difference.

Perhaps the most glaring example of the episode's conservatism is the positioning of Soren as a female. This defamiliarization may make viewers see that being discriminated against because of your sexual orientation is unfair. However, casting all the J'naii as women and Soren as feminine reifies heterosexuality. Our sympathy is directed toward Soren, whose happiness seems to depend on her rejection of homosexuality. Her gendered, feminine self is more appealing than the stern, unemotional rigidity of the other J'naii. Our sympathy is directed toward what Soren has lost—her feminine self—rather than with what she becomes, an ungendered, androgynous self.

As usual with *Star Trek: The Next Generation,* the scientific problem mirrors the show's social themes. The space that captures the J'naii shuttle is "null" space; that is, space that is outside normal space and time. Null space can be read as an analogue to sexual difference because homosexuality, at least in the terms of this show, is outside the traditional sexual behaviors. Null space is identified as "an anomaly." The language Riker and Soren use to describe null space suggests the parallel to homosexuality. "All the energy is bent around it. . . . [It is] naturally crooked." If Riker and Soren stay in null space for too long, they will die. So too if Soren remains in the role of sexual deviant, she will die—or at least, the self that is deviant will "die," to be replaced by a "normal," adjusted individual. Together, Riker and Soren use weapons to map out and "penetrate" null space. This gendering of the scientific problem reinforces the description of homosexuality as abnormal and anomalous.

Worf disproves Beverly's easy assurance of male and female equality when he makes disparaging remarks about women during a staff poker game. He expresses homophobic prejudice when he criticizes the J'naii's lack of sexual differentiation. In response, Beverly must acknowledge that "only this afternoon I was claiming such [sexist] attitudes were defunct." Although the characters want to pretend that men and women or J'naii and humans can be equal, the images tell another story. The camera angles reinforce Riker's male dominance and superiority over Soren. First, she is thrown to the floor of the shuttle and injured, not he. Second, as they have their discussion/confession of Soren's female identity, Riker stands over her. As Soren moves under the controls, Riker looms over Soren. He literally looks down on Soren. As Soren confesses an attraction to him, Riker stands there, his arms crossed over his chest. She reaches out and gently touches his cheek. When they kiss, he is much taller than Soren, and their kiss is a traditional passionate embrace, with the man dominating. This traditional image of a man and a woman kissing presents no challenge to our compulsory heterosexuality, as Frakes, the actor who plays Riker, noted.

Similarly, the environment reinforces heterosexuality as natural. Passion is represented through the setting of the lush forest on Soren's world. It is in the forest that Riker and Soren embrace—a long, passionate, traditional film kiss, in which Riker looms over Soren. The naturalness of this dark forest setting evokes the illicit passion of, for example, the minister and Hester Prynne in *The Scarlet Letter*. Soren gives Riker a tour of the forest, offering a flower that blooms only one day of the year. The flower prefigures the brevity of Riker and Soren's relationship and the uniqueness of Soren's "deviation" from the sexual norms of her planet. Soren's favorite tree is one that changes colors, a parallel to Soren's own changeability in sexual orientation. The episode may seem to present an argument *for* sexual difference, but using the signifier of the natural (the forest) as it does, it evokes the arguments *against* homosexuality as unnatural.

Whereas in some science fiction androgyny appears as a solution to sexism, in this episode androgyny is part of the problem. The J'naii clothes and buildings suggest an androgyny that is sterile and unattractive. Because of the costuming, androgyny cannot be seen as a viable alternative. The drab beige of Soren's attire suggests a similarly drab existence. The costume is cut so as to disguise her body—there are flaps where in a human female we would find the rise of breasts. Her short cropped hair unattractively frames her head, a simple and unadorned style. The parallel is borne out by Soren's comments about her society in which she reveals the J'naii's emphasis on utility and conformity. She tells Riker a horrifying tale of witnessing the persecution and brainwashing of another child, deviant like Soren herself. The child was attacked by other children and forced to confess its sexual deviancy; this incident persuaded Soren that she must always keep her sexual orientation hidden, lest she suffer the same fate. In addition, the buildings also reflect an image of constriction and imprisonment. Their bare rooms are seen twice from the perspective of the lush forest, first by Riker and Soren and then by Riker and Worf, when they return to rescue Soren. Both times we see a bright light framing the interior of the building like a picture frame. The framing resembles the imprisonment cells aboard the *Enterprise*—a bright band of light bisecting the space and separating the prisoner from the outside, and freedom. Riker's comments reinforce this sterile sense of confinement when, sitting alone on a concrete patio, he explains to Soren, "I needed some air." Yet he and Soren "have air" only for a few moments and both return to sterile environments—Soren to her new "adjusted" role and Riker to the lonely bridge of the *Enterprise.*

This episode's depiction of sexual orientation does seem to advance the final official policy of the White House with regard to gays and lesbians in the military: "don't ask, don't tell." But this weak compromise is finally unsatisfactory, as this episode shows. Furthermore, the "don't ask, don't tell" policy belies the danger and fear that one must continually live with under such a policy. "The Outcast" vividly conveys the psychic cost of living in the closet. Riker's somber expression at the end of the episode reveals the human pain that denying and separating same-sex lovers creates. In this regard, at least, "The Outcast" lives up to its advertisement as "'*The* gay episode'" (Tulloch and Jenkins 255).

But as Jenkins notes, these episodes have not answered the Gaylaxians' call for a continuing gay character on *Star Trek: The Next Generation.* By excluding a gay, lesbian, or bisexual character from the crew, the show suggests that although men and women, people of different races, and even alien races can work amicably together on the *Enterprise,* gay men, lesbians, and bisexuals will still be excluded. This exclusion leads the Gaylaxians and other viewers to look for hidden or closeted gay characters. As with so-called slash literature, written and read primarily by female fans of classic *Trek,* fans of *Star Trek: The Next Generation* look to *Enterprise* crew members who may present textual clues to their hidden gayness. Leading contenders include Data (whose sexual orientation is discussed in chapter 4), Geordi La Forge, and the alien Q. Taking characters whose sexual orientation seems ambiguous and extrapolating a hidden sexuality is one response to gay and lesbian sexuality that reflects American society's unease with this subject. And although it can be fun and subversive and inclusive to discuss Geordi's difficulty with women and the alien Q's desire for Captain Picard and Q's ability to assume any bodily form he chooses, finally that kind of reading throws the impetus for exploring sexual orientation back on the viewer and out of the text's responsibility. As Jenkins argues, "In refusing to demarcate a certain denotative space for homosexuality within the text, they left *Star Trek* open to wholesale reclamation. . . . Soon, all of the characters are potentially queer—at least on the level of connotation" (261). But as Jenkins also acknowledges, "Sometimes, resistant reading isn't enough" (262). As the next three chapters demonstrate, *Star Trek: The Next Generation* uses a version of this strategy to deal with race, abortion, and rape. Yet the series proves more able to deal explicitly with these topics than with sexual orientation, suggesting that sexual orientation is the most complicated and resistant social issue.

6

"We Weren't Meant to Know Each Other at All": Race

At first glance, *Star Trek: The Next Generation* might appear more explicit and progressive on race than about sexual orientation, discussed in chapter 5. After all, the original *Star Trek* introduced the first interracial kiss to television, and the character of Lieutenant Uhura, the communications officer, was considered by no less a personage than Martin Luther King Jr. to be an important role model (Nichols 164–65). *Star Trek: The Next Generation* shows a keen cognizance of this legacy in its casting of two major characters: Lieutenant Worf, a Klingon, and Geordi La Forge, the ship's engineer, both played by African-American actors. Significantly, Worf's heritage is depicted as literally alien, whereas La Forge has an overtly African heritage. Race politics appear not only in the casting of male crew members, but also in the depiction of female characters who are bispecies. In *Star Trek: The Next Generation*, alien species function as a parallel for human race.

As Daniel Bernardi brilliantly demonstrates in *Star Trek and History: Racing toward a White Future*, all the Star Trek series provide examples of how "popular culture is the terrain on which the meaning of race most forcefully penetrates common sense" (20). In his thorough analyses of classic *Trek, The Next Generation*, and fan online discussions of race, Bernardi persuasively argues the centrality of race to the construction of the Star Trek universe. Drawing on his ground-breaking book, this chapter concentrates on the intersection of gender and race in *Star Trek: The Next Generation*.

Racial differences, though downplayed, still exist among humans in the twenty-fourth-century world of *Star Trek: The Next Generation*. Although the series suggests that in the twenty-fourth century there are no racial categories for humans and that race exists only for aliens, *race in Star Trek:*

The Next Generation really carries the same double meaning that it does in the late twentieth century. That is, race signifies both *species* race and *color and culturally coded* race. In different characters and episodes, race can carry one or the other or both meanings.

As decades of scholarship on race attest, the categories of race are socially constructed; as Bernardi explains in his discussion, race is "a historically specific system of meanings that has a profound impact on social organizations, political movements, cultural articulations, and individual identity" (5). Whiteness presented as the default setting for the human race reifies white supremacy without overtly acknowledging the constructedness of racial categories. Indeed, scientific scholarship suggests that all racial differences among humans are superficial. "'Race has no basic biological reality'" according to Jonathan Marks, a biologist at Yale University (qtd. in Boyd 8A). Race, then, as many critics have noted, is about culture. As Michael Omi, professor of ethnic studies, explains, "'In a social sense, race is a reality; in a scientific sense, it is not" (qtd. in Boyd 8A). And through the figure of the alien, race can be considered from this perspective as a fictional (cultural) reality. As Barbara Jeanne Fields argues, race is a phenomenon, a cultural, not biological fact: "If race lives on today, [it is] because we continue to create it today" (117).

Star Trek: The Next Generation participates in the recreation and reinscription of race. It does so in part through the science fiction quality of defamiliarization. Race is addressed through the casting of actors who are African American or Asian American, but it also appears in *Star Trek: The Next Generation* through the figure of the alien, who is more literally a racial Other. All humans are of one race, but beings from another galaxy, even if they are played by humans, are comfortably depicted as Other, different. Aliens exemplify that: "Race has become a trope of ultimate, irreducible difference between cultures, linguistic groups or adherents of specific belief systems which . . . have fundamentally opposed economic interests" (Gates 5).

In his insightful book *Star Trek and History,* Daniel Bernardi argues that "the imaginary time of Trek speaks to real space–time of race relations" (3). Though critical of *Star Trek*'s treatment of race, Bernardi acknowledges that the series is "a valuable site for studying the ways race is produced, performed and perpetuated" (11), and he stresses that science fiction in general is well suited for exploring issues of race. However, Bernardi faults the series for failing to challenge dominant discourse about race. His criticism, like Heller's about sexual orientation, cannot be refuted. But in this chapter I explore the ways in which discussing race in *Star Trek: The Next Generation* is complicated by considering gender at the same time.

Adding gender to the mix reveals that *Star Trek: The Next Generation* depicts blackness as male. As the famous title of an early feminist anthology suggests, *All the Women Are White, All the Blacks Are Men . . .* (Hull). The absence of continuing major characters who are female and of color reveals assumptions about race. As I began to think about race in *Star Trek: The Next Generation*, the episodes involving La Forge and Worf first came to mind.* The series depicts racial otherness primarily through male characters.

Race operates in several overlapping ways in the series, not only in the casting of male actors, but also through the representation of alien species. In a bewildering but significant fashion, a doubling occurs as species themselves can be read as racially different. Then as actors of various racial and ethnic groups play the various species, another level of complexity emerges. While overtly denying racial conflict, *Star Trek: The Next Generation* plays out racial difference. As the series does with gender differences, *Star Trek: The Next Generation* reflects contemporary anxieties about racial roles and tensions. When gender and race intersect, as they do with Guinan, Keiko, and other noncontinuing alien characters, the representation becomes even more complex and troubling. Untangling these knots reveals the special positioning of women in racial tension.

As the examples of Worf's and Geordi La Forge's casting suggest, race operates most obviously at the level of casting. Casting raises issues about how race is presented in a universe where there are intelligent species other than humans. But casting of actors also affects how other species are depicted. For example, despite the fact that Klingons are sometimes played by European-American actors, the most prominent and central Klingon, Worf, is played by Michael Dorn, an African-American actor. While viewers see Worf as a member of an alien species, we also see that he is African American because we see the human actor's color.† This double filter complicates the racial reading of the show. Casting Dorn makes us read all Klingons racially, not only because they are an alien species, but also because the casting positions the character as an American racial "minority." The character of Guinan, added in the second season and played by Whoopi Goldberg, reifies the sense of African Ameri-

---

*Although *Star Trek: Deep Space Nine* occasionally showcases Keiko, a female Asian-American scientist, *DS9* and *Voyager* continue *Star Trek: The Next Generation*'s representation of racial otherness as primarily masculine. See Bernardi's discussion of Keiko (130).

†See Bernardi (132–34) for a discussion of Worf's assimilation.

can as almost literally alien. A famous Academy Award–winning actress, Goldberg invited herself to the show because the character of Lieutenant Uhura on classic *Star Trek* meant so much to her. As Patrick Stewart, who plays Captain Picard, describes it, "As a child in New York she watched the original *Star Trek*. And there she would see a black woman in an authority position on the ship, and she said to herself, 'Well, one of us made it'" ("Twenty Questions"). But the word "one" is perhaps the most important in terms of the depiction of race in both series. There are positive elements in the production of a role model, but there are also some problems with tokenism.

That there are so few actors of color in *Star Trek: The Next Generation* draws viewers' attention to the paucity of roles for any other than European-American actors. As in the notorious casting of all white actors to play the role of soldiers in *Star Wars*, this casting of whites in *Star Trek: The Next Generation* reifies American racism by suggesting that not only America, but also the universe, is primarily white. As Bernardi points out, even the aliens who have godlike powers are literally white (125).

In his assessment of the changes from classic *Star Trek* to *Star Trek: The Next Generation*, Clyde Wilcox optimistically asserts, "The role of blacks has changed in the new show" (92). Although there are a few more black performers in *Star Trek: The Next Generation*, the show's attitude toward race has not changed dramatically. As Wilcox points out later in his article, "Although science fiction often seeks to extrapolate current trends into the future, the assumptions of a culture are usually projected as well" (99). And *Star Trek: The Next Generation* reflects racial attitudes of the 1980s. Though certainly more challenged (at least in public and legal arenas) than in the late 1960s, when classic *Trek* aired, white supremacist attitudes still prevail, as shown by the casting of white actors in most roles.

Even whites get to play the racial Other through the casting of whites as aliens. Many Klingons are literally black-faced, as in the minstrel tradition, in which white actors donned black makeup to play African Americans. Heavy makeup is used to delineate the otherness of alien species; color, morphing, raised ridges, and tattooing signify species differences. Yet with the emphasis on visual difference, characters who are Klingons, Bajorans, or Vulcans are humanoid but different. The various violent conflicts, struggles, and prejudices faced by these aliens inevitably evoke the conflicts between different racial and ethnic groups on Earth. So race issues appear, safely distanced in time from the viewers, as conflicts between different species, the humans presumably having solved racial conflicts hundreds of years ago. As Judith Roof explains, "*Star Trek's* difference blindness is a liberal humanist vision of a society in which race, gender, class, ethnicity, and national origin are only insignificant variations of an essentially human common identity" (4). But what she describes is the superficial narrative; as the episodes discussed in this chapter reveal, *Star Trek: The Next Generation* deals explicitly with race through aliens.

Finally, and perhaps most telling in terms of the series' racial politics, is the intersection of race and gender in the series. The racial Other often appears in the myth of the tragic mulatta, the female figure of mixed race who ends up caught between two cultures. Bernardi discusses the biologically unlikely interbreeding of aliens (126) but does not focus on the special position of the female alien of mixed origin. Customarily represented as a white/black mix, the mulatta can pass in either world, but rather than seeing this flexibility as positive, writers and critics have depicted this hybridity as a psychological tragedy. Written by African Americans and European Americans, narratives about the mulatta have a long history. As Nancy Bentley describes it, the liminal position of the biracial human is viewed with "a combination of sympathy, revulsion, and fascination" because the mulatta "stood precisely at the place where nature and culture could come unbound" (198). Mulatta narratives, then, function to reassure the reader that such categories as "white" and "black" could and would be enforced. By showing women of mixed race who could not find a place in society, mulatta narratives reify the importance of racial distinctions, even as the figure of the mulatta itself acknowledges the arbitrariness and social construction of race.

But the mulatta's gender is absolutely central to her function as a reinforcer of race distinctions. There are many fewer fictional depictions of male mulattos, reinforcing the notion that "all the men are black" (Bentley 198). And mulattas are almost always a black-white mixture, shutting other races out of the idea of miscegenation. The mulatta represents race (and slavery) most powerfully because she is female and sexually desirable. As Bentley explains, "the Mulatta is granted her most pronounced symbolic power by virtue of her worldly suffering—her sexual exploitation and the betrayals and abuse she endures" (199). This figure appears in *Star Trek: The Next Generation* reconfigured through the coding of race in alien species.

In *Star Trek: The Next Generation*, there are many such "mulatta" women: Deanna Troi, half-human, half-Betazoid; K'Ehleyr, half-human, half-Klingon. Even Guinan, a survivor of a race exterminated by the Borg, can fit this role. Their femaleness suits these characters' subordinate and conflicted roles. Depicted as likable figures, they nevertheless pose no challenge to the male-dominated white hierarchy of Starfleet. Always outside the power structure, these women have the role of advisor, but never of leader. (Guinan advises the captain, but never commands the *Enterprise.*) Sexually desirable, these characters figure in plots that emphasize their sexuality. (Guinan's past sexual relationship with Picard is often hinted at, and in "The Dauphin," she and Riker engage in sexual banter.) Again, the sexual allure of the tragic mulatta, made beautiful and exotic by her mingling of racial otherness, appears. But her tragic nature means she exists only to stimulate the male characters by her beauty. Raising the issue of racial purity by their existence, the characters are used to suggest that the mingling of races causes problems. For example, throughout the series, much is made of Deanna Troi and Will Riker's failed love affair. Although they have mated, it is in the past; their relationship has ended, doomed, presumably, by her otherness. Similarly, the series hints that Picard and Guinan have had a love affair that ended long ago. The female mulattas' existence thus valorizes racial segregation. Nowhere is this clearer than in the depiction of the Klingon Empire, a fierce opponent to the Federation in the original series, now uneasy allies with Starfleet. Klingons' centrality to issues of race and miscegenation appears in a famous joke by Roseanne Barr: "My first marriage was a mixed marriage: I was an Earthling, he was a Klingon" (qtd. in McConnell 652).

How Klingons themselves view race is in itself a revealing part of the series. As race politics changed in America, so did the depiction of race on *Star Trek.* In the original *Star Trek,* Klingons were played by European-American actors wearing black face, their features unaltered, minstrel style. In the original *Star Trek,* we saw no Klingon females at all. Klingons in classic *Star Trek,* especially the "Trouble with Tribbles" episode, are depicted as arch-enemies who are a bit buffoonish. In a special episode of *Deep Space Nine,* actors from the original series interact with those from *The Next Generation* years. The contrast between an updated Klingon played by Michael Dorn, an African-American performer who also sports heavy ridges on his forehead, and the black-face European-American actors playing Klingons creates a humorous exchange. Although it is true that makeup techniques have improved, to the viewer, the original Klingons and the Klingons from *Star Trek: The Next Generation* seem to be different species. Asked about the apparent racial difference between different generations of Klingons, Worf gruffly replies that it is a matter that

Klingons do not discuss with outsiders. In a parallel to the different shades of blackness present in the African-American community, this difference shows how race and color can play out within a cultural group. That is, within a racial group, distinctions symbolically racial, such as appearance, carry weight and provide the criteria for discrimination. Worf's huffy dismissal of bizarre racial disparity within Klingons suggests how arbitrary racial distinctions are, especially when viewed from the perspective of race as a performance. That is, the Klingons from classic *Trek* and Worf himself are constructions, their "race" clearly artificial. Although no other episode deals as explicitly with race, the Klingons are noted for their gruff attitude of superiority toward all other races. They despise the Ferengi and laud their own people as warlike, honorable, and admirable.

This episode of *Star Trek: Deep Space Nine* reveals how much, and how little, matters of race have changed in America in the intervening thirty years. An African-American actor can have a major role, but his racial otherness must be presented as that of an alien species and he plays an *alien*, reifying his place in American culture as Other. Although Klingons are not invariably played by blacks, *Star Trek* does have a pattern of casting African-American actors in roles such as Vulcan or Klingon. Even LeVar Burton, though human, is presented as Other because of the odd eyepiece he wears. His altered vision and appearance emphasize his otherness. All people of color who are regulars on *Star Trek: The Next Generation* are set off in some such fashion; the only other major performer, Guinan, wears bizarre hats and is marked off by her extreme age and her status as one of the few survivors of a people destroyed by the Borg.

This particular episode of *Deep Space Nine* foregrounds our double vision as viewers. Federation reality may assume that race is no longer a factor in society or personal relationships, but our late-twentieth-century perspective informs us that race is one of the major influences, along with gender, that shapes our reading of character and situations. Because Klingons as an alien species evoke race, especially through the casting of African-American actors, any episode about Klingons is more about race than an episode about other aliens. Similarly, any episode about Geordi La Forge is an episode about race because of the prominence of the African-American performers playing these roles. LeVar Burton established his acting reputation through a key role in the miniseries *Roots,* which explored the history of an African-American family. Both Worf and La Forge evoke African-American masculinity through their characters. But these characters do not deal with the feminine, showing that the series leaves out gender through these male characters' central performance of racial otherness. But what of the intersection of race and gender, what of femininity, so critical to the series, as the other chapters demonstrate?

Examining the way in which African-American women in particular, and race in general, are treated in *Star Trek: The Next Generation* reveals much about the intersection of race and gender in American culture. Women of color appear in several small roles, such as the biologist Keiko, who is Asian American, but many of the early episodes deal with race and gender primarily through Worf and La Forge's heterosexual partners. It wasn't until the second season that Whoopi Goldberg joined the show as the immensely ancient alien, Guinan, who tends bar and dispenses wisdom in Ten-Forward, the *Enterprise*'s lounge. Although Guinan became a respected member of the crew, she never appears as prominently as Worf or La Forge.*

In "Code of Honor," chief of security Tasha Yar battles an alien wife played by an African-American actress. On Ligon II, women battle for the honor of winning and retaining a husband. Because all Ligonians are played by African-American performers and because their culture is described as having "remarkable similarities" to our own, this episode addresses issues of race and gender on Earth in the late twentieth century. In "The Emissary" Worf meets an old friend who becomes his lover. Half-human, half-Klingon, K'Ehleyr is played by a European-American actress, but her struggle with Worf for control and love reflects on race and gender. She reappears in "Reunion," leaving him their son. In "Yesterday's *Enterprise*" Guinan, alone of all the people aboard the *Enterprise*, realizes that the ship has altered history by going through a temporal rift. Her special position as a member of a ancient exterminated race privileges her and shows that the African-American figure of the wisewoman should be respected.

Race also appears through the depiction of Data as another race. This parallel is discussed in chapter 4. In particular, the episodes of *Star Trek: The Next Generation* that reflect social interest in racial intermarriage and in the relationship of African-American men to African-American women explicitly are dealt with here.

In "Code of Honor," race and gender are played out as signs of cultural difference. Written by Kathryn Powers and Michael Baron, "Code of Honor" first aired the week of October 12, 1987. A terrible plague on Styris

*The rarity of her appearances may be due to Goldberg's heavy movie schedule.

IV threatens to kill millions, and only Ligon II has the vaccine necessary to save these lives. Because the vaccine cannot be synthesized, the *Enterprise* crew must enter into a treaty to obtain the vaccine from the less technologically advanced Ligonians (who are still far ahead of twentieth-century Earth technology). The Ligonian chief, Lutan, boards the *Enterprise* to present a sample of the vaccine to Captain Picard. As he does so, Lieutenant Tasha Yar, chief of security, intercepts the package, flipping Lutan's guard as he attempts to deliver the vaccine directly to Picard. "A woman—your Chief of Security???" Lutan asks incredulously. Lutan seems both amused and impressed by Yar. The apparently less socially progressive society of Ligon affords women no such roles. As Lutan's lieutenant, Hagon, explains, "On our world, it is the duty of women to own the land and the duty of men to protect and rule it."

The original draft of the episode cast the alien Ligonians as reptiles, but the final version depicts them as African-Arabic. The switch suggests the depiction of alien as defamiliarized. Played by black performers, the characters appear in African-Arabic dress, with turbans, balloon pants, and sashes. The chief apparently has many wives, as we are introduced to one partner as his "First One." Although the script explicitly parallels the society to the Soong dynasty from thirteenth-century China, the city appears Egyptian or Arabic, with turrets and spires. But the costumes and casting evoke what one *Star Trek: Next Generation* staffer called "1940s tribal Africa view of blacks" (Nemecek 34). Bernardi identifies several "intertexts" that reinforce the raced parallel, "including spears, 'counting coup,' images of the safari, and disco-like clothing" (111). The Federation customs are presented as being superior, and eventually, through clever use of their more advanced technology, the *Enterprise* crew defeats Lutan and gets all the vaccine needed.

But first we are treated to notions of the desirability of white women and the attractiveness of black men to white women. Bernardi explains but does not fully develop this aspect of the plot: "The chief wants to use the white-human female to acquire more power at the expense of the black-alien female" (109). Lutan displays an interest in Yar, abducting her to his planet. Analyzing the situation, Deanna Troi, ship's counselor, announces that there was "some sexual attraction from all the males" toward Yar, but that Lutan also evinced "avarice or ambition." This hints at a more complicated plot than mere desire. But Lutan announces his sexual desire when, at the banquet when he has promised to return Yar, he refuses, saying, "This is not an act of war but of love." Lutan says he wants Yar to be his "First One." An attractive blonde woman, Yar seems to exemplify traditional European beauty. And she admits a certain attraction for Lutan. Troi prompts Yar's confession by saying, "But it was a thrill—Lutan is such, such a *basic* male image and having him say he wants you. . . ." Yar responds, "Well, yes, of course it made me feel good when he—" and then she breaks off, realizing what she's said. "Troi, I'm your friend and you tricked me!" Of course, what they have both presented is a basic racist stereotype of African-American masculinity.

What ensues is a challenge from Lutan's current "First One"—a challenge to the death. Feeling her honor threatened by her husband's expression of preference for Yar, Yareena, his "First One," issues a ritual challenge to Yar; they will fight to the death, the winner becoming "First One." Because the wife, Yareena, is played by an African-American actress, this fight seems a literal embodiment of a struggle between black women and white women for black men. The similarity in their names "Yar" and "Yareena" suggests that perhaps the women have something in common besides desire for the same man. Yar arranges a meeting and tries to explain that she is not interested in becoming "First One," but Yareena stalks out, refusing to listen to Yar. That the struggle has been prompted by men is made clear, first when Captain Picard initially refuses the challenge on behalf of Yar, not even letting her speak. Then later, because the vaccine is so desperately needed, Picard tells Lutan that he will order Yar to fight Yareena. So women are ordered to fight, or not fight, based on what the male authorities deem needful.

So far, the episode seems irredeemably racist and sexist. But the plot twists in such a way to suggest that women have opportunities to exercise power even in sexist hierarchies such as Starfleet or societies such as Ligon II. Dr. Beverly Crusher devises a plan to elide the life or death dilemma. (As in the notorious "Pon Farr" episode of classic *Star Trek,* in which Spock and Kirk must fight to the death for a Vulcan woman, medical science enables a pseudo-death.) After a protracted battle, Yar strikes Yareena with the poisoned claw club, then as Yareena falls, Yar throws her body on top of Yareena's, and both are beamed aboard the *Enterprise.* Brought back to life, Yareena becomes a free woman, and she chooses to reject Lutan, whom she realizes engineered the fight to obtain Yareena's lands. Significantly, Lutan objects to this proceeding, saying, "This is witchcraft." Lutan's objection echoes French feminists' insistence on the power of the witch; the claim historically was used to discredit and massacre women, but by Cixous and Clément, it is reclaimed. Having heard

Tasha Yar and Yareena battle.

Hagon cheering for her, Yareena chooses Hagon to be *her* "First One," relegating Lutan to the status of "Number Two." She does so by removing an ornate collar from Lutan's neck and placing it around Hagon's.

This turnabout suggests the triumph of feminine power. The agency is all female: Beverly, Tasha Yar, and Yareena. This episode provides an important exception to Bernardi's claim that the female characters on *Star Trek: The Next Generation* are "either helpers or fetishized objects" (112); in "Code of Honor" the females are active agents. That it is the white women who empower the black woman reifies the problem of white supremacy, even as the plot points to the value of sisterhood. Describing the activity as "witchcraft" only makes it clearer that the feminine has triumphed here. The women have not fought as men would do, but have drawn upon apparently magical, medical means to defeat the men who try to have them kill each other. That the collar that identified Lutan as the leader can be taken off by his wife and given to another again reifies the feminine: Jewelry rather than a gun functions as a weapon. The women of the *Enterprise* end up working with a woman from another species against her male leader. And the fight of a white woman and a black woman over a black man is depicted as a waste of time because the black man they were fighting for is not worth the fight. Graciously, Yareena asks Tasha whether she wants Lutan, and we hear Tasha refuse, before Yareena names him to be her "Number Two." Encoding the racism and sexism, this exchange reminds viewers of the desirability of blackness, and that blackness is represented as male. Although she is white and alien, and has almost killed the black woman, Yar is treated with respect by Yareena. They seem to have bonded through the experience, and Yareena regains her status and offers Tasha something in return for saving her life.

"The Emissary" also deals with mixed-race male-female relationships, but this time with a Klingon and a half-Klingon. In "The Emissary" Worf, who is a rare Klingon raised by human foster parents and serving with the Federation, shows his sexual side. His partner, a half-human, half-Klingon named K'Ehleyr, reflects many of the attributes of a female alien discussed in chapter 1. She has extraordinary powers: Her mission as an emissary for Starfleet causes the *Enterprise* to be used as a carrier ship, diverted to pick her up in space. In addition, a female admiral tells Captain Picard to "cooperate fully" with the envoy. "The Emissary" was written by Richard Manning and Hans Beimier; the show first aired the week of June 26, 1989.

The plot deals with a Klingon ship of "sleeping beauties," but in this updated fairy tale, the "beauties" are male warriors. As part of their war with the Federation, these Klingons were put in "cold storage," on reserve to be awakened when they were needed to fight. Forgotten after the war has ended, and cryogenically asleep for over seventy-five years, these Klingons have emerged in Federation space and they mistakenly think that the Klingon Empire is still at war with the Federation and are therefore hostile. It is the envoy's task to make sure that these Klingons do not destroy helpless Federation outposts. This plot is subordinated to K'Ehleyr's reunion with Worf. The back-and-forth of their relationship culminates in their cooperating to trick the Klingons into surrendering. But first they wage a battle of their own, about sex and control. As subordinates on a Federation ship, Worf and K'Ehleyr have only temporary control of this mission because their appearance will enable them to fool the Klingons into surrendering.

First, however, K'Ehleyr and Deanna Troi have a revealing exchange about being caught between cultures. Like Deanna, whose father was human but whose mother is Betazoid, K'Ehleyr is half-human (on her mother's side) and half-Klingon (on her father's side). But because she appears very

Klingon, with dark coloring and prominent facial ridges, K'Ehleyr has little choice about self-identifying with a race; her appearance determines that for her. As the Klingons were "defeated" in their war with the Federation, K'Ehleyr's appearance thus identifies her with a subordinate group. She and Worf are also clearly subordinate in terms of both their rank and their minority status on the *Enterprise.* Conversely, Deanna appears to be completely human and European American and therefore a member of the dominant group, humans. Her ability to pass as completely human enables her to reveal her racial mix on her terms, when she chooses to do so. Because she looks like a member of the dominant group, she is treated like one of them most of the time. Whereas Deanna has happy feelings about her mixed status, K'Ehleyr admits to feeling "trapped between two cultures." Deanna, by contrast, mouths pieties about "experienc[ing] the richness and diversity of the two worlds" her parents came from. That the plot revolves around K'Ehleyr also supports the idea that for a racially mixed woman, race and culture present choices, but also conflict. When the racial mix is visibly white, the character benefits from white privilege, which can present itself as annoyingly Pollyannish. Deanna can be positive about racial difference because she rarely experiences racial prejudice. That these choices depend heavily on the woman's appearance reveals the central tension of racial difference presented and perceived as appearance. There are fewer choices for the female character whose appearance is that of the oppressed race or species.

Significantly, however, major characters who are mixed-race tend to be female, like Troi and K'Ehleyr. What does this suggest about race and gender? It may be that the series is suggesting or adopting the notion that the "tragic mulatto" figure is, as she is in the film versions of Fannie Hurst's *Imitation of Life,* inherently female. The tragedy of being of mixed race is more of a problem for female characters than male characters because women's identity and acceptance is more closely related to appearance than it is for men. Although race may appear as a cultural test in the plot, in no episodes do white men mate with Klingon females.* In fact, the Duras sisters, the only Klingon females seen in any depth, are depicted as hideous, as is discussed later in this chapter.

K'Ehleyr seems unlikely to be dominated by Worf as she dominates him conversationally. Furthermore, her height allows her to look directly into his eyes, challenging him and meeting his gaze. She wins Worf's affec-

---

*However, Worf mates with K'Ehleyr, who is half-human, and toward the end of the series he has a relationship with Deanna, who is half-human.

K'Ehleyr and Deanna share a moment of sympathy.

tion when she engages a holodeck program of fighting that he has devised. Though outnumbered, K'Ehleyr kills her three monstrous opponents, thus capturing Worf's attention and interest. They then mate in the same holodeck setting, after they fight against more aliens. Worf then attempts to make their union permanent by reciting a Klingon oath of marriage.

Vehemently, K'Ehleyr refuses. "I am not going to become your wife," she tells him. In a role reversal, she admits that mating with him was "glorious and wonderful" but says that because of their careers, she is not ready to marry. Worf comments about the Klingons who slept for seventy-five years, "Klingons do not surrender," but Worf and K'Ehleyr each go through a process in which they surrender to the other. Putting aside their differences, they work together on a strategy by which they pretend that they, not the white folks, run the *Enterprise*. Through their complicated relationship, this episode suggests the importance of members of subordinated groups working together to subvert the prejudices and control of the dominant group.

Worf names himself Captain and K'Ehleyr acts as "Number One," supplanting the white characters who actually run the ship, Picard and Riker. Ironically, this phrase echoes the naming of the "First One" in the species played by African-American actors in "Code of Honor." And similarly, K'Ehleyr has some secondary power. After the Klingons acknowledge Worf's authority, he sends K'Ehleyr to take over their ship. But as she departs, they acknowledge their love for each other. Their mutual admiration and strength show a sexual side of the heretofore asexual but very masculine Worf. He needs a woman of strength and courage. That she is half-human seems to matter less because she can master the Klingon challenges. Here, then, race is presented as a cultural test rather than as a matter of appearance or physical difference. That K'Ehleyr herself is a hybrid implies that humans as a species can learn from another race. But that her role is played by an apparently "white" actress suggests that *Star Trek: The Next Generation* views the world from a Eurocentric lens.

Although Whoopi Goldberg is undoubtedly the most famous and powerful member of *Star Trek: The Next Generation*'s cast, her character, Guinan, rarely assumes center stage. An ambiguous figure, Guinan is immensely old, one of the few surviving members of her species. In "Yesterday's *Enterprise*" she uses her intuition to change the course of history. The episode casts light on the intersection of race and gender, as Guinan's special knowledge and privileged position take precedence over Captain Picard's power and authority. Written by Ira Steven Behr, Richard Manning, Hans Beimier, and Ronald Moore, "Yesterday's *Enterprise*" first aired the week of February 19, 1990. "Continually cited as one of TNG's most popular and powerful" (Nemecek 116), this episode depicts Guinan as mysterious, all-knowing, and finally all-powerful, as she determines the course of history.

When a temporal rift appears and a previous *Enterprise, Enterprise C,* emerges, only Guinan notices that the universe has changed. Before, the *Enterprise* was on a peaceful mission to explore; after, the *Enterprise* is involved in a war. Before, Worf was on the bridge of the *Enterprise,* the embodiment of the treaty between the Federation and the Klingon Empire. After, Worf disappears, to be replaced by Tasha Yar, who had been killed after the first season. Guinan senses the change and tells the captain that he must force the *Enterprise C* back into the rift, to certain destruction, so that the timeline can be restored. If the *Enterprise C* returns to its rightful time (two decades earlier) and defends a Klingon outpost, the Klingons will be so impressed with the humans' honor in dying to defend them that they will sign a treaty; the war, and the death of 40 billion beings, will be averted. As an incentive to the female captain to take this suicide mission, Captain Picard informs the female captain of *Enterprise*

C that the Federation is losing the war with the Klingons, and expects to surrender within six months.

Here in the very premise is a reinforcement of the Federation's white patriarchal order: the plot reveals that a black woman, Guinan, must reinscribe the history in which the Federation (white) triumphs over the Klingons (black). Furthermore, two white women—Tasha Yar, the *Enterprise*'s original chief of security, and the *Enterprise C*'s Captain Garrett—must both die in order to restore the Federation's primacy. And these two white women willingly make this sacrifice. Like the women rulers in "Angel One" and the eponymous "perfect mate," women here sacrifice themselves for the patriarchal order. Captain Garrett orders her crew to return through the temporal rift, where she knows that they face certain death. But Garrett is killed even before they return, so Tasha Yar, who has been informed by Guinan that she dies a meaningless death in the original timeline, volunteers to go on the *Enterprise C*, preferring to die a death in honorable battle. That she has also fallen in love with a crew member on *Enterprise C* makes her sacrifice additionally maudlin and stereotypically feminine.

The setting and her behavior remind us of Guinan's femininity. Goldberg plays a traditional wise woman, a serious version of the psychic she played in *Ghost*. Repeatedly through the episode, Guinan and others describe her knowledge of previous timelines as feminine, in contrast to the masculinity of Starfleet. "Somehow this is all wrong," she tells the captain as she shocks him, and the viewers, by entering the bridge, a masculine Starfleet space that she rarely enters. Hers is the domestic space of Ten-Forward, the ship's meeting lounge and bar. And her comments emphasize the domestic, the private. She tells the captain that what's wrong, what's changed is that there are no families on the *Enterprise*. In an observation that underscores her maternal aspect, she tells Captain Picard, "There should be children here." Picard, who in other episodes complains about the children on the *Enterprise*, can't quite believe her. And why should he? The *Enterprise* is a powerful warship, no place for families. Captain Picard has no family aboard, even in the other timeline.

Guinan's ability to make these events happen is based on traditional feminine power of intuition, a power that at first the captain and others resist. "How can I ask them to sacrifice themselves based solely on your intuition?" he asks Guinan. Tasha Yar, the tough chief of security, is disturbed when she realizes that Guinan is affected. "I've never seen anything bother her before," Tasha explains. That the normally imperturb-

Focus reveals the separation of white and black women.

able Guinan is upset influences the captain. Guinan offers no proofs when asked for them. "I only know I am right," she says, insisting that the captain must send the other *Enterprise* back in time. Data reifies her wisdom by identifying her racial otherness. It's not just that she is racially other (African American), but also that she is gendered as the other—her sense of time is nonpatriarchal, feminine. It is logical Data who suggests that "perhaps her species has a perception that goes beyond linear time." Yet this brief endorsement of feminine time, as described by Julia Kristeva in "Women's Time," is quickly undercut as Captain Picard's reason for trusting Guinan becomes clear. She functions as the woman behind the powerful man. "We've known each other a long time," she reminds Captain Picard. And he tells the crew in a briefing that "She has a special wisdom. I have learned to trust it." That the show later hints even more broadly at their previous love affair reinforces Guinan's traditionally feminine position as the behind-the-scenes advisor to a great male leader. Guinan is not present at the briefing, and with the exception of her trip to the bridge and the captain's ready room, she remains in the lounge.

"Yesterday's *Enterprise*" begins and opens with Guinan at a table in Ten-Forward. In both instances, she is with a character played by another African American—first Worf, then, at the end of the episode, with Geordi. The placement with Worf sets her up as a mother figure, as she gives him prune juice to drink and then advises him to look for a girlfriend. Worf disappears as the timeline changes, for with the Federation and the Klingon empire at war, Worf never gets a chance to join Starfleet. The entire episode can be read, then, as a black woman's struggle to return the black man to a position of power and authority within the white power structure of Starfleet. That Guinan ends the episode asking Geordi La Forge about Tasha Yar, whom Guinan has sent to her death so that Worf might return and literally replace her as chief of security, reinforces this reading. Guinan has explained to Tasha, "We weren't meant to know each other at all," meaning that Tasha had died before Guinan joins the *Enterprise* crew. But the statement also signifies that the black and white woman are not meant to be colleagues, an interpretation supported by "Code of Honor," in which Tasha fights a black woman to the death for her black husband. Reading "Yesterday's *Enterprise*" through the prism of gender and race reveals the ways in which the Federation and Starfleet are built on women's sacrifices. In return, they receive the power of indirect influence accorded Guinan.

"Yesterday's *Enterprise*," "Code of Honor," and "The Emissary" show that race is perhaps the most complicated and compelling subtext in the show. The depiction of race and gender is particularly complicated, drawing on the figure of the mulatta and displacing race onto alien species. Gender seems a stronger commonality than race, at first, as the female characters share special feminine powers such as intuition and empathy. But the female characters end up using these qualities to support the men of their races. *Star Trek: The Next Generation* reflects the ways in which black and white women are separated by race and by men, while only hinting at the possibility of women working together.

7

"The Right to Exercise Control": Reproductive Politics

In America, the struggle over who controls reproduction in all its forms—conception, birth, birth control, and abortion—is becoming increasingly volatile and heated. It is not surprising, then, to find representations of reproductive politics in popular culture. Such representations are usually coded and implicit because the subject matter is too controversial to be tackled directly. Popular culture always reflects the concerns and issues of the nation and time period in which it is produced, and *Star Trek: The Next Generation* provides an excellent example of popular culture reflecting a social issue: abortion. *Star Trek: The Next Generation* was created and ran during years in which public discussions and conflicts about reproductive politics were at new highs. As the previous chapters demonstrate, *Star Trek: The Next Generation* merits the scrutiny of feminists. At the same time, *Star Trek* fans will not be surprised to see the myriad and particular ways that *Star Trek: The Next Generation* functions as a litmus to contemporary American culture. After all, the show's ability to deal with complex issues is one of the main reasons for its popularity. Television shows such as *Baywatch*, another extremely popular syndicated show, are popular for very different and less admirable reasons. *Star Trek: The Next Generation* consciously deals with serious social concerns, such as reproductive rights, that other shows eschew completely.

Between 1987 and 1994 legal abortion faced a series of attacks. An explicitly antichoice president, Ronald Reagan, was in office and *Roe* v. *Wade*, the Supreme Court decision legalizing abortion, came under attack by the neoconservative government. Attorney General Edwin Meese "attacked *Roe* v. *Wade* as a wrong decision that should be overturned and asserted that states should have the right to make abortion a crime" (Eisenstein

160). Even earlier, in 1979, the Hyde Amendment stopped Medicaid-funded abortion for indigent women. In 1985 "federal funding to international family planning organizations that offer or support abortion was cut off" (Eisenstein 188). By executive order, doctors who worked in publicly funded clinics were forbidden to even mention abortion to their patients. A promising new drug that produced an abortion, RU-486, was not allowed into the country. The number of violent attacks on clinics and abortion providers increased sharply, leading to the murders of doctors in Florida in 1993.

Zillah Eisenstein connects these attacks to the Reagan administration's backlash against women. As she describes, "First, control was established over parents/women as mothers, for example, in issues of child custody and compulsory fetal or neonatal surgery. Second, the authority of parents/men as fathers was reinforced, for instance, in parental notification or consent requirements regarding abortion, birth control for minors" (125). She further explains, "Women's absence from the Reagan administration represented and reflected the administration's rejection and dismissal of the idea of equality for women" (141). Until 1993, when President Clinton signed a parental leave bill, the United States was the only industrialized nation without a national pregnancy policy. Even now the current American law guarantees only twelve weeks parental leave, without pay, and is the least generous of any industrialized country.

These facts of everyday life in America filled not only the front pages of newspapers, but also, as Judith Wilt notes, "the plots of novels" (xi). In an insightful analysis of the treatment of abortion in contemporary fiction, Wilt raises many issues that are germane to the emergence of abortion in *Star Trek: The Next Generation*. Wilt explains why abortion appears repeatedly in fiction: "Debate about abortion may begin with reasons, proceed to statistics, but it always comes down, really, to stories" (3). In her study of abortion in public discourse from 1960 to 1985, Celeste Michelle Condit explains the power and importance of public narratives. In a chapter on television, she stresses that "television's depiction of a culture of abortion was of great consequence. This pervasive cultural medium helped to translate the abstractions of political discourse into terms of real life practices" (141). Describing rhetorical narratives in general, Condit also supplies an analysis that fits *Star Trek: The Next Generation*: "To be broadly successful in challenging existing beliefs . . . , rhetorical narratives must produce personal involvement and emotional arousal of a large audience" (25).

Although literary scholars tend to privilege the stories of realistic narratives (as Condit does) and traditional narratives such as novels (as Wilt does), the stories of *Star Trek: The Next Generation* reach millions more people, and hence deserve similar scrutiny about the same political issues. As discussed in the introduction to this book, science fiction has a unique role to play in discussions of gender politics. Only in science fiction are certain settings permissible, such as the female-dominated world discussed in chapter 2, or in this case, defamiliarization of the familiar, such as abortion. By placing pregnancy and abortion in alien characters or within an altered context, we can perhaps begin to discuss abortion without as many assumptions, preconceptions, and emotional baggage. In her insightful discussion of abortion rhetoric, Condit claims that "programs directed at teenagers (largely *science fiction* [emphasis added], action programs, and situation comedies) are not 'appropriate' for dealing with a controversial issue like abortion" (140). Condit's statement is too sweeping, for even the original *Star Trek* dealt with abortion (see "The Mark of Gideon"), and as this chapter demonstrates, *Star Trek: The Next Generation* deals with abortion in a number of episodes. Condit does raise many important issues about the use of rhetoric in what she describes as "the American *argument* about abortion" (1). Like other literary critics, Condit sees that "the meaning and practice of abortion is central to the reproduction of the human species, to our understandings of gender, and to our life ethics" (1).

Similarly, in her study of abortion in contemporary fiction, Wilt singles out abortion as raising "the whole vexed process of human sexuality and maternity" and describes both contemporary writers and feminism as "conflicted" (32). Yet the core of the abortion debate for her is about control. She typifies maternity as "retain[ing] an edge of its original nature, its original wildness, not fully captured even by the huge apparatus of idealization, repression, reduction, and manipulation, which culture has applied to it" (2). In her Kristevan depiction of feminine maternal power, Wilt reflects the edge of maternity that appears in *Star Trek: The Next Generation*. As Julia Kristeva explains in *Powers of Horror: An Essay on Abjection*, the maternal functions as the abject, the horrific, because of its uncontrollable power over all human life. In a historical rather than psychoanalytic context, Adrienne Rich (*Woman*) sees this same power in the maternal because every human depends on a human mother who carries him or her until birth. This overwhelming power of the mother over the fetus makes maternal power threatening and abject. In our culture, this power has been taken over by doctors, as Rich details in *Of Woman Born*, and by the gross sentimentalization of the mother-child bond.

Only science fiction can present maternity in a new, defamiliarized perspective. By presenting a mother who is male, as Octavia Butler does in "Bloodchild" or as *Star Trek: The Next Generation* does in "The Offspring," in which the male android Data has a child, science fiction can remove the traditional responses and sentimental conditioning about mothering. Because it is science fiction, the show can preserve more of the wild, untamed power of maternity by presenting it in new forms, such as a machine giving birth or a woman reproducing an alien. These unique qualities of science fiction enable it to depict maternity in all its potential power. As science fiction evokes maternal power of reproduction, however, it also evokes the issue of abortion. Plots about reproduction inevitably raise the issue of maternal choice.

As important as plot is to the discussion of abortion in narrative, the language used is even more revealing. As Wilt explains, "Choice may not always result in abortion, but rhetorically it is abortion" (3). When episodes of *Star Trek: The Next Generation* present choice in a pregnancy, the show is perforce "proabortion," rhetorically. Presenting an abortion as a possibility makes choice a matter of discussion, debate, and concern. Focusing on rhetoric is crucial to the abortion debate, as the ways that words such as *prolife* have been used to bolster an antichoice position. Who, after all, wants to be "antilife" or "prodeath"?

Not only word choice but also the use of rhetorical figures can shape our reaction to an abortion. In "Apostrophe, Animation, and Abortion" Barbara Johnson explains, "Because of the ineradicable tendency of language to animate whatever it addresses, rhetoric itself can always have already answered 'yes' to the question of whether a fetus is a human being" (34). In Gwendolyn Brooks's "the mother," for example, the speaker addresses the fetuses she has aborted, expressing regret but also explaining why she chose abortion. Johnson points out that "the fact that the apostrophe allows one to animate the inanimate, the dead, or the absent implies that whenever a being is apostrophized, it is thereby automatically animated, anthropomorphized, 'person-ified'" (34). "It is no accident" Johnson explains, "that the anti-abortion film most often shown in the United States should be entitled 'The Silent Scream.' By activating the imagination to believe in the anthropomorphized embryo's mute responsiveness" (34), the film uses rhetorical presentation to "person-ify" the fetus. In movies such as *The Silent Scream* and *Eclipse of Reason*, fetuses are represented as having consciousness and voice in an attempt to persuade viewers to oppose abortion rights. As Robert James Branham explains in "The Role of the Convert in *Eclipse of Reason* and *The Silent Scream*," "The power of these films results not only from the graphic imagery they feature, but also from the situation of these images in a narrative context" (408). The "narrative descriptions of the ultra-sound image [of a fetus] are used to interpret and dramatize images that in themselves are less vivid" (Branham 417). Condit more specifically explains the use of metonymy, the process by which a name that emphasizes a quality of something is substituted for a more specific and precise name. She points out that the depiction of a fetus as an unborn baby is one of the "prolife" movement's more successful strategies, as this takes the "blastocyst, embryo, fetus, viable baby" (82) and reduces the range to unborn baby. *The Silent Scream* and still photographs reinforce this rhetorical move through pictures of a two- or three-month-old fetus. As Condit describes it, "in the pictures the fetus was largely independent of its placenta and umbilical cord. The photographs featured no blood or placental tissue to turn stomachs queasy, and they focused on head and feet" (83). *Star Trek: The Next Generation* picks up on this rhetorical move, as the "fetuses" in the episodes can speak and are conscious. Yet this device is used in ways that are finally prochoice.

Given this context of rhetoric, abortion, and cultural conflict, then, we can expect to find in *Star Trek: The Next Generation* reactions to this public debate. "Galaxy's Child" (discussed in chapter 1), "Up the Long Ladder," "The Child," and "The Offspring" all deal with pregnancy, childbearing and childrearing, and control, especially control of one's own body. "The Child" and "Up the Long Ladder" are episodes from the second season. "The Child" was written by Jaron Summers, Jon Povill, and Maurice Hurley, and first aired in November 1988; Melinda M. Snodgrass wrote "Up the Long Ladder," which aired in May 1989. "The Offspring" was written by René Echevarria and ran in March 1990.

These three episodes illustrate the nature of debate about reproductive choice and present feminist responses to abortion by drawing on science fiction's quality of defamiliarization. "Galaxy's Child" focuses on the danger posed to the *Enterprise* after it becomes a surrogate mother to an alien fetus. Seemingly incapable of surviving on its own, the alien latches on to the *Enterprise* and threatens the ship's existence by draining it of power. One of the strategies discussed by the crew parallels a suction abortion, and the alien finally detaches only after the energy is made unpalatable to it. The plot suggests that when a mother's (*Enterprise*'s) life is in danger, an abortion is justified. But because the mother-fetus pair are a ship and an alien, the abortion theme is muted, in contrast to other episodes discussed here in greater detail. Like the other episodes, however, "Galaxy's Child" provides a solution in which the fetus develops on its own, and other aliens arrive to assume the role of parents. Although an abortion is presented as possible, another solution is found.

"The Child," "Up the Long Ladder," and "The Offspring" deal with human or humanoid issues of reproductive choice. "The Child" opened the second season of the show; because season premieres are usually greeted with great interest, the episode undoubtedly had more impact than if it had aired later in the season. In "The Child," Deanna Troi is impregnated by an alien as she sleeps. The impregnation can be seen as a result of a rape because Deanna has no chance to consent. Bizarre as the circumstances are, the pregnancy is depicted as benign. It is a remarkable pregnancy that takes just thirty-six hours to come to term and Deanna suffers no pangs of childbirth. The beautiful child also grows quickly, aging eight years in twenty-seven hours. Meanwhile, the ship faces a problem when samples of a plague it is carrying to a Federation lab begin to grow and threaten to break out of their containers; simultaneously, Wesley Crusher, a young ensign and the only nonadult in a recurring role, tries to decide whether he should stay on the *Enterprise*. The child proves to be crucial to these subplots; through his presence, and Deanna's and the crew's reaction to him, many issues of reproductive politics are discussed in both explicit and implicit fashion.

"Up the Long Ladder" can be seen as a counterpoint to "The Child." The former's title refers to the long ladder of evolution, a journey of species development fueled by sexual reproduction. Although the episode was penned by a woman, the main character is not a pregnant woman, as in "The Child," but a man whose control of his own body, because of its literal reproduction as a clone, is in question. Lieutenant Riker, the officer so concerned about the paternity of Troi's child in "The Child," faces a rape and reproduction of his own. Riker and Dr. Pulaski (Beverly Crusher's brief replacement) visit a long-lost human colony to discover that the settlement has survived only through cloning. The original colony ship had crashed on a planet named Mariposa, leaving only five survivors, who used their technology to reproduce asexually. Another nearby colony, Bringloidi, has prospered, but as a primitive agricultural society. The *Enterprise* enters the space sector in answer to a distress beacon triggered by the Bringloidi's sun. The dying sun forces all colonists to evacuate to the *Enterprise.* The episode contrasts the physical and earthy Bringloidi to the antiseptic and highly technological Mariposans. The desperate Mariposans kidnap Riker and Dr. Pulaski to steal cells from them for cloning. According to *The Star Trek: The Next Generation Companion,* screenwriter Snodgrass recalls that "Right-to-life advocates objected to the prochoice 'I'm in charge of my body' sentiment espoused by Riker (intended) in denying the Mariposan permission to use his body for cloning" (Nemecek 88). The next episode to raise issues of reproductive choice also focuses on a male character, moving us from a reluctant father to a male "mother," Data.

In "The Offspring" Data, the male android, has a child. Although his gestation process differs from Deanna Troi's biological gestation, Data too uses his body, in this case his positronic pathways, to create a child who is a part of him, but also different. Data names his child Lal, which means beloved in Hindi, but he allows Lal to choose for itself what its appearance will be—what sex, and what species. Lal chooses to be a human female. Data's achievement is remarkable because no one else has been able to create androids after Data's creator, Dr. Soong, died. The Federation bureaucracy then decides that it should have custody of Lal, and a fight for her ensues. Lal's emotions are agitated by this conflict, and she dies at the end of the episode. As Data educates Lal and as the Federation bureaucrats try to wrest control of her from Data, many issues about reproduction, childbirth, and parental rights emerge. As discussed later in this chapter, Data himself is feminized in relation to the humans on the ship, and he functions as a parallel to human mothers in this episode.

In these narratives, the debate over who has the right to control a nascent or new life, and reproductive rights in general, reveals the subtle and overt ways arguments about gender and abortion appear in science fiction. "The Child" sneakily casts the possibility of an abortion in terms that are overtly antichoice; abortion is suggested only by the gruff and forbidding chief of security, Worf. The mother, Deanna, appears to communicate telepathically with the fetus and she appears to decide to keep the pregnancy. Yet the depiction is complex, because although Deanna overtly makes the decision, she is influenced by the fetus, and Worf's assessment of the situation turns out to be accurate. "Up the Long Ladder" presents an overtly prochoice position through Riker's adoption of prochoice rhetoric. "We certainly have the right to exercise control over our own bodies," he declaims. But despite his strong words and compelling delivery of them, he claims this right only in the context of rape. Riker and Dr. Pulaski are drugged, kidnapped, and their bodies violated when cells are removed from their stomachs. The episode focuses more on Riker—he is given the dramatic dialogues and he terminates the growing clones—than on Pulaski.

This emphasis on the male victim rather than on the female suggests a way in which science fiction's defamiliarization can work. Placing the male in the position of reluctant reproducer makes the injustice of the position easier to see. "The Offspring" functions similarly. Because "The Offspring" sympathetically depicts Data's resistance to a hierarchy that disregards his views on reproduction, this episode defamiliarizes the debate about abortion: The "mother," Data, is male. Because the episode argues for his right to control his offspring, the show presents a prochoice position. Whereas "The Child" denies choice to women, Riker's position in "Up the Long Ladder" and Data's threatened disenfranchisement in "The Offspring" suggest the ways in which their real-life parallel, a human mother, are similarly kept outside decision-making structures. It might seem problematic to discuss abortion through a male character, but doing so enables viewers to see through the injustice of antichoice attitudes that do not give the woman any choice or control of her body. Unameliorated by sentimental attitudes toward mothering, this episode defamiliarizes maternity. The appearance of reproductive politics in *Star Trek: The Next Generation* shows that popular culture in general, and science fiction in particular, should be studied for what they reveal about issues of concern to women.

On the other hand, as happens with other political issues such as sexual orientation (discussed in chapter 5), *Star Trek* reveals that popular representations more comfortably espouse freedom when a normally dominant group is oppressed. For example, in "Angel One," Riker advocates male-female equality on a planet where men are legally and culturally subordinate to women. This role-reversal message works in the overt level of these shows. In the area of reproductive freedom, these episodes reveal that in our world, whereas a father has a right to control his body and his child, a mother has no such option. Although *Star Trek: The Next Generation* differs from the original series in a change in the famous voiceover—"to boldly go where no *one* has gone before" instead of "where no *man* has gone before"—*The Next Generation* fails to do so. Yet its journey provides a fascinating study of abortion debates in America.

As does every episode, "The Child" opens with the most famous voiceover in television. In episodes that focus on reproductive rights, however, the voiceover evokes more than its denotation. These phrases resonate: "to seek out new life . . . to boldly go where no one has gone before." In *The Next Generation,* the "new life" can refer to crew members' offspring, a decided change from the childlessness of the original series. The substitution of "one" for "man" in the original *Star Trek*'s "to boldly go where no *man* has gone before" has particular resonance in episodes where female reproduction is the focus. As "The Child" opens, completion of a module to keep medical specimens alive has just been accomplished when a strange starlike entity follows and then invades the *Enterprise.* Its movement is marked by ominous, heavy music similar to the theme for the shark in *Jaws.* Cruising through the ship, the alien hovers over a male figure, then moves to another cabin. It sidles up a blanket that is then shown to be covering a recumbent Deanna Troi, fast asleep. Deanna breathes heavily and then sits up abruptly, startled. Her expression conveys a combination of dismay and apprehension. Almost immediately thereafter, the ship's officers assemble, and they are informed of an unusual pregnancy—Counselor Troi's alien encounter was an impregnation. What should be done about her pregnancy? This question dominates the plot.

As the officers discuss the situation, Deanna Troi appears to have little to say, although she is the subject of their debate and she too is an officer. She sits a few chairs apart from the other officers, at the end of a long table. She doesn't meet their eyes, and she takes deep breaths and frowns. Her arms are held tightly to her sides, her hands hidden in her lap, as the other officers, including Dr. Katherine Pulaski and Lieutenant Worf, discuss options. As Dr. Pulaski explains the unusual pregnancy, she shows a huge projected video of the fetus, which she identifies as male. Its sex is important because in other regards, the fetus is half human, half Betazoid, like Deanna. The fetus might be a clone, virgin birth, or parthenogenesis, and the crew considers parthenogenesis, because Deanna disclaims any humanoid partner or father. However, if the child were a clone, it would also be female, not male. Lieutenant Riker, the second-in-command and Deanna's former lover, barks out, "Who's the father?" Patrilineage is all important here, and not just to Riker. Who or what the father is might threaten the whole ship. Over their heads looms an image of the fetus and the heavy, portentous sound of its heartbeat as the officers' voices diminish. The camera then moves into alternating extreme close-ups of first Deanna, and then the fetus, giving the sense that the two are communicating. We see Deanna's troubled expression and then the expressionless eye and translucent face of the fetus. As Condit describes in "prolife" images, the fetus appears autonomous, independent of the mother. No umbilical cord or placenta is shown. Deanna reaches down to her stomach, seemingly controlled by the contact with the fetus. The communication is expressed by the close-ups of her and her fetus and the visuals, but of course regular viewers of the show also know that Deanna, as half-Betazoid ship's counselor, is genetically empathic. Her role on the ship is to provide the captain with feedback about crew members' and aliens' state of mind and mood. Although the security chief strenuously argues for an abortion, Deanna decides to continue the pregnancy.

The patriarchal hierarchy of the ship is clear, and the pregnancy does not challenge male dominance. Only Deanna and the doctor are female, and visually, and through the plot, the alien male fetus dominates. The officers discuss possible actions while the fetus's heartbeat overwhelms the voices. As the captain acknowledges that the child will be born, the image of the fetus is projected over his head, his hands reaching down to the captain's head. Curiously and significantly, the captain and the fetus are both bald, emphasizing the power struggle for control over the ship, a struggle Captain Picard loses to the more powerful alien being. The fetal image's huge size and its overpowering heartbeat reflect its dominance.

The pregnancy is clearly the result of what must be called a rape, an issue discussed in other episodes in chapter 8. As the representative of the stereotypical feminine values of nurturance and empathy, Deanna Troi suffers throughout the series. In this episode, her reproductive capacity is key: The alien first floats over a male crew member, but then rejects him, presumably because he cannot gestate the fetus. The alien enters Deanna's body while she is asleep and her consent is not obtained. When Riker, the ship's first officer and her former lover, exclaims, "This is a surprise," she replies, "More so for me." She is clearly not happy. Her serious expression and intonation make it clear that the pregnancy is unwelcome. Deanna's options are further limited by the pregnancy's accelerated progress. As Dr. Pulaski explains, the fetus was halfway through the first trimester when the pregnancy was first diagnosed, the morning after the rape. When the officers meet, only an hour later, the fetus is already several weeks further developed. So the legally acceptable first trimester abortion is already impossible. The issue of choice is further obscured by the rapidity of the fetus's development and the lack of any discomfort to Deanna Troi. When asked how she's feeling, Deanna says "I should be feeling uncomfortable [at this point she looks nine months pregnant] with

The alien fetus looms over Captain Picard and Riker.

all the changes in my body, but I don't. I feel fine, better than fine—wonderful." As if that were not enough of a reward for her "choice" of motherhood, she experiences no pain during labor. Her lack of choice and her acquiescence to an unplanned pregnancy are vindicated by her ease of labor and the brevity of the pregnancy itself. Like the ads by the Arthur Moss Foundation showing beautiful, healthy, happy, well-dressed children that proclaim "Life, what a beautiful choice," implying that these model children were all unplanned pregnancies that turned out picture perfect, Deanna's situation elides the actual bloody, painful process of reproduction. I need hardly point out that both the antichoice Moss ads and Deanna's science fiction pregnancy are possible only in a fantasy, a television ad campaign and a television science fiction show. But in the *Star Trek: The Next Generation* episode the cognitive estrangement that is science fiction's most pronounced quality is here used for potentially deleterious ends. Unlike a real pregnancy and more like a woman's body shortly after an abortion, Deanna Troi's body bears no signs of pregnancy or delivery. It is impossible for the doctor to tell that she has had a child, just as it is impossible for a doctor to tell whether a woman has had an abortion. As in the Moss ads, Deanna's child is beautiful. His deceptive charm makes Worf look like a brute for calling for an abortion for security reasons.

However, Worf was right—not just in the general argument, but in specifics. The alien child's presence affects the medical supplies that the *Enterprise* is carrying. As usual in *Star Trek: The Next Generation,* there are subplots, and these too focus on reproduction. The radiation that the alien child exudes allows one of the specimens the ship carries to grow, endangering the entire crew. By the end of the episode, the alien child itself recognizes the danger to the crew's health and kills itself. But before expiring it makes Deanna smile as it thanks her for its life. By the end of the episode, the alien life has been removed, but it is the child rather than the mother who makes the choice. The mother and other adults are relieved of having to make the emotional decision of life or death for the unwanted child. The show could be read as supporting the prolife position, which would forbid abortion completely, even when the mother's life is at stake, even in cases of rape and incest, and prohibit many forms of birth control because a fertilized egg might be destroyed.

In another subplot about life choices, the adolescent son of the ship's former chief medical officer, Dr. Crusher, makes a decision to stay on the *Enterprise* rather than explore other career options. Throughout the series, Wesley is extraordinarily privileged in that he, like the alien child, gets whatever he wants (a position on the bridge of the *Enterprise,* for example). Wesley makes this choice after consulting the wise and ancient alien Guinan, who in terms that surely bear ethically upon the abortion debate, advises Wesley, "Sometimes the game is to know when to consider yourself before others. Give yourself permission to be selfish." It is a permission never offered to Deanna, who must give up her body to the alien fetus, which is, not coincidentally, male.

When Deanna gives birth, she has no partner, so Data stands in for the father. Data's involvement in the birth emphasizes the necessity of accepting and bonding with different forms of life. As a unique android, subject to discrimination, he is shown in earlier episodes as deserving respect and life. Dr. Pulaski, the ship's chief medical officer, objects that Data is an inappropriate substitute because he is an android, but Deanna insists on his presence and Data is fascinated by the birth process. As the baby emerges, Data asks questions about when the mother acknowledges the fetus's consciousness—in short, he queries when life begins. He is hushed when the baby is born, so these questions, so pertinent to the issues raised by the show, are never answered. Data says, "Thank you for allowing me to participate. It was remarkable." It is, but no more remarkable than Data's own "pregnancy," which occurs in the next season. A parent without a partner like Deanna, Data also uses his body to give birth to another. These two parents without partners enable viewers to play out issues about parenting and the divergent roles the sexes are allowed to perform, especially in terms of abortion.

"Up the Long Ladder" functions as a bridge between these two episodes. In fact, the bridge motif dominates the episode, as do references to marriage and compulsory heterosexuality. It is as though being daringly and explicitly prochoice, the show needs then to reassure its viewers that being prochoice does not mean challenging all of society's conventions. This parallels what Condit describes in realistic television dramas, which usually deal only with abortions that "did not conflict with the values of family and motherhood" (138). In the examples she provides, the values of childbearing are stressed, as they are in this episode of *Star Trek: The Next Generation.* Unlike realistic dramas, however, science fiction shows focus on characters who eschew the traditional nuclear family. Only Chief O'Brien, later transferred to a more stable space station, actually has a nuclear family. The episode opens with Worf, the aggressively masculine Klingon, fainting on the bridge. Dr. Pulaski hides Worf's shame at having contracted a childhood disease and pretends that he has passed out from a fasting ritual. This engaging exchange sets the tone for Riker's masculine posturing later in the episode. The crew then decodes and follows the distress beacon, and they rescue the Bringloidi colonists, who insist on fleeing with their animals. Cloistered in a cargo hold, they present a stark contrast to the high-tech *Enterprise.* Their social patterns also contrast strikingly with the male-dominated ship. Whereas Captain Picard and his "Number One," Riker, actually do run the ship, the colonists' titular head is only a figurehead; his spirited daughter actually makes decisions and looks after the colony. The young, attractive woman finds Riker attractive; she pursues him unsuccessfully until she asks, "Do you not like girls?" to which he responds energetically, "'Course I do." The scene fades as they embrace. This heterosexual act and the emphasis on it prepare for Riker's prochoice position—he is proheterosexuality as well as prochoice. A chance comment of the father leads the ship to look for "the other colony" on Mariposa, which turns out to be as high-tech as the Bringloidi are low-tech. When Riker and Dr. Pulaski realize the Mariposans are clones, the doctor asks, "How did you suppress the natural sexual drives? Drugs? Punitive laws?" The prime minister's response positions his people as unnatural.

He explains, "The entire concept of sexual reproduction is a little repugnant to us." Pulaski's reply is revealing and judgmental: "You have got a problem." Left unresolved is whether they have sexual activity of any kind. Clearly, however, the robust heterosexual sexuality of Riker and the Bringloidi is preferable from the show's perspective. The attitude toward the Mariposans is negative and judgmental; the Bringloidi prosper on their own, using "natural" reproductive urges; the Mariposans interfere with traditional heterosexual reproduction. The Bringloidi are depicted as healthy and vibrant, the Mariposans as sterile, unfriendly, and cold.

The issue of reproductive rights comes up not with Riker's sex with the Bringloidi woman (they don't appear to use birth control), but when the Mariposans first request, then steal DNA from Riker and Pulaski. At first, the prime minister of Mariposa makes a plea: "We need an infusion of fresh DNA," because the clones are deteriorating after being reproduced for many generations. Outspoken Riker objects strenuously: "No way! Not me!" As the prime minister argues his case, suggesting the advantages of cloning, Riker asserts, "Human beings have other ways of doing that [preserving themselves]. We have children." Rather than setting the tone for the discussion as he usually does, the captain merely echoes Riker and claims, "I think that you would find that attitude prevalent" among the crew. When the prime minister asks whether they are sure they will not reconsider, Riker again takes command: "Out of the question!"

The scene in which the DNA is stolen clearly evokes a rape, both through the visual images and through the music. Although they are drugged, Riker and Pulaski's eyes are wide open, blankly staring as though they are in a coma. One at a time, a needle is slowly pressed down toward and then slowly into their abdomens. We do not see a technician's face, only gloved hands. As the needle thrusts down, the music is harsh and eerie. Their bodies are being violated against their will. The large phallic needle is inserted and then plunged like a syringe. Although Pulaski later explains that stomach cells are the best ones for cloning, there is no escaping the vaginal implications of the site of their penetration. Like Deanna Troi invaded by the alien, Riker and Pulaski have no choice. But unlike Deanna, her two crewmates have already said "no," especially Riker, who has repeatedly and vociferously refused the opportunity to donate cells. The rape aura is underlined when Geordi La Forge, their crewmate, asks, "What happened to you on Mariposa? Is everything all right?" They then realize they have lost time, and discover the missing cells. Riker then leads Pulaski back to the lab.

Riker destroys a "fetus," an incubator clone, as Pulaksi and La Forge look on.

It is here that the parallel to abortion is most striking. In the lab they find two glass artificial wombs. Riker approaches them and looks into the boxes to see flesh growing. As he lifts the lid, there is a sound like suction, a seal being broken. The bodies are not fully developed—all we see is a piece of quivering flesh. Using his phaser, Riker terminates one body. Then he turns to Pulaski, who doesn't speak but only nods for him to destroy the other "fetus." Here Riker seeks and obtains a woman's consent before performing an "abortion." This action suggests the importance of individual choice. Although she is the doctor, she turns away as he performs the operation. As he finishes, the prime minister bursts in and screams, "Murderers!" His accusation is the most common cry heard at abortion clinics, as protesters accuse everyone of entering a clinic where abortions are performed of being "murderers." The neutral figure here, despite her own victimization, Pulaski attempts to stop their fight with a "Gentlemen, please." On the ship as the crew discusses the problem, Deanna similarly seems sympathetic to the Mariposans, displaying the empathy that so often makes her a victim. The defining line, again, is Riker's. Like Worf's position in "The Child," the prochoice position is enunciated by a male character. Riker vehemently insists that no matter what the Mariposans believe, "We certainly have the right to exercise control over our own bodies." The dilemma is resolved by a "shotgun wedding," as Riker characterizes it, between the Mariposans and the Bringloidi. When Riker's Bringloidi lover hears the captain's suggestion that the two colonies merge, she says "I don't know if I want to be Eve." In a response tailored also to the abortion question, the captain tells her, "It's your choice." The Bringloidi, run by this woman, and the Mariposans, represented by the male prime minister, will breed the old-fashioned way. The prime minister's awe at an extremely pregnant Bringloidi reveals his fear of female reproduction. This character (who has no other lines, and who was actually the two-weeks-overdue pregnant wife of a prop man; Nemecek 88), moves toward the prime minister as his hand reaches toward her stomach. But the prime minister cannot completely overcome his distrust, and he pulls his hand away. This episode shows the centrality of reproduction to *Star Trek: The Next Generation*'s definition of what it means to be human. It presents a prochoice position, but through a male character and a male perspective, for men. Pulaski only goes along obediently and with mixed feelings. "Up the Long Ladder" also looks forward to another male character's brush with reproductive rights in "The Offspring."

"The Offspring" opens with Data's crewmates Geordi La Forge, Deanna Troi, and Wesley Crusher proceeding to the lab to which Data, mysteriously, has invited them. They are unsure of the reason for the invitation and they comment on Data's cautious and secretive demeanor of late. As they enter, Data makes an adjustment and pulls a humanoid form from the ceiling. Nude, roughly formed, with sketchy facial features and no genitalia, this creature is introduced as Data's "child."

This wonderfully bizarre introduction presents the viewer with a creature who is unformed and whose sex is uncertain, or as it is described in the episode, "neuter." Although human embryos are sexed from the beginning of fertilization, like Data's child, whom he has named Lal, they are usually not definitively identified as male or female until the emergence from the womb. Lal, because it is incompletely separated from its gestating parent (as we shall see) and is unsexed, represents a fetus. As Captain Picard says of Lal, "The umbilical cord is virtually uncut. The child depends on him." Lal is described as being in the "formative stages of her development." As Data says, "until all of the transfers are complete, we won't know for certain" whether Lal's brain can function like Data's. Although Lal can walk and talk, she still must undergo a series of trans-

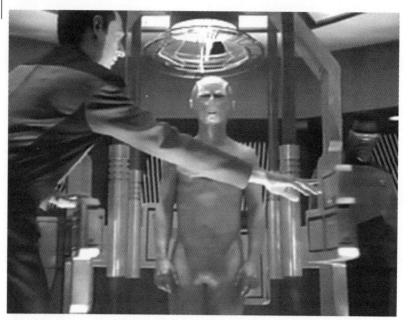

Data introduces Lal.

fusions from Data's positronic brain in order to exist and have consciousness. The captain explains Lal's parasitic dependence on Data by declaring, "I'm convinced the damage will be irreparable if they are separated," an assertion that is borne out by the story's conclusion, in which Lal dies from distress at the prospect of being separated from her father. Lal relies on Data not only for direction and socialization, but also for mental functioning. Lal's positronic brain is incomplete until the final neural transfers, which take place almost at the end of the episode. Lal's brain *is* Data's, transferred in a series of steps. In this regard, then, Lal's dependency on Data is parasitic, like that of a fetus to its mother. As Deanna Troi observes, Lal is "a new life out of his own being." The fetus cannot survive without its mother, and Lal, as we shall see, cannot survive without Data.

For most of the episode, viewers are confronted with what can be described as a walking, talking fetus. In this regard, *Star Trek: The Next Generation* is no less a fantasy than the popular films *Look Who's Talking* (1989) and *Look Who's Talking Too* (1990) and television series *Baby Talk* (1990–92). Why should television shows want to play with ideas about fetal development and parenting? Both *Look Who's Talking* and this episode of *Star*

Trek: The Next Generation blur the boundaries between the fetus and the child. In both cases a fetus is presented as a child—thinking, vocalizing, expressing a personality, and engaging with the world. In this regard they reflect the complications of fetal viability, which in the period 1987–94, when *Star Trek: The Next Generation* aired, kept changing to earlier in the pregnancy as new advances such as drugs to stimulate very premature lungs into breathing earlier were developed and their use became widespread. These medical developments challenged *Roe* v. *Wade*'s definition of fetal life as legally and completely under the mother's control until after the first three months of pregnancy.

Yet this episode is finely complicated and ultimately reassuring about the prospect of abortion, in part because of the emphasis placed on Data's choice. As an android, Data has a unique and subordinate relationship to the rest of the crew. Although he is a unique being and highly skilled, he is often called on to risk his life to protect humans and he is often asked to perform particularly dangerous tasks (such as plugging an interdimensional hole in space) while the rest of the crew waits in relative safety. Especially when he tries to reproduce, his subordinate position reflects that of women. In an insightful analysis of Data's function, Rhonda V. Wilcox argues that Data represents the "oppressed, particularly African Americans" ("Data" 265). Although she makes a convincing case for Data's function as a stand-in for African Americans, she also admits that "the character should not be oversimplified" (265). An equally strong case can be made for Data's representing another oppressed group, women. Especially when he tries to reproduce, Data's subordinate position reflects that of women. He spends much of "The Offspring" caring for his daughter and he consults the crew's only other parent, a mother, on childrearing strategies. When the captain chastises him for reproducing without consulting anyone (especially him), Data replies, "I have not observed anyone else on board consulting you about procreation, Captain." Data defends himself by characterizing himself as having a "primordial instinct to perpetuate." And he teaches his daughter not only facts, but also mannerisms such as simulated blinking. Yet obliging, accommodating Lal can be turned off and returned to a recess in the ceiling (prefiguring her reabsorption into Data's "womb"). When her questions grow too bothersome or too frequent, Data literally turns her off. Data has a control over his child that is more far-reaching than that of a mother over a child and more like that of a mother over a fetus. Data can terminate Lal, and he also realizes that she depends upon him for everything. Data seems to acknowledge Lal's fetuslike dependency on him. When the captain first objects to Lal's existence, Data asks, "Do you wish me to deactivate Lal?"—a termination that can be compared to an abortion.

Despite his control over Lal, Data's own reproductive freedom is threatened throughout the episode. The captain is quite angry when presented with the evidence of Data's fecundity and he yells at him, a rare loss of control for the normally restrained Captain Picard. Later, however, the captain becomes Data's staunch defender against an admiral, the outsider who wishes to spirit Lal away from Data and into the research labs of Star Fleet. Data asserts his parental rights in terms that we are more accustomed to hearing from mothers—perhaps even an echo of Mary Beth Whitehead, the surrogate mother who made international headlines when she tried to keep her biological child. Data says, "You ask that I give her up. I cannot. No one can relieve me from my obligation. I am her father." The issue of choice is raised repeatedly through the idea that reproduction should not have been Data's choice alone and that separation is not his choice either. The episode pushes the idea that the parent alone should control reproduction. The viewer is directed to sympathize with Data when the outsider, the cruel and heartless admiral, accuses the captain of being "sentimental" about Data and Lal. Furthermore, Data and the captain are vindicated by Lal's demise. She withers away at the prospect of being separated from Data.

Lal's sentimental death makes a fascinating futuristic version of an abortion. Here the fetus, though dying from incomplete sustenance, is able to declaim, "I feel. I love you father," and the parent has the opportunity to bid the fetus farewell. "We must say good-bye now," Data tenderly informs Lal. The scene evokes Gwendolyn Brooks's moving poem, in which she addresses her aborted fetuses and asks for their understanding. When Data says, "I wish I could feel it with you," Lal replies, "I feel it for both of us. Thank you for my life. Female. Human." Her last words exonerate Data and (by implication) present a rosy depiction of the termination of a fetus. Data turns Lal off and exits the lab to declare not "It's a girl," as he did earlier in the episode, but "I have deactivated the unit." Through reabsorption, Lal lives on in Data's mind. As he explains at the end of the show, "She is here. Her presence so enriched my life that I incorporated her programs back into my own. I have transferred her memories to me." Data's actions thus make clear Lal's parasitic relationship to him and justify his act of creation. Like Deanna's son's, Lal's gratitude for her brief life provides permission and exoneration for a termination.

Deanna's, Riker's, and Data's pregnancies raise the issue of abortion, an issue currently dividing American society. What is fascinating about these representations is the way they inoculate the idea of abortion, safely dealing with cultural forms in a mild, nonthreatening form. In Deanna's and Data's cases, both the mother and father are exonerated by the plot. Their children die, but they are not held accountable. They do not choose abortion, even when it might be sensible or wise. Instead, the fetuses make that choice for them. These two versions offer no signposts for real women making the decision whether to have a child or to abort. Even Riker's brusque termination of his "offspring" may be presented as his right, but it is also presented as disturbing and distressing, as Dr. Pulaski's averted eyes and grimace suggest. Nor do the episodes provide any ethical insights into the legality of abortion. Indeed, "The Child" is most pernicious for the way it elides any discussion of rape, which is often considered an appropriate reason to have an abortion. The genuine physical sacrifices that mothers make for their children are also elided because Deanna, Riker, and Data suffer no physical pain or personal inconvenience as a result of their pregnancies. Curiously, only with a male android can *Star Trek: The Next Generation* advocate the importance of personal choice and individual freedom. It seems that only with an impossible case involving a male character can a parent control his or her own reproduction. What is especially clear in the emphasis on forgiveness and even saintliness of the fetuses is that reproductive choice makes our culture uneasy and we yearn for an easy, uncomplicated, and guilt-free solution.

8

"No, I Won't Let You": Rape, Romance, and Consent

As might be expected, episodes that focus on female characters in *Star Trek: The Next Generation* highlight problems particularly faced by women, such as rape. Two episodes in this series focus directly and explicitly on rape. Although an early episode, "The Child" from the second season, briefly depicts Deanna Troi becoming pregnant from a rape by an alien, that show focuses primarily on abortion. It is not until the sixth and seventh seasons that entire shows are devoted to rape. Perhaps because rape is such a controversial social problem, the series could not deal with it until *Star Trek: The Next Generation* was well established and able to take such a risk. As it was, "Sub Rosa," an episode from the final season that deals with rape, received much criticism from fans. Telewriter Brannon Braga notes, "The show was not a favorite of . . . 'hard-core fans.' . . . I've come to notice that whenever you infuse a show with sexual themes, some of these fans seem to short-circuit" (qtd. in Nemecek 280).

Braga's comment, though revealing, does not tell the full story. It is not sexual themes per se, but the unsettling, thought-provoking, and even feminist angles that emerge from explicit treatment of topics such as rape that disturb some fans. Without being pedantic or preachy, the series deals with issues in such a way that the viewer must confront real-life problems without the pat answers and stereotypes that affect and comfort conventional social attitudes. For example, in these episodes there is no way to say that the female characters invited the rape, were "asking for it," or behaved unwisely. The conventional patriarchal platitudes that reassure women that it won't happen to them and reassure men that it's not their fault simply won't work in this science fiction setting.

As with issues such as sexual orientation and abortion, science fiction has a unique way of dealing with the topic of rape. The quality of defamiliarization enables the viewer to see rape from a new perspective. Defamiliarization, or placing the known into an unfamiliar setting, thus "estranging" it from conventional reactions and responses, to use Darko Suvin's terms, works especially well with disturbing crimes such as rape. By depicting men as well as women as victims of sexual assaults, *Star Trek: The Next Generation* minimizes the conventional sexist reactions to rape narratives (questions such as "What was she wearing?" and "Did she want it?"). By making the rapes mental rather than literally physical, the episodes emphasize that rape is a crime of violence rather than sexuality. The psychic rape also enables an exploration of the psychological cost of rape and how rape is used, as Susan Brownmiller claims, as "a conscious process by which *all men* keep *all women* in a state of fear" (15). The rapes depicted in *Star Trek: The Next Generation* support Brownmiller's analysis of rape as "a societal problem resulting from a distorted masculine philosophy of aggression" (400). Specifically, *Star Trek: The Next Generation*'s depiction of rape emphasizes a feminist perspective on recovered memory and battered women who kill in self-defense.

The show's depiction of rape should be placed in the context of backlash against women, especially as it appeared in the mass media in the 1980s, just before the series' depiction of rape. Like any mass culture text, *Star Trek: The Next Generation* reflects the period and society in which it was produced. During the years that the series ran, a dramatic increase in the number of reported rapes made the crime more visible and more discussed. Several prominent rape trials, including the New Bedford gang rape and the Rideout trial on marital rape, brought rape to the attention of the American public in new and forceful ways. The New Bedford trial (1984) focused on the gang rape of a woman who went into a bar to buy cigarettes and was raped by a group of men. It was later presented as a fictional case in the film *The Accused*. The Rideout trial (1978) was the first to draw attention to the crime of marital rape. Greta Rideout's husband was the first man to be tried for raping his wife while they were still living together, and the trial attracted tremendous media attention. Coverage of rape trials and television movies and books about rape increased.

As amply documented by Susan Faludi in *Backlash: The Undeclared War against American Women,* some groups attempted to reverse the changes in attitudes toward rape that exposed the crime's sexual politics—a crime committed primarily against women by men. The reactionary attitudes of the Reagan and Bush administrations included the proposal by the U.S.

Attorney General's Commission on Pornography "that women's professional advancement might be responsible for rising rape rates. With more women in college and at work now, the commission members reasoned in their report, women just have more opportunities to be raped" (Faludi xii). Reports of rape rose dramatically in the years just before *Star Trek: The Next Generation.* From the 1970s to the late 1980s, "Reported rapes more than doubled . . . [rising] at nearly twice the rate of all other violent crimes and four times the overall crime rate in the United States" (Faludi xvii). Increasing focus on rape in well-publicized cases such as the Central Park gang rape (1989) and the more recent William Kennedy Smith and Mike Tyson rape trials (1991) made rape a controversial and well-discussed phenomenon, especially on television news and talk shows.

In two important books, anthropologist Peggy Reeves Sanday explores the ritualization of rape in American culture. Many of the issues that she identifies as central to rape culture are addressed in *Star Trek: The Next Generation.* In *Fraternity Gang Rape: Sex, Brotherhood, and Privilege on Campus,* Sanday emphasizes the importance of discourse in our understanding of what constitutes rape (9–10). By showing how attitudes toward rape change over time and how rape is defined differently in different cultures, Sanday brings an anthropologist's perspective to bear on what are falsely presented as "natural" or common-sense attitudes about sexual violence. How we describe a sexual encounter affects our evaluation of it. And rape is most often presented as being the woman's fault. While she specifically explores the discourse community in a fraternity setting—a discourse that encourages rape—her emphasis on discourse explains why it is important to examine popular culture texts, for there, too, we find the construction of discourse that explains and shapes our understanding of what rape means. Sanday reveals that popular misconceptions about rape still abound and stresses that the legal definition includes coercion, not limited to a use or threat of force. This legal definition of consent dominates the episodes discussed in this chapter. In *A Woman Scorned,* Sanday examines acquaintance rape and explores the necessity of honest and direct communication between men and women to avoid date rape. Again, Sanday's feminist analysis applies to these episodes of *Star Trek: The Next Generation.*

In her discussion of the notorious St. John's rape case (1991), in which a group of college men raped a young woman and then were acquitted, Sanday emphasizes that "the polarization of the American sexual culture is reflected not only in the sexual behavior . . . but in the subsequent reactions to that behavior in the courtroom and the media" (*Fraternity* 17). Because both assailants were upper-class, otherwise noncriminals, the blame was placed on the woman. Similarly, in both episodes, the *Enterprise* crew members assume that the bizarre changes that Deanna Troi and Beverly Crusher undergo after they are raped are a result of choice rather than coercion. Sanday explores how we have a "sexual culture that victimizes women and seduces males with its addictive power" (*Fraternity* 18). The rapists in each episode are serial rapists; they have raped before and cannot stop assaulting women. Indeed, Ronan, Beverly's assailant, must "rape" to survive. In *A Woman Scorned,* Sanday focuses on acquaintance rape, a phrase coined in the 1970s "to distinguish forced, nonconsensual sex involving people who knew one another from rape involving strangers" (19). This is the type of rape explored in "Violations" and "Sub Rosa." Sanday calls for further public discussion of our rape-prone society, and these two episodes of *Star Trek: The Next Generation* expose the hideousness of acquaintance rape. Deanna Troi befriends a man who later rapes her and Beverly Crusher is entranced by the alien who takes over her body and who has been her grandmother's lover. In dialogue with other media discussions of rape, "Violations" and "Sub Rosa" expose the social misconceptions about rape and the dangers to women.

The discussion of rape in popular culture also appears in newspapers, television reportage, and even in the broadcasting of trials. In *Rape on Trial: How the Mass Media Construct Legal Reform and Social Change,* Lisa Cuklanz discusses the importance of examining popular media. Although she focuses on television movies and newspaper coverage, what she argues applies equally well to popular fictional series such as *Star Trek: The Next Generation.* She argues that "the battle for rape law reform . . . extends into the realm of public communication and consciousness" and insists that "it is on this rhetorical terrain that much real social change takes place" (6). Examining made-for-television movies about rape, Cuklanz points to the largely female audiences for these texts and suggests that these movies contain "room for the articulation of reform views" (86). She discusses how "the fictional mode enabled the elimination and distillation of key issues for consideration" (111), compared to the journalistic accounts of rape trials. This firsthand mode is even more intensified in *Star Trek: The Next Generation* because there the writers are not bound by a factual plot; they are free to set up the rape scenario in the way that makes the most effective statement. In addition, the futuristic science fiction setting enables the crew to express shock and horror at rape, a common crime in the late twentieth century, but rare in the more enlightened future. The target audience for *Star Trek: The Next Generation* (men ages eighteen to forty-nine) means also that instead of being directed at possible *victims*— women—these episodes reach the potential *rapists*. Keeping Sanday's and Cuklanz's feminist readings of rape and culture in mind makes clearer the positive feminist import of both episodes. "Violations" and "Sub Rosa" expose rape culture, debunk sexist myths about rape survivors, and let the viewers see and identify with pain and anguish caused by rape.

In "Violations," from the sixth season, Deanna becomes the victim when she is mentally raped. "Violations" was written by Pamela Gray and Jeri Taylor, and the episode first aired the week of February 3, 1992. A family of aliens—an overbearing father, his wife, and his browbeaten son—travel on the *Enterprise* en route to another planet. Called Ullians, they are skilled telepaths who are able to stimulate and collect memories. Identifying with the son's difficulties with his overbearing parent, Deanna is friendly and sympathetic to Jev. (Deanna's own mother is a full telepath who is quite obnoxious, and Deanna's difficulties with her mother are often featured in the series.) Deanna's friendliness is rewarded with rape, a classic acquaintance rape scenario.

Deanna seems to be safe as she exits the elevator she shared with Jev, but he pursues her to her quarters, using his mental powers to attack her. Jev viciously invades Deanna's mind, forcing her to relive a sexual encounter with Will Riker. In the flashback, Jev replaces Riker and the sexual encounter turns into a sexual assault. The experience leaves Deanna catatonic. Her physical isolation and trauma reflect the emotional trauma experienced by rape victims. In similar violations, Jev then "rapes" Riker and Beverly Crusher, but Deanna recovers. Because, as Sarah Projansky notes, "the major mystery of the episode" (41) is Deanna Troi's coma, these secondary "rapes" serve only to create sympathy for Troi's violation. Finally, the crew figures out what has happened; Jev is taken away to be punished. The episode concludes with the father and Captain Picard lamenting the violent nature of sentient beings. The show's title and dialogue make the connection with human rape explicit and unambiguous. Rape is defined as a violation.

"Violations" is not the first time that Deanna Troi has been featured as the victim of a rape. In "The Child" Deanna is visited, as she lies sleeping, by an alien who impregnates her. In both "The Child" and "Violations" Deanna does not provide her consent. Whereas she is physically invaded in "The Child," in "Violations" it is her mind, more specifically her memory, that is violated. Making rape a mental rather than a physical crime emphasizes it as an exercise of control and dominance, rather than a crime of passion. In a perceptive analysis of "Violations" and "The Child," Projansky argues that these rape narratives "function symbiotically with the neocolonialist system [of the Federation] itself" (46). She demonstrates how the rapes function to reify the "paternalistic militarism" of the Starfleet hierarchy. This reading of "Violations" makes sense, but it does not preclude a more specific and sympathetic reading of how the rape affects an interpretation of rape itself. The particular kind of rape shown in "Violations" reflects a concern with memory that is the particular provenance of survivors of sexual abuse, the majority of whom are female.

The specifics of the rape also evoke the controversy of "recovered memory," the process by which, through therapy, adults recall memories of childhood sexual abuse. Several prominent cases have made recovered memory a public controversy (see Franklin; Gorman; Klass; Testa). The show opens with an example that points to recovered memory: The Ullian father, Tarmin, assists Keiko, a female crew member, in recalling an early childhood memory. Although the memory is a pleasant one of her grandmother, the process evokes the recovery of repressed memory. Tarmin has Keiko focus on an object she remembers vividly, but without understanding its significance. Keiko does not realize the importance of the object she remembers, a cup, until Tarmin leads her through a step-by-step evocation of events. Although the notion of recovered memory is controversial because its critics claim that it can be manipulated by the therapist, proponents insist that the process is a legitimate way to deal with the repression of unpleasant memories such as sexual abuse. In a number of notorious cases, men have been convicted of sexual assault and even of murder by a witness testifying to repressed but now recovered memories (see Franklin; Gorman; Klass; Testa). Significantly, the criminals have been men and the witnesses women. Legitimizing recovered memory may be seen as a valorization of feminine knowledge, heretofore denied by the legal system, but now achieving acceptance. In "Violations," a sympathetic depiction of recovered memory as a scientific and valid activity lends credence to the proponents of recovered memory.

Recovered memory stands at a crux of feminism and backlash. Most of those who have used recovered memory to discover sexual abuse have been women. Because recovered memory works on a model of feminine time, as described by Julia Kristeva, its very process valorizes the feminine. Instead of the masculinist logic of linear time or the rigid rationality of the legal system's need for proof, recovered memory acknowledges the fluidity of time and memory. The limited acceptance of recovered memory, then, validates some women's later remembrances of abuse by men, especially fathers and male authority figures. At the same time, as recent books and articles show, there has also been a backlash against recovered memory (Gorman; Testa). Its opponents claim that recovered memory is a hoax perpetuated by angry and bitter feminists who want to create crimes where none exist. By suggesting the validity of recovered memory, "Violations" supports *one* feminist view of the mind. Like all science fiction, *Star Trek: The Next Generation* uses patterns such as a futuristic setting and extrapolation of existing science to legitimize certain controversial present-day issues such as recovered memory. What the show does with the plot is important and is discussed later in this chapter, but first it is crucial to note that through its very structure, an episode can make strong political statements. The assumptions and acceptance of recovered memory make the antirape message of the episode even stronger.

The episode also deals with broad categories of masculine and feminine through aliens and humans, underscoring the problem of rape as one of masculinity and aggression. Deanna represents femininity through her position as ship's counselor, her concern for others, her empathic ability, her long beautiful hair, her form-fitting costumes. That she and Keiko, both women, are the first participants in recovered memory and that their femininity makes them appropriate subjects for memory recall is emphasized by the reactions of the male crew members to the process. Worf, the aggressive and macho chief of security who represents quintessential masculinity as Deanna represents femininity, brusquely rejects the idea of memory recall for him in language that evokes rape. "Klingons do not allow themselves to be *probed*," he gruffly asserts. When Beverly Crusher coyly suggests that Captain Picard have his memories probed, he grimaces and rejects the idea. Riker tells La Forge that *he* wouldn't want to share his memories with an audience. The men's rejection of being "probed" reinforces the gendering of rape as a crime committed primarily by men against women. Although the Ullian female, Inad, can also enter another's thoughts, we are shown only Jev and his father Tarmin invading another person's mind, as Projansky points out (49, n11).

The femininity of having one's memories "probed" is contrasted in the plot. As first Deanna and then Riker and then Beverly Crusher fall mysteriously into comas, Geordi La Forge, the ship's engineer, and Data, the analytical android, try to solve the puzzle through masculine logic. Using the computer, they search for parallels and clues as to what might have caused the illnesses. Through deduction, the pair discovers that only Jev visited every planet where others similarly fell into unexplained comas. The duo's detective work contrasts the femininity of "memory"—chaotic, unregulated, unknown—to the masculinity of technology and the scientific mind and process represented by La Forge and Data.

Mysteriously, Jev's victims fall into comas, and they cannot explain what has happened to them. But what appears to be a coma is really a trauma induced by being mentally raped (like the notorious "date rape" drug that obliterates its victims' memories). That the activity is a rape is made clear by Deanna's experience. After sympathizing with Jev about his difficult father, she returns to her quarters and gets ready for bed. Dressed in a seductive off the-shoulder nightgown, she lets down her long dark hair and begins brushing it. Then the flashbacks occur. She frowns, and we see a man pushing her down. She tells him—Will Riker—"We can't, not while we're serving on the same ship." She repeats her rejection, "Will—don't!" They kiss, but then she pushes him away, saying "You mustn't do this" and cries out. Then Riker's face changes to that of Jev, and she yells, "NO! NO! DON'T!" She screams, "NO!" again and then passes out. Jev has entered her memory, what appears to be a pleasant memory, and then turns it into a sexual assault. The camera repeats the violation as it pulls up from her body to a shot from the ceiling. We see her body seductively posed on the floor as she lies unconscious.

The flashback appears to be an actual memory of Deanna's, but it is altered by Jev. What isn't clear is how assaultive Riker himself was in the original incident. Although there has been sexual tension between the two, by this point in the series they have settled into the role of comfortable comrades. Yet given Riker's reputation as a sexual predator, delineated in other episodes, the viewer must at least wonder about the possibility of Riker, too, having posed a danger to Deanna's sexual autonomy. Projansky even describes this scene as one of "(attempted) rape" (39) and emphasizes how the rape is repeated through the memory and Jev's repeated invasion of Troi's mind. Again, it is the danger of those known that is emphasized: acquaintance rape. More generally, the memory of Riker and Jev's use of it evokes Brownmiller's famous precept that rape is "a conscious process by which *all men* keep *all women* in a state of fear" (15).

In a bizarre fashion, by watching these rapes, the audience, too, is im-

Riker forces Deanna to the floor.

plicated in rape culture. As Laura Mulvey suggests in her much-cited "Visual Pleasure and the Narrative Cinema," the process of film itself is voyeuristic and fosters dominance. Exploring the psychoanalytic dynamic between spectator and film, Mulvey argues that classic Hollywood film privileges a masculine perspective by making women the object of a "male gaze." Female characters are filmed in such a way as to emphasize their objectification, as objects in a frame. This sequence of Deanna's struggle and her inanimate body creates a male gaze, to use Mulvey's famous phrase. Deanna's violation is redoubled as we watch it happen, and view her body from a privileged angle of spectatorship. The viewer's dominance is reinforced by the shot from the perspective of the ceiling, providing us with an omniscient view of the room, and a sexualized perspective of her unconscious body, seductively posed.

Deanna is clearly victimized and damaged here. She recovers from the coma on her own, but she displays many signs of a rape survivor. She cannot recall what happened to her—why she passed out. "Why do I feel so frightened?" she asks. "What happened to me?" When Jev suggests that he comb her memories, and the Captain rejects the idea as being too traumatic, Deanna insists on "testifying." The parallel to a rape survivor's testifying in court is made clear by the female Ullian. She says "If we are ac-

Camera pans Deanna's supine form.

cused, surely we are entitled to a defense." Deanna, like a courageous rape survivor, agrees. "I want to do it Captain. Something awful happened to me and I don't even know what it was." She fights back by trying to understand what happened to her. At first Jev implants a false memory that it was his father, Tarmin, who assaulted her. But when Deanna is alone with Jev in her quarters, she realizes that it was Jev who attacked her. She fights back.

In moves that are straight out of self-defense classes for women, Deanna reacts strongly to Jev's assault. She identifies him as her attacker, and as he rips off her communicator badge, pinned to her clothes, she yells "NO!" Although he prevents her from communicating with others and seeking help, she does not let him silence her. She knees him in the groin, yelling, "No, I won't let you," and hits him. He throws her to the ground. It seems an equal battle, the outcome unclear, as Worf enters the room. Jev's brutal physical assault on Deanna makes the parallel to rape inescapable. Although her resistance is valiant, it is male deduction that saves the day. Data and Geordi have figured out that Jev was the culprit and they have come with Worf to apprehend him. Significantly, Data helps her up off the floor, underscoring his centrality, and that of masculine logic, in aiding Deanna.

Deanna fights back.

Riker and Beverly Crusher also lapse into comas, but their encounters with Jev are briefer and not sexual—Riker relives an instance when he had to order a door shut in an emergency, killing a crew person, and Beverly has to relive identifying her husband's corpse. In both instances, these unwelcome memories deal with violent death and conflict. Riker's and Beverly's violations reinforce the horror of a rape. Their abuse is not given as much narrative space, but their parallel "rapes" provide more sympathy for the victim by presenting another female and even a male experiencing the same trauma. The science fiction setting enables a male character to experience what in our world is predominantly a female trauma. This defamiliarization promotes the sympathetic identification of male viewers with an essentially female problem. Given the male target audience for *Star Trek: The Next Generation*, this situating of a male character is a clever rhetorical move to persuade male viewers to see a feminist issue in a new light.

Although Beverly's and Riker's experiences support the interpretation of the violations as rape, both incidents are subordinated to Deanna's narrative, both in order of presentation and in the amount of time devoted to them. This subordination stresses the feminist analysis of rape. After all, it is Deanna who identifies and confronts Jev. All three incidents are named by Jev's father as "this form of rape." In the concluding scene we see both the patriarchs—Tarmin, Jev's father, and Picard, Deanna's "father"—discussing the sorry situation. Picard identifies violence as something that sentient races must evolve away from, and he warns the viewers that "violence is capable of consuming us." This pat conclusion does not belay the issue of consent raised in this moving and frightening episode. It is choice, and the invasion of an intimate part of the self—in this case memory as a synecdoche for the body's private parts—that make the horror of rape clear. Its gendering is also made clear through the rapist's gender as well as that of the victims—Deanna primarily, but also Beverly. Riker appears here, as he does in "Up the Long Ladder" (where he experiences the theft of his DNA), to be a stand-in so that the male viewer can empathize with a woman's situation. Using a male character to create empathy for a female plight—rape—might seem antifeminist, but it can also be seen as a rhetorical displacement that enables the predominantly male viewers to understand and sympathize with a rape survivor. This is science fiction functioning as a thought experiment, or defamiliarization—seeing the familiar, rape, from a new perspective. This displacement onto a male character, then, can promote a feminist expose of, and distaste for, rape.

In "Sub Rosa" from the final season, Beverly Crusher is again assaulted. Written by Brannon Braga, the teleplay is based on a story by Jeri Taylor, who cowrote "Violations." The show first aired the week of January 31, 1994. Attending her grandmother's funeral and closing up her grandmother's house, Beverly discovers that her 100-year-old grandmother had a young lover. The lover, a "ghost" or alien life form, sexually manipulates Beverly. He needs human lovers as symbionts. Without a human host, he cannot survive. Beverly faces the loss of her identity and physical autonomy as the creature merges with her, telling her they will become "one." At the same time the creature, whose name is Ronan, threatens the planet's ecological balance and the lives of Beverly's crewmates. Eventually, after Ronan almost kills Captain Picard, Beverly regains her independence, fights back, and eventually destroys the creature. Although Beverly experiences some sexual pleasure, this episode identifies and explores rape's essential feature as coercion.

The show's title, "Sub Rosa," points to one of the episode's major themes, the dangers of hidden or repressed sexuality (the phrase means "in secret"). More specifically, the episode exposes a major social problem, the secrecy surrounding rape and sexual abuse within families. Although Beverly is an adult, her position in her family and in relation to the creature makes him a father figure. He has been the lover and dominator of her grandmother and previous generations of her family's women. The relationship is incestuous, and this is emphasized through the episode's exploration of Beverly's ethnic and family heritage. Beverly's consent to this sexual relationship is never obtained, and Ronan attempts to coerce her by threatening and even killing her friends and violating her grandmother's corpse.

As the episode evokes the sexual abuse of females by family members, it also overtly introduces the idea of domestic violence, or spousal abuse. The culture of romance (and romance novels in particular) is exposed for encouraging a climate that is a psychological setup for the cycle of abuse. The psychology of battering is quite well known and involves a particular pattern of conditioning. Coercion and threats, intimidation, isolation, economic abuse, male privilege, minimizing, denying, and blaming are all strategies a batterer uses to control a woman (see Celani); as we will see, Ronan uses each of these tactics against Beverly. An important way in which the abuser maintains control over the battered woman is to alternate abuse with what is called the honeymoon phase. The batterer will be terrifyingly violent and damaging, but he will alternate the abuse with loving, caring, even excessively romantic attentions. He will promise his victim anything. This alternation deceives the woman into thinking that the abuse is the aberration and that, as he has promised, she will be happy and loved. Batterers use our society's emphasis on romance, on being one with a partner, to make the woman think that she is loved and that she should stay with the abuser, neglecting all others for this primary relationship of "love."

Like other battered women, Beverly changes after Ronan enters her life. He controls and dominates her actions, cutting her off from her friends and her work. In a calculated isolation on Ronan's part, Beverly loses her identity. He becomes the focal point of her existence, as she spends all her time with him, neglecting friends and her job. He abuses her, but then assures her of his love. His insistence on making love and giving her physical pleasure after he abuses her is a classic batterer's move. She ignores warnings from others (her grandmother's friend, Ned, and the captain). Beverly threatens to call the *Enterprise*, the representative of legal authority, but Ronan tricks her into avoiding that escape route. Seeing Beverly, the accomplished professional woman, caught in the snares of a batterer makes it clear that any woman can be susceptible to this socially sanctioned form of sexism; it is sexism, compulsory heterosexuality, and the socially conditioned desire of a woman to be loved that make her vulnerable to battering.

Hidden sexuality dominates romance fiction and the episode exposes the myriad dangers of the romance plot. Romance rarely appears as a plot device in *Star Trek: The Next Generation*. The episode typifies Ann Snitow's identification of romance novels as pornography for women. In "Mass Market Romance: Pornography for Women is Different," Snitow explores the use of sexuality in romance fiction. She cites the critic Peter Parisi, who identifies the process in romances as "'trying to convert rape into love-making'" (194). In Snitow's words, "How different [from men's pornography] is the pornography for women, in which sex is bathed in romance, diffused, always implied rather than enacted at all! This pornography is the Harlequin romance" (195). Snitow cites Joanna Russ's description of the situation of Gothic heroines, who, like babies, are loved "simply because they exist" (196). These heroines reify the traditional feminine prescription of passivity. This criticism of romance novels suggests that these fictions disarm women, teaching them to fantasize dependency and even a type of rape. But "Sub Rosa" shows battery and rape as brutal and dangerous. The episode does not fault Beverly for yearning for romance, but identifies the guilt as the perpetrator's. Furthermore, the episode presents a model of resistance to feminine passivity, which can lead to life-threatening situations.

Passive femininity is strenuously resisted in both rape episodes of *Star Trek: The Next Generation,* but particularly in "Sub Rosa." Beverly Crusher must struggle with an embodied Harlequin romance when she encounters a magical but demanding lover. As Snitow points out, "romance is a primary category of the female imagination" (200). A typical romance plot features an older, more powerful hero, punishing kisses, the "need" of the heroine to be overwhelmed. By presenting Beverly's confrontation with a seductive but dangerous and soul-destroying romantic figure, "Sub Rosa" criticizes the romance plot. The writers set up a typical romance scenario and let Beverly resist. Her resistance is effective in combating the romance plot because she is a highly visible and admirable role model.

In "Sub Rosa" Beverly is taken over by a strong romantic figure from Gothic literature. In a feature typical of romances, Beverly explores her family and ethnic heritage, which happens to be Scottish. The planet Caldos, on which her grandmother lived, is a recreation of Scotland, down to authentic Scottish cornerstones. The inhabitants dress in traditional Scottish attire. Beverly inherits a mysterious candle from her grandmother—and it turns out—a ghostly lover who has dominated generations of her family's women. Jeri Taylor, who concocted the story, identifies herself as an "addict of a number of trashy genres" (Nemecek 280), including romances and historical novels, and their influence can be seen in this romantic setting.

The crucial issue in romance fiction and in rape is that of consent. Although there is abundant evidence that Beverly enjoys the physical sensations from Ronan, the plasma-based symbiont, she does not consent. Like Deanna's alien impregnator in "The Child," Ronan visits Beverly first while she is asleep. Furthermore, their relationship is incestuous, given that Ronan has been the lover of over 200 years of Howard women. (Although Beverly does not initially object to their relationship as incestuous, the viewer realizes the sickness of the alien preying sexually on generations of the same family.) Ronan epitomizes a romance hero: He is an older man and his expression of physical passion involves punishing kisses and embraces. He overwhelms Beverly. His language and the changes in Beverly show that she is not fully herself. Ronan tells her that they will become "one," traditional romance language, but ironically, also the language of domestic violence. Ronan's use of "one" also evokes *couverture,* the legal process by which a husband and wife became legally one person in the early modern European legal tradition. For example, in the contemporaneous film about domestic violence, *Sleeping with the Enemy,* the abusive husband tells his wife, "We are one and will always be one." What Beverly does not realize, at first, is that her lover means this literally. Without her body, Ronan cannot survive. His dependency on her for physical survival signifies how patriarchal society depends on the labor and bodies of women to survive.

The plot exposes the dangers of a woman's submerging herself in a male partner. Becoming one with Ronan changes Beverly. She loses interest in work although she has always been a consummate professional and a superb doctor. Typifying economic abuse, Ronan convinces her to quit her job on the *Enterprise,* thus making her more dependent on him. Ned Quint, a friend of her grandmother, repeatedly warns her about the candle that houses Ronan's spirit. However, being warned about the dangers of a relationship with a batterer does not help Beverly see the problem. She is even warned by conventional superstitious belief. When Beverly first sees Ronan's visage in a mirror, she is frightened and drops the mirror, breaking it. And she does indeed get the traditional bad luck. When she returns alone to her grandmother's cottage, she senses Ronan's presence and threatens to call the *Enterprise.* She realizes he is dangerous.

Over the next few days, she succumbs to his dominating personality. Although she feels physical pleasure, it is a pleasure that she has not chosen deliberately and it has many character-altering effects. Inexplicably to her friends, she resigns from Starfleet and abruptly leaves the ship. The cost of this sensuality with Ronan is her self, her identity. In this way, the experience parallels a rape. She does not consent, and she is even physically altered; at the end of the episode, her eyes turn a strange brilliant green—a color that symbolizes Ronan's dominance because his basic physical manifestation is a greenish cloud. The change in her eye color represents his control over her. Like other rapes, this mental rape leaves physical traces. As he attempts to get her to turn against her friends, he pulls her down to her knees, so that she kneels before him in obeisance. These physical signs reveal that he is a negative, controlling, and dominating presence. Like Deanna's deterioration, Beverly's shows the cost to women of rape and male dominance.

This mental invasion is paralleled by an invisible physical assault. Although Ronan has no visible body, he forces her around the cottage. As she is buffeted around the room, Beverly finally says, "What's happening to me? I feel so strange." The language evokes Deanna's words after she is raped by Jev. She gasps, "Who are you?" Pulled around the room and up the stairs, she pushes herself down and away, resisting him. She asks again, "What's happening to me?" and cries out, "I don't understand—stop it!" Using the language of romances, Ronan tells her he loves her and again repeats that they will become one. In repayment, he tells her that she will feel physical pleasure more intensely than she ever has before. But at a tremendous price.

Ronan also causes a disruption on the planet, another rape. His presence disrupts the weather systems, resulting in violent storms. We witness a struggle between technology, represented by the *Enterprise,* and physicality (male sexuality) represented by Ronan. Beverly's experiences with Ronan are intercut with scenes of Geordi La Forge and Data struggling to correct the planet's weather systems. They use the *Enterprise,* which sends a beam down to the planet. These shots of the *Enterprise* set up the struggle as masculine technology versus a primitive natural force. These are the forces warring inside Beverly—her body versus her trained intellect.

Finally, like Deanna, Beverly fights against the man who possesses her. After Ronan zaps Picard, Beverly chooses to use her medical kit to save Picard's life rather than help Ronan escape. She yells "No!" as he strikes Picard. When Ronan reanimates Beverly's dead grandmother, she again screams "No!" She rejects Ronan, identifying him as "infusing" (raping) her with plasmic energy. She identifies his attack on her entire family— "You've been using me, my entire family"—she tells him. Screaming "No, No!" again, she grabs La Forge's phaser and destroys his candle home, an unsubtle phallic symbol of his masculinity. Ordering Riker to close all plasma conduits, Beverly aims the phaser at Ronan, warning him to keep away from her and destroying his humanoid body. Only she can destroy Ronan because he has disabled Picard and La Forge. Here the episode reveals its most feminist premise: that women can and will fight back against rapists. Picard and Geordi's figurative impotence suggests that a woman cannot and should not rely on men to protect her.

As in *Sleeping with the Enemy*, this episode depicts a woman's killing her abuser in self-defense. Even the camera angles are similar—the male figure threateningly moving toward her and the victorious woman shaking and sinking to her knees after killing the predator. But we have moved here away from the male gaze that dominates "Violations." Here the camera angles stress Beverly as an agent rather than as an object. At the episode's climax, she is presented as *the* active force, while her normally dominant male colleagues, from the captain on down the ship hierarchy, are incapacitated. They literally lie unconscious at her feet.

This episode warns of the dangers of romance as pornography for women. It may be seductive and appealing, but it is finally soul-destroying. Ronan's use of force parallels and reinforces societal constraints on women's achievements and mobility. Beverly cannot be a professional woman and have traditional romance, too. The two are antithetical. In a voiceover, Picard warns that Crusher's recovery from the illness will be slow—and the final scene shows Beverly healing as she talks with Deanna about her regrets. She admits to missing Ronan and the pleasures he provided. Like Deanna's experiences with the alien who impregnates her and with Jev, Beverly's experience focuses on choice and freedom. With Ronan, Beverly had none. Her rejection of him and his possession of her is a rejection of sexuality without full, informed consent. The plot shows her rejecting Ronan's domination and her loss of identity.

In this regard, at least, "Sub Rosa" should be seen as positive from a feminist perspective. The episode does reject rape culture, and it points to the dangers of romance. Yet the dilemma of the professional woman is not resolved. Must Beverly remain sexless? Because none of the major crew members has a permanent sexual relationship, Beverly's solitary situation is less sexist than it might seem in another setting. In its sophisticated replaying of the romance plot, the show does seem to assert that science fiction is more liberating for women than romances. In this way, the episode might be read as enacting a conflict between two of the most popular fiction genres.

As both "Sub Rosa" and "Violations" show, science fiction as a genre—and *Star Trek: The Next Generation* in particular—has the potential to challenge its viewers' comfortable or traditional assumptions about controversial subjects such as rape. Both episodes sympathetically depict rape survivors fighting back. Deanna and Beverly provide strong role models of successful, assertive women who choose their careers over traditional femininity. Indeed, their very survival seems predicated on their careers. That they have a strong history of independence and supportive colleagues helps each break out of her victimization. Both episodes indirectly suggest the importance of careers for women. That they have to make a choice between career and romance is more a function of the sexism of traditional relationships than an ideal supported by the show. For both characters, the possibility of an egalitarian relationship with a man remains a desirable option, possible but clearly difficult to achieve, as it is for everyone on the *Enterprise.* These characters and these particular two episodes should send us back to the "real" world questioning and resisting the problematic nature of work, love, and sexuality for women.

The two most recent books on *Star Trek*, Thomas Richards's *The Meaning of Star Trek* and Jeff Greenwald's *Future Perfect*, hardly mention gender at all, and seem little concerned with the importance of feminism for *Star Trek* or *Star Trek*'s importance for feminism. As preceding chapters attest, however, *Star Trek* covers almost every area of interest to feminists. From classic *Trek* to the most recent series, *Voyager*, women have been the series' loyal fans, as Camille Bacon-Smith's research shows. I agree with Ferguson, Ashkenazi, and Schultz when they claim that "a strong subgroup of feminist viewers is underestimated, and underappreciated" (231). If you read only *The Meaning of Star Trek* or *Future Perfect*, however, such devotion would seem inexplicable.

Sexual Generations reveals the ways feminist issues are addressed and developed over the series' seven-year run; careful attention to *The Next Generation*'s treatment of feminist issues makes the breakthroughs in the succeeding series, *Deep Space Nine* and *Voyager*, seem almost inevitable. Finally we have an African American and a woman in leadership positions and main characters. Like *The Next Generation*, these two series reflect complicated and contradictory positions on race, gender, and sexual orientation.

In its use of a major character who is a Trill, the wormlike symbiont with a humanoid body that changes (and thus can change its sex, as in "The Host"), *Deep Space Nine* advances the depiction of sexual orientation, including an intense lesbian kiss that was featured in a recent special on the *Star Trek* series. In its use of Odo, a Changeling who, like Data, functions as an isolate among humans, the series explores issues of race. But despite its setting on a space station, in many ways *Deep Space Nine* challenges traditional notions of gender less than the latest series, *Voyager.*

Voyager finally realizes Gene Roddenberry's vision of a female space captain. In its inclusion of a Native American, an Asian American, and a woman who is half-Klingon, half-human, as well as a Vulcan played by an African-American actor, the series contains a more complicated racial mixture. Specific episodes have dealt with rape and abortion, in much the same way as in *The Next Generation.* Two episodes that focused on repressed memory involved male characters, but reflecting a retrenchment from this notion, were critical of implanted memories. Overall the series has extended the treatment of feminist issues without changing the approach described in *Sexual Generations.*

Where *Voyager* departs from this script is in its depiction of female scientists, an important and promising development. Captain Kathryn Janeway is not only a Federation captain, but also a scientist. *Voyager's* chief of engineering, B'Elanna Torres, is also a scientist. Through these characters' collegiality, camaraderie, and conflict, as well as numerous plots that focus on feminist ethics, the series presents a version of science that embraces feminist ideas about how women can alter the practice of science.

I use *science* to include both what is considered "pure" science—research—and its sister—technology. In *Whose Science? Whose Knowledge?: Thinking from Women's Lives,* Sandra Harding discusses the problem caused by an "insistence on the separation between the work of pure scientific inquiry and the work of technology and applied science." She describes the separation of science and technology as being the "attempt of Western elites to avoid taking responsibility for the origins and consequences of the sciences" (2). *Voyager* follows Harding's feminist call to consider science in its broadest sense, from research about the universe and its inhabitants to technological and engineering problems.

Through her usually dispassionate command of the ship, Captain Kathryn Janeway represents science at its most abstract and objective; B'Elanna, because of her passionate, half-Klingon nature and her training as an applied scientist, represents the other end of the spectrum of science. Captain Janeway is Starfleet by the book, a hierarchical leader who demands and receives respect. B'Elanna Torres, on the other hand, is a renegade who belonged to the Maquis, a terrorist group. When circumstances land *Voyager* and the Maquis in Delta Quadrant, the Maquis are stranded, their ship destroyed by the alien who transported them there.

The future of Star Trek? Captain Janeway (top) and the Queen Borg (bottom).

Forced to join the *Voyager* crew, B'Elanna does so reluctantly (as do the other Maquis). But eventually, B'Elanna adapts to Starfleet regulations and Janeway appoints her chief of engineering. The women's different career paths reflect their racial differences; Janeway is a European American with an upper-class demeanor, whereas B'Elanna comes from a mixed background, part Klingon (known for their warriorlike temperament) and part human. Janeway is light-complexioned, whereas B'Elanna is a swarthy brunette who sports a bony ridge down the center of her forehead. Their characters and physiques are very different, as are their approaches to science. Janeway practices a more traditional science, arguing for caution, circumspection, objectivity, detachment; Torres vehemently calls for advocacy, intervention, identification. That they so often work together (although they disagree and argue) shows not only that two very different characters can cooperate, but also that traditional science and a more feminist science can coexist.

That feminist science is the other in this equation is emphasized by B'Elanna's more immediate identification with a feminist approach to science. Choosing the woman who is literally alien to represent alternative science stresses the difference of this position. That B'Elanna occupies a lower position in the hierarchy and never completes Starfleet Academy makes the importance of listening to the outsider even more apparent. That B'Elanna and Janeway can work together so closely also suggests the importance of all women working together to overcome their ethnic, cultural, and political differences.

"Prototype," an episode from the 1996 season, presents these women as primary characters. Portraying B'Elanna Torres in a relationship with a robot, "Prototype" depicts feminist standpoint theory, which argues that women may practice science differently than men. According to this theory, a feminine perspective that emphasizes inclusiveness and interiority is contrasted to traditional scientific attitudes and practices, which stress objectivity and detachment, approaches typically associated with the masculine. That the two women work closely together shows how the series presents science as an integrated system (unlike the first *Star Trek*'s extreme separation of Spock, the science officer, from Scotty, the engineer). This holistic view of science is itself a significant perspective, but many individual episodes also deal directly with the intersection of feminism and science.

"Prototype" presents B'Elanna, Captain Janeway, and Security Chief Tuvok with a case in scientific ethics, complicated by gendering. In this episode, they encounter a robot in a pod and take the robot aboard *Voyager*. The robot's power supply is draining and they struggle to keep it alive; B'Elanna acts as a doctor. In a dramatic change from the customary use of camera angle, this episode opens with black and white footage, disrupted by static. The camera looks up at B'Elanna, Lieutenant Tuvok, and Ensign Kim as they study the robot, and we realize that the camera reflects the viewpoint of the object being studied, the robot. The camera angle produces a sense of disorientation and panic. Quite literally, this use of camera work provides the "feeling for the organism" that feminist historians of science call for. Color quickly reappears, and the camera soon resumes an angle suggesting the viewpoint of the crew members. Introducing the episode this way calls the audience's attention to the radical disruption of traditional perspective that supports the plot.

As B'Elanna wrestles with the engineering problems the robot represents, Tuvok argues against trying to save it. Although he agrees they should study the robot, he worries that it may pose a threat, and it should first be drained (killed), then studied. Tuvok's is a traditional scientific perspective, an approach that has led to natural history museums with stuffed and mounted specimens of animals and birds. B'Elanna, on the other hand, argues vehemently for doing whatever they can to maintain the creature's life. She interprets the sounds it makes as speech: "It is trying to communicate." She asks the robot, "What are you trying to say?" She insists, "We've got to figure out how to fix it" and describes the problem as being "a bleeding artery." Her language refers to a patient rather than a machine, and she uses an approach that suggests empathy, identification, and communication. Interconnectedness sharply contrasts to Tuvok's dispassionate approach. In fact, it is after consulting with the ship's doctor, himself a hologram, that B'Elanna cures the robot. B'Elanna's consultation with another alien "robot," the hologram doctor, reveals her openness toward other life forms. B'Elanna's empathic response reflects Barbara McClintock's "feeling for the organism." Through her insistence on communicating with the robot and trying to understand its perspective, B'Elanna succeeds in reviving it. Her success vindicates this alternative perspective, suggesting, as McClintock's 1983 Nobel Prize did, that a nontraditional approach can succeed where traditional science fails.

As an outsider, as she explicitly states, B'Elanna learns more about science on *Voyager* than she ever could have at Starfleet Academy. She gains new knowledge because she is far away from the Federation and because of the freedom that a female captain who is also a scientist gives her. The ship itself, and its exploration of uncharted and unknown territory in the Delta Quadrant, reflects the vindication of B'Elanna's alternative, feminist science. As a result, she is rewarded with scientific success and a relationship with a new life form. That her relationship to this race is presented and discussed in terms of the maternal reinforces the gendering and tremendous power of the alternative science she practices.

Part of the gendering appears in the emphasis on reproduction. Not only does B'Elanna give Unit 3947 new life, she also promises new life to its entire race. Its creators have died and the automated units face extinction as their power units run dry; they are unable to reproduce. The captain emphasizes the parallel between B'Elanna as mother and robots as children when she describes the automated units as having been left "to fend for themselves." The robots ask for B'Elanna's help in reproducing themselves. The captain objects, claiming that it is "a clear violation of the Prime Directive" of noninterference. Although B'Elanna vehemently argues the case with Janeway, she is refused permission to work with the robots. The robots abduct B'Elanna and force her to do the work she wanted to do. Finally, she succeeds in creating a new robot. As the robot, identified as Prototype 1001, enters consciousness, she delightedly grabs Unit 3947's hand; perplexedly, it asks, "What are you doing?" and she exclaims, "I am congratulating you. You are a father." Just as clearly, B'Elanna is the mother or, in the language of the robots, "a Builder."

This moment of triumph is short-lived; B'Elanna quickly discovers that the robots exterminated their original Builders. Now that she sees the robots as a threat to human life, B'Elanna's original advocacy changes. Unable to reproduce themselves without her technological expertise, the robots' very existence is at stake. They are so dependent on her that the parallel to mothering emerges again. This time, though, the robots are situated as dependent fetuses. That "termination" is the term used by the robots to describe what they did to their Builders underscores the abortion analogy. B'Elanna resolves to "terminate" the robots. Exclaiming, "My God! What have I done?" B'Elanna picks up a tool and attacks Prototype 1001, just as it says it's "Ready to accept programming." She apologizes to Unit 3947, the "father," as he is beamed back to Voyager.

This section of the plot clearly suggests abortion, but it is B'Elanna's discussion with the captain that makes the abortion analogy even clearer. The setting makes their close relationship and confidence evident. The captain usually remains seated in her captain's chair or at a table and gives orders, but here both women sit on a sofa, positioned as friends and equals rather than commanding officer and subordinate. This cozy domestic scene differs dramatically from the bonding that occurs on original *Star Trek* or even on *The Next Generation*. In those series, the male captain's bonding with his male officers is brief, usually on the bridge, never in the captain's living room. Distressed, B'Elanna says to Janeway, "I don't know what to say." Sympathetically, the captain uses the language of abortion counseling, providing B'Elanna with support: "As far as I'm concerned, you did what was necessary." The captain acknowledges the loss of life involved, but only after justifying B'Elanna's termination of the unit. "It must have been difficult," she says, "to destroy what you created." B'Elanna describes what happened, and the captain repeats, "As I said, it must have been difficult." Then, echoing the captain's words, B'Elanna replies, "It was necessary."

On one level, this exchange is simply that of a captain reviewing a subordinate's actions; at the same time, however, this episode of *Voyager* reflects the anxieties and complexities created by science that allows both the conception and the termination of life. That both the scientists are female and the science involves creation and reproduction emphasizes a conservative view of abortion, a position that justifies abortion when the fetus (robots) threatens the life of the mother (humans). The episode represents science as complex, conflicted, and unable to solve all the problems that the two women encounter. That B'Elanna did the right thing is unequivocal, reifying the idea of a woman's choice, though in very limited circumstances.

This brief discussion of *Voyager* reveals how the issues raised in *Sexual Generations*, and new issues, such as the depiction of women and science, can and should be discussed through the aegis of *Star Trek*. The title of this episode of *Voyager*, "Prototype," suggests a way to read all the *Star Trek* series, as prototypes that involve trying out new possibilities, performing other futures. That the trajectory from classic *Trek* to *Next Generation* and then to *Deep Space Nine* and now *Voyager* raises issues of gender, race, and sexuality is not surprising because Star Trek's journey has and always will be our own. It is my hope that *Sexual Generations* also can function as a prototype that will be succeeded by many other books on gender in the Star Trek universe.

WORKS CITED

Ashcroft, Bill, Gareth Griffiths, and Helen Tiffin, eds. *The Post-Colonial Studies Reader*. New York: Routledge, 1995.

Bacon-Smith, Camille. *Enterprising Women: Television Fandom and the Creation of Popular Myth*. Philadelphia: University of Pennsylvania Press, 1992.

Balsamo, Anne. *Technologies of the Gendered Body: Reading Cyborg, Reading Women*. Durham, N.C.: Duke University Press, 1996.

Barr, Marlene. *Alien to Femininity: Speculative Fiction and Feminist Theory*. New York: Greenwood Press, 1987.

———. "'All Good Things . . .': The End of *Star Trek: The Next Generation*, The End of Camelot—The End of the Tale about Woman as Handmaid to Patriarchy as Superman." In Taylor Harrison, Sarah Projansky, Kent A. Ono, and Elyce Rae Helford, eds. *Enterprise Zones: Critical Positions on Star Trek*. Boulder, Colo.: Westview, 1996. 231–43.

Beauvoir, Simone de. *The Second Sex*. 1952. New York: Vintage, 1972.

Belenky, Mary, et al. *Women's Ways of Knowing: The Development of Self, Voice, and Mind*. New York: Basic Books, 1986.

Bentley, Nancy. "White Slaves: The Mulatto Hero in Antebellum Fiction." In Michael Morrit and Cathy N. Davidson, eds. *Subjects and Citizens: Nation, Race, and Gender from Oroonoko to Anita Hill*. Durham, N.C.: Duke University Press, 1996. 195–216.

Bernardi, Daniel Leonard. *Star Trek and History: Race-ing toward a White Future*. New Brunswick, N.J.: Rutgers University Press, 1998.

Besant, Sir Walter. *The Revolt of Man*. London: Blackwood, 1882.

Bhabha, Homi. *Nation and Narration*. New York: Routledge, 1990.

Boyd, Robert S. "Science Rejecting Notion of Genetic Race." *The Sunday Advocate*, October 13, 1996, 8A.

Branham, Robert James. "The Role of the Convert in *Eclipse of Reason* and *The Silent Scream*." *Quarterly Journal of Speech* 77 (1991): 407–26.

Brooks, Gwendolyn. "the mother." In *Selected Poems*. New York: Harper & Row, 1963.

Brownmiller, Susan. *Against Our Will: Men, Women, and Rape*. New York: Simon & Schuster, 1975.

Bulwer-Lytton, Edward. *The Coming Race*. Philadelphia: John Wanamaker, 1871.

Butler, Octavia. "Bloodchild." In Pamela Sargent, ed. *Women of Wonder: The Contemporary Years*. New York: Harcourt Brace, 1995. 123–40.

Celani, David. *The Illusion of Love: Why the Battered Woman Returns to Her Abuser*. New York: Columbia University Press, 1996.

Chodorow, Nancy. *The Reproduction of Mothering*. Berkeley: University of California Press, 1978.

Cixous, Hélène, and Catherine Clément. *The Newly Born Woman*. Trans. Betsy Wing. Minneapolis: University of Minnesota Press, 1986.

Clareson, Thomas. "Lost Worlds, Lost Races: A Pagan Princess of Their Very Own." In Thomas Clareson, ed. *Many Futures, Many Worlds: Theme and Form in Science Fiction*. Kent, Ohio: Kent State University Press, 1977. 117–39.

Condit, Celeste Michelle. *Decoding Abortion Rhetoric: Communicating Social Change*. Urbana: University of Illinois Press, 1990.

Cuklanz, Lisa. *Rape on Trial: How the Mass Media Construct Legal Reform and Social Change*. Philadelphia: University of Pennsylvania Press, 1996.

Decarnin, Camilla, Eric Garber, and Lyn Paleo, eds. *Worlds Apart*. Boston: Alyson Publications, 1986.

Donawerth, Jane. *Frankenstein's Daughters: Women Writing Science Fiction*. Syracuse, N.Y.: Syracuse University Press, 1997.

Eisenstein, Zillah. *The Female Body and the Law*. Berkeley: University of California Press, 1988.

Eliot, Jeffrey M., ed. *Kindred Spirits*. Boston: Alyson Publications, 1984.

Faludi, Susan. *Backlash: The Undeclared War against American Women*. New York: Crown, 1991.

Farmer, Philip Jose. "The Lovers." *Startling Stories* 27 (1952): 12–63.

Ferguson, Kathy E., Gilad Ashkenazi, and Wendy Schultz. "Gender Identity in *Star Trek*." In Donald M. Hassler and Clyde Wilcox, eds. *Political Science Fiction*. Columbia: University of South Carolina Press, 1997. 214–33.

Fields, Barbara Jeanne. "Slavery, Race, and Ideology in the United States of America." *New Left Review* 181 (1990): 95–118.

Fox, Marcia. Introduction. In George Gissing, *The Odd Women*. New York: Norton, 1981.

Franklin, Eileen, with William Wright. "The Secret Too Terrible to Remember." *Good Housekeeping* 213 (1991): 82–86.

Garber, Eric, and Lyn Paleo. *Uranian Worlds: A Reader's Guide to Alternative Sexuality in Science Fiction and Horror*. 1983. New York: G. K. Hall, 1991.

Gates, Henry Louis, Jr. *"Race," Writing, and Difference*. Chicago: University of Chicago Press, 1986.

Gilligan, Carol. *In a Different Voice*. Cambridge, Mass.: Harvard University Press, 1982.

Gorman, Christine. "Memory on Trial." *Time* 145 (1996): 54–55.

Gould, Stephen Jay. *The Mismeasure of Man*. New York: Norton, 1981.

Greenwald, Jeff. *Future Perfect: How Star Trek Conquered Planet Earth*. New York: Viking, 1998.

Griffith, Nicola, and Stephen Pagel, eds. *Bending the Landscape: Fantasy*. Clarkston, Ga.: White Wolf Press, 1996.

Haraway, Donna. "A Manifesto for Cyborgs: Science Technology, and Socialist Feminism in the 1980s." *Socialist Review* 80 (1985): 65–108.

———. *Primate Visions: Gender, Race, and Nature in the World of Modern Science*. New York: Routledge, 1989.

Harding, Sandra. *Whose Science? Whose Knowledge? Thinking from Women's Lives*. Ithaca, N.Y.: Cornell University Press, 1991.

Harrison, Taylor. "Weaving the Cyborg Shroud: Mourning and Deferral in *Star Trek: The Next Generation*." In Taylor Harrison, Sarah Projansky, Kent A. Ono, and Elyce Rae Helford, eds. *Enterprise Zones: Critical Positions on Star Trek*. Boulder, Colo.: Westview, 1996. 245–58.

Harrison, Taylor, Sarah Projansky, Kent A. Ono, and Elyce Rae Helford, eds. *Enterprise Zones: Critical Positions on Star Trek*. Boulder, Colo.: Westview, 1996.

Hassler, Donald M., and Clyde Wilcox, eds. *Political Science Fiction*. Columbia: University of South Carolina Press, 1997.

Hastie, Amelie. "A Fabricated Space: Assimilating the Individual on *Star Trek: The Next Generation*." In Taylor Harrison, Sarah Projansky, Kent A. Ono, and Elyce Rae Helford, eds. *Enterprise Zones: Critical Positions on Star Trek*. Boulder, Colo.: Westview, 1996. 115–36.

Heller, Lee E. "The Persistence of Difference: Postfeminism, Popular Discourse, and Heterosexuality in *Star Trek*." *Science-Fiction Studies* 24:2 (1997): 226–44.

Hermann, Claudine. "Women in Space and Time." In Elaine Marks and Isabelle de Courtivron, eds. *New French Feminisms*. New York: Schocken, 1981. 168–73.

Hollinger, Veronica, ed. "On Star Trek." *Science-Fiction Studies* 24:2 (1997): 207–66.

Hull, Gloria, ed. *All the Women Are White, All the Blacks Are Men, but Some of Us Are Brave: Black Women's Studies*. Old Westbury, N.Y.: Feminist Press, 1982.

Hurst, Fannie. *Imitation of Life*. New York: Harper, 1933.

Huyssen, Andreas. *After the Great Divide: Modernism, Mass Culture, and Postmodernism*. Bloomington: Indiana University Press, 1986.

Ingelow, Jean. *Mopsa the Fairy*. In Nina Auerbach and U. C. Knoepflmacher, eds. *Forbidden Journeys*. Chicago: University of Chicago Press, 1992. 215–316.

Irigaray, Luce. "Is the Subject of Science Sexed?" *Cultural Critique* 1 (1985): 73–88.

———. *This Sex Which Is Not One*. Trans. Catherine Porter, with Carolyn Burke. Ithaca, N.Y.: Cornell University Press, 1985.

Jenkins, Henry. *Textual Poachers: Television Fans and Participatory Culture*. New York: Routledge, 1992.

Johnson, Barbara. "Apostrophe, Animation, and Abortion." *Diacritics* (Spring 1986): 29–57.

Joseph-Witham, Heather R. *Star Trek Fans and Costume Art.* Jackson: University Press of Mississippi, 1996.

Joyrich, Lynne. "Feminist Enterprise? *Star Trek: The Next Generation* and the Occupation of Femininity." *Cinema Journal* 35 (1996): 61–84.

———. *Re-viewing Reception: Television, Gender, and Postmodern Culture.* Bloomington: Indiana University Press, 1996.

Keller, Evelyn Fox. *Feminism and Science.* Oxford: Oxford University Press, 1996.

Klass, Tim. "'Delayed Memories' Divide Professionals and Some Families." *The Sunday Advocate* (Baton Rouge, La.), August 18, 1996, 19A.

Kolodny, Annette. *The Land before Her: Fantasy and the Experience of the American Frontiers, 1630–1860.* Chapel Hill: University of North Carolina Press, 1984.

Kristeva, Julia. *Powers of Horror: An Essay on Abjection.* New York: Columbia University Press, 1982.

———. "Women's Time." In Robyn R. Warhol and Diane Price Herndl, eds. *Feminisms: An Anthology of Literary Theory and Criticism.* New Brunswick, N.J.: Rutgers University Press, 1991. 443–62.

Lacan, Jacques. *The Four Fundamental Concepts of Psycho-Analysis.* New York: Norton, 1978.

Le Guin, Ursula. *The Left Hand of Darkness.* 1969. New York: Putnam, 1972.

Levin, Ira. *The Stepford Wives.* New York: Random House, 1972.

Lewontin, R. C., Steven Rose, and Leon J. Kamin, eds. *Not in Our Genes.* New York: Pantheon, 1986.

McConnell, Frank. "'Live Long and Prosper': The 'Trek' Goes On." *Commonweal* 118.19 (1991): 652–54.

Minkowitz, Donna. "Queers in Space." *The Village Voice,* February 5, 1991, 67–68.

Moskowitz, Sam. *When Women Rule.* New York: Walker, 1972.

Mulvey, Laura. "Visual Pleasure and the Narrative Cinema." *Screen* 16.3 (1975): 6–18.

Nemecek, Larry. *The Star Trek: The Next Generation Companion.* New York: Pocket Books, 1995.

Nichols, Nichelle. *Beyond Uhura: Star Trek and Other Memories.* New York: Putnam, 1994.

Penley, Constance. *NASA/TREK: Popular Science and Sex in America.* New York: Verso, 1997.

Piercy, Marge. *Woman on the Edge of Time.* New York: Fawcett, 1976.

Projanksy, Sarah. "When the Body Speaks: Deanna Troi's Tenuous Authority and the Rationalization of Federation Superiority in *Star Trek: The Next Generation* Rape Narratives." In Taylor Harrison, Sarah Projansky, Kent A. Ono, and Elyce Rae Helford, eds. *Enterprise Zones: Critical Positions on Star Trek.* Boulder, Colo.: Westview, 1996. 33–50.

Rich, Adrienne. "Compulsory Heterosexuality and Lesbian Existence." In *Adrienne Rich's Poetry and Prose*. New York: Norton, 1993. 203–23.

———. *Of Woman Born*. New York: Bantam, 1977.

Richards, Thomas. *The Meaning of Star Trek*. New York: Doubleday, 1997.

Roberts, Robin. *A New Species: Gender and Science in Science Fiction*. Urbana: University of Illinois Press, 1993.

———. "'No Woman Born': Immortality and Gender in Feminist Science Fiction." In George Slusser, Gary Westfahl, and Eric S. Rabkin, eds. *Immortal Engines: Life Extension and Immortality in Science Fiction and Fantasy*. Athens: University of Georgia Press, 1996. 135–44.

Roberts, Wes, and Bill Ross. *Make It So: Leadership Lessons from "Star Trek: The Next Generation."* New York: Pocket Books, 1995.

Roof, Judith. "Fiction Nation, or Fantasies of Future Normativity." *Ms.* 1995.

Rosenbloom, Rachel, ed. *Unspoken Rules: Sexual Orientation and Women's Rights*. New York: Cassell, 1996.

Rosinsky, Natalie. *Feminist Futures: Contemporary Women's Speculative Fiction* Ann Arbor, Mich.: University Microfilms International Research Press, 1984.

Russ, Joanna. "*Amor Vincit Foeminam:* The Battle of the Sexes in Science Fiction." *Science Fiction Studies* 7 (1980): 2–15.

Sanday, Peggy. *Fraternity Gang Rape: Sex, Brotherhood, and Privilege on Campus*. New York: New York University Press, 1990.

———. *A Woman Scorned: Acquaintance Rape on Trial*. New York: Doubleday, 1996.

Schuster, Hal, and Wendy Rathbone. *Trek: The Unauthorized A–Z*. New York: HarperPrism, 1994.

Shelley, Mary. *Frankenstein; or, The Modern Prometheus*. 1831. New York: Signet, 1965.

———. *The Last Man*. 1826. Lincoln: University of Nebraska Press, 1965.

Snitow, Ann. "Mass Market Romance: Pornography for Women Is Different." In Gail Dines and Jean M. Humez, eds. *Gender, Race, and Class in Media*. Thousand Oaks, Calif.: Sage, 1995.

Steffen-Fluhr, Nancy. "Women and the Inner Game of Don Siegel's *Invasion of the Body Snatchers*." *Science-Fiction Studies* 11.2 (1984): 139–54.

Suleri, Sara. "Women Skin Deep: Feminism and the Postcolonial Condition." In Bill Ashcroft, Gareth Griffiths, and Helen Tiffin, eds. *The Post-Colonial Studies Reader*. New York: Routledge, 1995. 273–82.

Suvin, Darko. *Metamorphoses of Science Fiction: On the Politics and History of a Genre*. New Haven, Conn.: Yale University Press, 1979.

Testa, Karen. "Family Settles Repressed Memory Suit." *The Advocate* (Baton Rouge, La.), November 16, 1996, 6A.

Tompkins, Jane. *West of Everything: The Inner Life of Westerns*. New York: Oxford University Press, 1992.

Tuana, Nancy, ed. *Feminism and Science*. Bloomington: Indiana University Press, 1989.

Tulloch, John, and Henry Jenkins. *Science Fiction Audiences: Watching Dr. Who and Star Trek.* New York: Routledge, 1995.

"Twenty Questions: Patrick Stewart." *Playboy* 139 (1992): 138–40.

Westfahl, Gary. "Where No Market Has Gone Before: 'The Science-Fiction Industry' and the Star Trek Industry." *Extrapolation* 37.4 (1996): 291–301.

Wilcox, Clyde. "To Boldly Go Where Others Have Gone Before: Cultural Change and the Old and New Star Treks." *Extrapolation* 33.1 (1992): 88–100.

Wilcox, Rhonda V. "Dating Data: Miscegenation in *Star Trek: The Next Generation.*" *Extrapolation* 34.3 (1993): 265–77.

———. "Shifting Roles and Synthetic Women in *Star Trek: The Next Generation.*" *Studies in Popular Culture* 13.2 (1991): 53–65.

Wilt, Judith. *Abortion, Choice, and Contemporary Fiction: The Armageddon of Maternal Instinct.* Chicago: University of Chicago Press, 1990.

Wittig, Monique. *Les Guérillières.* 1969. Boston: Beacon Press, 1971.

INDEX

Names preceded by an asterisk are *Star Trek* characters and places.

Abatemarco, Frank, 79

abortion: and backlash against women, 145; and control, 146–47; defamiliarization of, 146, 148–49, 151, 154, 163; and family values, 156; in fiction, 145–46; futuristic version of, 162, 163; in "Galaxy's Child," 21–24, 148–49; and gender, 150–51, 156; in media stories, 145; in "Prototype," 188–89; rape and, 151, 153, 155, 163, 164; reproductive politics and, 144–51, 153–55, 161–62, 163

abuse, sexual, 81–84, 85, 101–2, 169–70, 175–81

*Acamar III, in "The Vengeance Factor," 36

Accused, The (film), 165

acquaintance rape, 167, 168, 171

African Americans: actors, 125–32, 139, 184; as role models vs. tokens, 128; wisewoman figure, 132, 140. *See also specific roles;* race

aging, fear of, 39

alien, female. *See* female alien

alien fetus, 21–24, 148–49

Alien movies, 46, 63, 94, 114

alien societies: rapists from, 164, 168–69, 170, 171, 174, 175, 178, 179–80; sexual orientation of, 109–12, 114, 116–17, 118, 121; sorceress figures from, 18, 19, 20, 31, 33, 35, 41, 43, 48, 65. *See also* woman ruler

alien species. *See* race

*Alkar, in "Man of the People," 79–84, 86

*Alkar's mother, in "Man of the People," 80–84, 85, 87

"Allegiance," 39–40

*Alrik, in "The Perfect Mate," 73–75, 77–79

American society: gender as issue in, 7; Gulf War and, 74–75; hate crimes in, 119; marriage rates in, 75; power as issue in, 7, 20; race in, 127–32, 133, 137; rape as issue in, 164–68; reflected in mass culture, 7, 10, 13, 20, 35, 125, 130, 144, 151, 165–68; reproductive politics in, 144–50, 155, 161, 163; rights of disabled in, 70; romance in, 176–77; sexual orientation in, 108–9, 118–20, 123; social conditioning in, 74

androgyny, 117, 119, 122–23

androids: comparisons of, 107; creation of, 150; *Data, 91–98; parental rights of, 162, 163; qualities of, 106; reproductive rights of, 147, 161, 163; as stand-ins for women, 91, 92; use of term, 91. *See also* *Data

"Angel in the House, The" (Patmore), 47, 48, 64

of, 147; technology as masculine, 22, 23, 24, 26, 40, 171, 179
male bonding, 24, 43, 50–51, 189
male characters: African-American, 125, 127, 131–32; comparisons of, 35, 39, 79; defamiliarization and, 174, 175. *See also specific characters*
male gaze: in cinema, 20, 172; at female alien, 43; in "Violations," 172, 173, 180
Manning, Richard, 136, 139
"Man of the People," 69, 79–85, 100
*Maquis, in *Voyager* series, 184, 186
*Mariposa, in "Up the Long Ladder," 149–50, 156–59
"Mark of Gideon," 146
Marks, Jonathan, 126
*Marouk, in "The Vengeance Factor," 36–38
marriage, and reproductive politics, 156
marriage rates, 75
masculine ethos: aggression in, 165, 170, 171; blackness in, 127, 129, 131–32, 133, 136; competition in, 104; control in, 50, 64, 74, 96, 101–3; in frontier life, 104; of hierarchy, 31; of individuality, 24, 27, 29, 35, 50, 65; in legal system, 170; of logic, 31, 42; poker game in, 103–4, 122; rigidity of, 30, 31, 35, 96–97; science in, 8, 9, 186; of soldierhood, 24; and species difference, 27; technology in, 22, 23, 24, 26, 40, 171, 179; woman ruler converted to, 65. *See also* patriarchy
mass culture: feminization of, 5; male gaze in, 20, 172; poaching in, 5; society reflected in, 7, 10, 13, 20, 35, 125, 130, 144, 151, 165–68; strong political statements in, 170
Matthias, Jean, 28
McClintock, Barbara, 187
McFadden, Gates, 112
Meese, Edwin, 144
memory: as feminine, 171; recovered, 165, 169–70, 175; repressed, 169
metamorphosis: of female aliens, 19, 35,

41, 43, 63, 105; in feminine ethos, 51; of insects, 51–52; of perfect mate, 77; of woman ruler, 63, 65
metonymy, 148
Minkowitz, Donna, 110
*"Minuet," in "11001001," 98–100
Miodinow, Leonard, 59
mirrors: in "Man of the People," 82; in "The Most Toys," 102; in "The Perfect Mate," 77, 78, 79; in "Sub Rosa," 178–79
"Mismeasure of Man, The," 91–92
misogyny, in "Conspiracy," 53, 59
Mona Lisa (Leonardo da Vinci), 102, 103
Montgomery, Elizabeth, 31
Moore, Ronald D., 24, 139
*Moriarty, Professor, 93
Moskowitz, Sam, 45n
"Most Toys, The," 92, 100–103, 105
mother, 18–19, 23–24, 68; and decision making, 151, 152, 155; defamiliarization and, 151; fear of generative power of, 46; and fetal viability, 161–62; sacrifices of, 163; sentimentality about, 147, 151; separation from, 24, 27, 28, 39, 53; sexuality and maternity, 146
"Mother, The," 147
Mulvey, Laura, 20, 172

"Naked Now, The," 92, 94–97, 100
Native American characters, 184
nature, as feminine, 22, 24, 33
Nemecek, Larry, 112, 118, 150
"No Woman Born," 114
*null space, 117, 121

*O'Brien, Chief, 156
*Odan, in "The Host," 112–16
*Odin, The, in "Angel One," 54
*Odo, 183
*O'Donnell, Juliana, in "Inheritance," 92, 106–7
"Offspring, The," 147, 148, 150, 151, 156, 159–63

Robin Roberts, a professor of English and of Women's and Gender Studies at Louisiana State University, is a graduate of Mount Holyoke College and received a Ph.D. degree from the University of Pennsylvania. She is the author of *A New Species: Gender and Science in Science Fiction, Anne McCaffrey: A Critical Companion,* and *Ladies First: Women in Music Videos.*

Typeset in 9.5/13 Palatino
with Eras display
Designed by Erin Kirk New
Composed by Jim Proefrock
at the University of Illinois Press
Manufactured by Cushing-Malloy, Inc.

University of Illinois Press
1325 South Oak Street
Champaign, IL 61820-6903

www.press.uillinois.edu